The Great

Impressionists

Masterpieces from the Courtauld Collection of Impressionist and Post-Impressionist Paintings and Drawings

Australian National Gallery, Canberra,
in association with
The Courtauld Institute Galleries,
University of London

Foreword

The Courtauld Collection of French paintings and drawings of the late nineteenth and early twentieth centuries is acknowledged as one of the truly great collections of the art of that fertile period. A unique combination of circumstances has enabled the Australian National Gallery to join with the Courtauld Institute of the University of London to bring the Collection to Australia. The result is a rare chance for the people of Australia to enjoy outstanding works by the masters of Impressionist and Post-Impressionist painting. *The Great Impressionists* exhibition will be a significant experience for all its viewers.

A great deal of interest and enthusiasm, time and effort must be expended by many people to mount and make a success of an exhibition of this kind and the Government and the Gallery wish to express their warm appreciation of these efforts and commend the exhibition to all art lovers.

On behalf of the Australian Government I am delighted to welcome the Courtauld Collection to Australia.

Barry Cohen,
Minister for Home Affairs and Environment,
Canberra ACT February 1984.

Australian National Gallery

Published by the Australian National Gallery, Canberra, ACT, 2600, 1984.

Photography Courtesy of the Home House Society Trustees, Courtauld Institute Galleries.

Reproduction rights courtesy of S.P.A.D.E.M. — Pierre Bonnard, Aristide Maillol, Pablo Picasso, Paul Signac, Maurice Utrillo, Édouard Vuillard; A.D.A.G.P. — Pierre Bonnard, André Derain, Oskar Kokoschka.

Cataloguing-in-publication data

The Great Impressionists.

Bibliography.
Includes index.
ISBN 0 642 87465 4.

1. Courtauld, Samuel, 1876-1947 — Art collections
2. Australian National Gallery — Exhibitions.
3. Impressionism (Art) — France — Exhibitions.
4. Painting, French — Exhibitions. I. Australian National Gallery. II. Courtauld Institute Galleries.

759.4'074'099471

ISBN 0 642 87465 4

Publications Department, Australian National Gallery
Co-ordinator of Publications, Alan Dodge
Designer, Alistair Hay
Editor, Bruce Semler

Typesetting by Smith & Miles Ltd, Sydney

Printed by Dai Nippon Printing Company, Tokyo.

Contents

Preface

The Courtauld Institute of Art, University of London, celebrated its fiftieth anniversary in the academic year 1982-83. In celebrating our past achievements we have also looked to the future, and during the last few years have had to consider the best way to accommodate our greatly expanded art collections, our teaching staff and students, four specialist libraries, and the Department of Technology and Conservation; all need more space. The problem has become more acute now that the original lease of 20 Portman Square, made over to the University by Samuel Courtauld in 1931 for the housing of the Courtauld Institute of Art, expired in 1981. The Courtauld Institute Galleries at Woburn Square (opened in 1958) are no longer large enough for the collections and the original plan to erect a new building for the teaching departments next to the Galleries has ceased to be practicable.

The Fine Rooms on the Strand, or northern, side of Somerset House next to King's College, London, have remained empty since the 1970s and adjoining space which can be converted to suit the Institute's teaching activities will also become available. The Fine Rooms were opened in 1780 and once housed the Royal Society, the Royal Academy of Arts, and the Society of Antiquaries. They formed part of a major architectural scheme for government offices and learned societies designed by Sir William Chambers and built between 1776 and 1780. Negotiations between the University of London, on behalf of the Courtauld Institute, and the British Government to enable both the Institute and its collections to occupy the whole of the Strand Block are now at an advanced stage. Preliminary detailed design work has been commissioned from two architects, Mr Christopher Firmstone and Mr Paul Hampton, and the Courtauld Institute of Art Trust has been formed to raise the money needed to pay for the conversion.

We were therefore delighted when the opportunity was offered by *Nihon Keizai Shimbun (Japan Economic Journal)* to show our collection of Impressionist and Post-Impressionist pictures for the first time in Japan, at Tokyo, Kyoto, and Osaka, in January-May 1984. The Home House Society Trustees, to whom control of the collection had been given under Samuel Courtauld's original foundation, recognized that the substantial financial contribution made by our sponsors in Japan would to some extent justify the risks of sending such precious objects across the world. There was also the well known interest of the Japanese people in French nineteenth and early twentieth century art, and the enjoyment that we hope will be given to visitors to the exhibition was a strong incentive.

Georges Seurat 1859-1891
The bridge at Courbevoie. *(detail)* **1886**
oil on canvas 46.4 x 55.3cm

When plans for the exhibition had reached an advanced stage in early summer 1983 the Australian National Gallery expressed keen interest in showing it in Canberra after the Japanese tour. We greatly welcomed this chance to show the Courtauld Collections for the first time in Australia, in the fine surroundings of the Australian National Gallery, opened by Her Majesty the Queen in October 1982. We thank the Chairman and Council of the Australian National Gallery for their initiative and join with them in expressing our warmest gratitude to the Australian Government and the sponsors of the exhibition, without whose guarantee of indemnity and generous financial support the Australian showing could not have taken place.

We therefore hope that we can give pleasure to the peoples of Japan and Australia by showing our pictures, many of which are world famous, and at the same time help to secure their future accommodation in Somerset House.

We are most grateful to the present owner of Picasso's *Child with Dove,* formerly in Samuel Courtauld's collection, for agreeing to lend this picture as a substitute for Van Gogh's *Self-Portrait with bandaged Ear,* which is in too fragile a state to travel and we also thank Sir Michael Levey, Director of the National Gallery, London, where *Child with Dove* has been on loan for some years, for his kind collaboration. We gratefully acknowledge help given us by Mr Michael Wilson of the National Gallery and by Miss Frances Carey, Department of Prints and Drawings, British Museum.

The English text of the catalogue has been edited by Dr Dennis Farr, who also wrote the introductory essay on Samuel Courtauld and his collection and the entries for most of the paintings. He was assisted by Mr William Bradford, who wrote all the entries for the watercolours, drawings and prints, and Mrs Helen Braham, who wrote the entries for the paintings in the Princes Gate Collection which have been included in the exhibition (except no.15, Cézanne). They in turn would like to acknowledge the help they received from Dr John House and Mrs Juliet Wilson Bareau and colleagues in the Department of Technology and the Photographic Service of the Courtauld Institute. They are grateful to the University's Senate House technical staff, particularly Mr Michael Newman, and to Mr William Clarke, paper conservator at the Courtauld.

At the Australian National Gallery we have received every assistance from Mr James Mollison, Director, Mr David Jaffé, Curator of European Art before 1900, and their colleagues in all the detailed arrangements that a major enterprise such as this necessarily entails. To them and the many others in Japan and Australia who have helped to bring this exhibition into being we express our warmest thanks.

Jeanne Courtauld	Peter Lasko
Chairman,	*Director,*
Home House Society Trustees	*Courtauld Institute of Art*

Samuel Courtauld and the Courtauld Collections

Britain has been very fortunate in its rich artistic heritage, its magnificent medieval cathedrals and the peerless art collections built up over the past four hundred years or so by men and women of taste and wealth. Many of the paintings, drawings, sculptures and other *objets d'art* which once formed part of a royal or a nobleman's collection are now in our public museums and galleries. Others remain in great country houses, a glittering record of patronage, sometimes of sheer ostentation, and a part of our social and economic history as well as of the history of taste, a subject of increasing interest to art historians. The change from the patronage of the Church, as the principal employer of architects, artists and craftsmen, to the patronage of royalty and, eventually, the newly-ennobled or land-owning classes was a process precipitated by the Protestant Reformation in the sixteenth century. The following century was the heyday of royal patronage, together with that of a few discerning aristocratic connoisseurs. Political stability in the eighteenth century, coupled with the creation of new wealth based on an expanding overseas empire and the entrepreneurial skills of a new and rapidly developing class of industrialists, created favourable conditions for the cultivation of the arts. The first public museum, the Ashmolean, was founded at Oxford in 1683 and was followed by the British Museum in 1753, but it was not until the nineteenth century that the majority of our national and municipal museums and galleries came into being, partly as a response to the needs of the urban population and partly as a tangible expression of national pride and scientific enquiry. The National Gallery, London, was founded in 1824 with the purchase of a group of paintings from the international banker, John Julius Angerstein.

Samuel Courtauld

The support of living artists in England differed markedly from that in France. State support in France had been much more developed and systematic since the reign of Louis XIV. Although the Royal Academy of Arts was established in London by George III in 1768, this was in emulation of a French prototype. The French founded the Musée du Luxembourg by royal decree as early as 1818, as a 'museum of living artists', whereas England had to wait until Sir Henry Tate's benefaction and the opening of the Tate Gallery in 1897 for a national gallery of historic and modern British art. Recent modern foreign art was not admitted at the Tate until 1917 and no work by a living artist, whether British or foreign, could be accepted by the National Gallery.

Mr Douglas Cooper, in his pioneering study of the history of public response to the Impressionists and Post-Impressionists in this country and elsewhere, shows how British collectors, with a few honourable exceptions, were quite unwilling to buy their work, despite many opportunities to see pictures by Manet, Monet, Degas, Pissarro, Sisley, Gauguin, Van Gogh and Cézanne, between 1870 and 1912[1]. The French were hardly more receptive to the merits of their artists: Monet did not begin to win recognition until the early 1890s when he was over fifty years old; Manet died in 1883 at the age of fifty-one, tardily honoured by the French State in 1882; Gauguin's *Ia Orana Maria* (1891, Metropolitan Museum of Art, New York) a major painting from his first visit to Tahiti, was refused as a gift by Léonce Bénédite, Director of the Musée du Luxembourg, in 1893;[2] and Cézanne's true stature had barely begun to be recognized before 1895, when Ambroise Vollard began to sell his work to Count Camondo and Auguste Pellerin. Even so, it took the memorial retrospective exhibition of 1907, held within a year of his death, to establish his reputation as one of the great masters of the nineteenth century. Yet there were French collectors like Gustave Caillebotte and Etienne Moreau-Nélaton, who supported the Impressionists during their lifetime. The first bequeathed his collection to the French State in 1894, while in 1906 Moreau-Nélaton gave thirty-four paintings, including the *Déjeuner sur l'Herbe* by Manet, and bequeathed additional works in 1927. These collections are now among the chief glories of the Musée du Louvre and the Musée de l'Impressionisme, but they were not so esteemed when first offered to France.[3]

By contrast, American collectors like Mr and Mrs Potter-Palmer of Chicago, Erwin Davis and H. O. Havemeyer of New York, to name only a few of the principal buyers, reacted enthusiastically to Paul Durand-Ruel's first exhibition of Impressionist art in New York in 1886. They began a love-affair with French art that was carried on by succeeding generations of collectors, like Michael and Gertrude Stein, Etta and Claribel Cone of Baltimore, Dr Alfred Barnes of Philadelphia, and Walter Arensberg, who bought Matisse, Picasso, and Cézanne; and the tradition has been continued through to our own day by, for example, Mr and Mrs John Hay Whitney and Mr and Mrs Paul Mellon. German and Russian collectors, too, were very active from the late 1890s to 1914, as the public collections in Munich, Bremen, Hamburg, Berlin, Essen, Leningrad and Moscow bear eloquent witness.

It is within this historical context that Samuel Courtauld's own achievements as a collector must be seen. His early career gave no hint of an adventurous artistic taste, and as a collector he was by no means a pioneer in this country. If one has to award that title it must go to Miss Gwendoline Davies, who in 1912 began to collect modern French pictures on an appreciable scale. She not only took over from where Sir Hugh Lane had left off at his death in 1915, that is Impressionist art of the 1860s to 1890s, but extended her taste to include artists of the next generation.[4] Where Courtauld surpassed his predecessors was in scale and sheer quality. If he was slow to start (he was forty-six in 1922 when he began seriously to collect), he more than made up for this by speed and decisiveness. Within eight to ten years he built up not only his own collection; in 1923 he gave £50 000 to the Tate Gallery as a trust fund (the Courtauld Fund) for the purchase of Impressionist and Post-Impressionist paintings. He had quickly realized how poorly represented these were in the national collection and that it would soon no longer be possible to acquire first-class works at comparatively reasonable prices. By this most generous act, Courtauld totally changed the national collection. He brought to his collecting that combination of flair, energy, and sense of public duty that had marked his successful career as a leading industrialist.

Born in 1876, Samuel Courtauld was the second of four sons of Sydney and Sarah (née Sharpe) Courtauld. He was descended on his father's side from a Huguenot family of distinguished silversmiths and silk-weavers, while his mother's family included the poet-banker, Samuel Rogers, and an eminent archaeologist and classical scholar, Samuel Sharpe. The first immigrant, Augustin Courtauld, left his home on the Isle d'Oléron off the west coast of France after the Revocation of the Edict of Nantes in 1685 and settled in London in about 1690. There, as a Protestant, he could remain free from religious persecution.[5] The Courtaulds switched from silversmithing to silk-weaving in the nineteenth century and for almost one hundred years their factory at Pebmarsh, Essex, flourished as a small-scale family business. This was transformed during World War I and the years immediately after it by the development of the synthetic fibre rayon silk, made from cellulose. Largely under Samuel Courtauld's guidance (after leaving Rugby School he entered the family business) the firm became a vast international concern of which he was Chairman from 1921 until his death in December 1947.

The Courtaulds were Unitarians[6] and, although like many other successful merchants and industrialists they had become absorbed into the landowning classes by the later nineteenth century, their religious beliefs and puritanical way of life set them apart from their neighbours. Like others of their faith and the Quakers (Society of Friends) with whom they had some affinities, they took a deep interest in social problems and supported the arts, especially music. Courtauld's father was fond of music and played the violin, but the arts were respected rather than actively cultivated in the Courtauld household, and young Samuel enjoyed a fairly conventional middle-class Victorian upbringing. In some autobiographical notes written at the end of his life Courtauld recalled that his occasional visits to the National Gallery as an eighteen-year old youth 'damped my spirits' because of 'the rarified atmosphere of education and sanctity' which he felt there.[7] He enjoyed the rich colours of Turner's *Fighting Téméraire* and *Ulysses deriding Polyphemus* in the National Gallery, but much more enjoyed his visits to the Royal Academy as 'a genuine pleasure, if not a very deep one. There was little of schoolroom austerity and piety to be seen on those walls, . . .' His first real quickening of interest came when he went to Krefeld and Paris to study weaving and his understanding of the Old Masters was deepened by what he saw in the Louvre. Of contemporary artists' work, he 'noted with approval' some ballet paintings by Degas; interestingly, this taste for Degas was shared by an older generation of English artists, notably Walter Sickert, and collectors, although Courtauld was probably unaware of this.

After his marriage in 1901 to Elizabeth Kelsey, who was to share his interest in art and music, they visited Italy and here he was profoundly affected by the great Renaissance masterpieces to be seen in Florence and Rome: 'The old masters had come alive to me, and British academic art died. In the former I now perceived a wonderful mastery allied with strong emotion and with life itself; I felt strong and exciting currents still flowing beneath the surface of the paint. In the latter I felt nothing but artificiality and convention, and could detect no progress in technique.' Gradually Courtauld realized that the emotion and vitality of the old masters was to be found again in the modern French School. He began to be aware of Manet and Monet, as well as Degas, but still could not appreciate Cézanne and Seurat. Roger Fry's two Post-Impressionist exhibitions in London in 1910 and 1912 seemed to hinder his awakening, for he derided the Fauves and their precursors attracted some of the same odium.

The next stage of his conversion came in 1917 when he saw Sir Hugh Lane's collection on exhibition at the Tate Gallery. This was, he said, 'my second real "eye-opener" . . . I remember especially Renoir's *Parapluies,* Manet's *Musique des Tuileries* and Degas' *Plage á Trouville,* . . . I knew nothing yet of Cézanne, but I was initiated in a curious way.' He then recounts the infectious enthusiasm of a young portrait painter friend (probably Glyn Philpot, R.A.) who led him to Cézanne's *Provençal Landscape,* which had been lent by Gwendoline Davies to an exhibition of French art at the Burlington Fine Arts Club in May 1922. He made Courtauld 'at that moment' feel 'the magic, . . . and I have felt it in Cézanne's work ever since.'[8] That exhibition contained seventy-one works by all the major French artists of the last hundred years: from Corot, Daumier and Delacroix through Courbet, Manet and Degas to Renoir, Cézanne, Gauguin and Seurat. The loans came principally from English and French private owners, with some contributions from London dealers such as Oliver Brown of the Leicester Galleries and Percy Moore Turner of the Independent Gallery, whose Renoir, *Le Printemps, Chatou,* Courtauld was to buy five years later.

From May 1922 Courtauld began his career as a collector in earnest and over the next ten years or so he acquired some superb masterpieces. In 1921 he had bought two Thomas Gainsborough portraits which had once belonged to his mother's family. One of these, *Portrait of Mrs Gainsborough c.*1779, not only represents a leading eighteenth-century master but is a tender work with a delicate handling of paint that accords well with Renoir's *La Loge* (no. 75), which Courtauld was to buy in 1925. Already, surely, some idea of what he looked for in a painting was beginning to emerge. Apart from the Gainsboroughs, he started modestly by buying a Toulouse-Lautrec drawing *Woman in Bed* (no. 93), a late Renoir oil *Woman tying her Shoe* (no. 77), and a recent landscape of St Paul, 1921, by Jean Marchand (1883-1941), a painter then much admired by London art critics. The last two works came from Percy Moore Turner, who was to be a helpful guide and adviser.

It has been emphasized by those who knew him that Courtauld always made the final decision about buying a picture himself, and he would frequently look through a dealer's stock room. He often preferred to have paintings hanging for some weeks in his lovely Robert Adam house (built 1773-75) in Portman Square to make sure, before completing a purchase, that his choice was the right one. He greatly valued his wife's taste and judgement and the collection is very much the joint creation of Samuel and Elizabeth Courtauld.

P.M. Turner, who had run picture galleries in Paris from 1906 to 1914 before setting up in London in 1921, was a friend of Roger Fry, and the shape of the Courtaulds' collection, with its strong emphasis on Cézanne (twelve oils, if one includes the paintings acquired for the Tate Gallery

Henri de Toulouse-Lautrec 1864-1901
A woman lying in bed. 1896
soft pencil, watercolour wash on paper 30.3 x 48cm

through the Courtauld Fund), Seurat (twelve oils, including the monumental *Baignade* bought for the Tate in 1924 and now in the National Gallery); eight Degas oils and pastels and two bronzes; and five oils by Manet, plus important graphic works by him, seems to show at the very least that the Courtaulds shared with Fry a remarkable similarity of taste. Although Samuel Courtauld's tastes were much less austere than Fry's there are other interesting pointers.

Fry was born into a Quaker family; his father, Sir Edward Fry, had been a judge and at first opposed his son's wish to become a painter, after Roger had graduated from King's College, Cambridge, with a first-class honours degree in the natural sciences. Ten years older than Courtauld, Fry shared with him a nonconformist religious background, and after establishing a high reputation as an old master expert he underwent a conversion to modern art when he discovered Cézanne in 1906.[9] In 1916 he began to recognize the importance of Seurat but did not write a full-scale essay on him until 1926.[10] Fry and his friend the economist Maynard Keynes also obtained Courtauld's financial support for an artists' co-operative exhibition society, the London Artists' Association, formed in 1925. While it seems inconceivable that Courtauld was unaware of Fry's critical opinions, he was, like Fry, a most independent-minded man who would not care whether the 'experts' agreed with him once he had made up his mind about a picture.

Edgar Degas 1834-1917
Seated woman adjusting her hair. c.1884
chalk and pastel on paper 63 x 59.9cm

During 1923 Courtauld quickened his pace of acquisition, laid the foundation of his collection and defined its scope. He bought Daumier's *Don Quixote* (no.19); two small Degas bronzes of dancers and the pastel of *Seated Woman adjusting her Hair* (no.25); Manet's *Bord de la Seine à Argenteuil;* two Monets, the *Antibes* landscape (no.66) and the *Vase of Flowers* (no.65); two Cézannes, *L'Etang des Soeurs* (no.7) and the *Still Life with Plaster Cast* (no.13), the first truly major work to enter the collection; Gauguin's *Haymaking* (no.30) and the splendid early Seurat drawing *Standing Female Nude* (no.86), once doubted but now regarded as authentic.

In three successive years, 1924, 1925 and 1926, Courtauld bought three superb Cézannes: *Les Grands Arbres au Jas de Bouffan* (no.8), *La Montagne Sainte-Victoire* (no.9), and *Lac d'Annecy* (no.14); sometime in 1926 he acquired the finest of his three Gauguins, *Nevermore* (no.31); earlier, in 1924, he had bought two Manets, one through the Courtauld Fund, *La Serveuse de Bocks* (now in the National Gallery, London), the other for himself, the beautiful *Les Paveurs, Rue de Berne* (on loan from the Courtauld heirs to the Fitzwilliam Museum, Cambridge). The crowning glory of the Courtauld Collection, Manet's famous last great masterpiece, *A Bar at the Folies Bergère* (no.49), was bought in 1926 along with that strangely haunting and faintly comic image of Madeleine Knobloch in *A Young Woman Powdering Herself* by Seurat (no.84), one of three works by this artist acquired that same year.

This bare recital of names and titles gives some idea of the vigour with which Courtauld pursued his purpose. It is no accident that many of the paintings in his collection have become acknowledged by historians as key works in the careers of the artists who painted them, but Courtauld followed no set programme, he was guided by a natural taste of quite remarkable consistency. There were limitations to it, the only Picasso oil in the collection is the early oil *Child with Dove* of 1901 (no.70, on loan from a descendant), and the Picasso drawings are both from his neo-classical phase of the early 1920s (e.g. no.71, *Seated Female Nude*). There are no fauve or cubist paintings and the two Matisse drawings do not belong to the most adventurous period of the artist's career. Yet how appropriate it is that Courtauld should own Renoir's *Portrait of Ambroise Vollard* of 1908 (no.76), which he bought direct from Vollard in 1927, and thus preserve in company with his Impressionist paintings a portrait of the dealer who did so much to promote them. Mr and Mrs Courtauld continued to acquire important paintings such as the two Degas oils: *Woman at a Window* (no.22) and *Two Dancers on the Stage* (no.23), both bought in 1927, as was the Van Gogh *Peach Blossom in the Crau* (no.98). The following year they purchased the Van Gogh *Self-Portrait* and the Toulouse-Lautrec *Tête-à-Tête Supper* (no.92) as well as the intriguing Manet sketch for *Le Déjeuner sur L'Herbe* (no.48). Then came another painting by Gauguin, more small oil sketches by Seurat, a Bonnard (no.1) and a Vuillard (no.100), all of the highest quality.

Apart from an exquisite early Camillè Pissarro, *Lordship Lane Station* (no.72), a Cézanne and a Monet all acquired in 1936, Courtauld bought very little after 1930, except for work by a few young English artists who exhibited at the London Artists' Association; some old masters, a number of which were bequeathed to his family, were mainly bought during the last ten years of his life.

In 1931 Elizabeth Courtauld died and Samuel Courtauld's plans to establish a university department of art history were given new impetus by this sad event. For some years previously, Courtauld had been urged by his friends, Viscount Lee of Fareham and Sir Robert Witt, to endow such an institution, and in September 1929 he made a formal offer to the University of London which was accepted the following year. After his wife's death he gave the remainder of the lease of his house, 20 Portman Square, to the University, and in October 1932 the first students were admitted to the Courtauld Institute of Art. In 1932, 1934 and 1938 he gave a substantial part of his private collection to the Institute and his bequest of further works of art became effective in January 1948. His view of the purpose of the new institute and of the art historian appears in an unpublished essay:

> Today we need teachers and leaders for the great host of laymen whose interest in art might be awakened, or further stimulated. It is obvious that we must train enough scholars and experts to teach these more popular teachers of tomorrow, for though the purpose of him who aspires to enrich the lives of the laity cannot be to turn them into specialists, yet he himself must have been taught something more than the mere rudiments of art

Edgar Degas 1834-1917
Woman at a window. c.1871-72
oil on paper, mounted on linen 61.3 x 45.9cm

history; especially must he be able to judge whether such 'facts' as he has to make use of are really entitled to that name.[11]

Stimulated by Samuel Courtauld's munificent example, other benefactors have since enriched the collections of the Courtauld Institute. In 1934 Roger Fry died and in accordance with his wishes his family gave many of his paintings, Omega Workshop designs and West African sculpture to the Institute. We have included three of his Post-Impressionist paintings in this exhibition: the two Bonnards (nos.2 and 3) and the Derain (no.27) which he bought from the first Post-Impressionist exhibition. In 1952 Sir Robert Witt bequeathed his incomparable photographic archive and a collection of over 4000 old master prints and drawings, of which we have included a Boudin (no.6) and a Rodin (no.79). Further gifts and bequests followed, notably Mark Gambier-Parry's bequest of his grandfather's important collection of early Italian masters (in 1966) and Lord Lee of Fareham's bequest, which became effective in 1958 on the opening of the new Courtauld Galleries, to the cost of which Courtauld had made a handsome benefaction. A group of fine eighteenth and nineteenth century English watercolours was bequeathed and given by William Spooner and his wife in 1967.

Perhaps the most magnificent bequest, rivalling Samuel Courtauld's collection in quality, came to us from Count Antoine Seilern in July 1978. This was first put on public display at the Galleries, as the Princes Gate Collection, in July 1981. Count Seilern never wanted his name attached to his collection, yet it is of astonishing range and variety and reflects his personal taste in no uncertain manner.[12] Its strengths lie in the early Flemish and Italian schools, in the thirty-two Rubens paintings and studies and the group of Tiepolo oil studies. He also admired nineteenth and twentieth century artists; thus we have included from his collection works by Cézanne (no.15), Degas (no.26), three Kokoschkas (nos.44-46), a Manet oil sketch (no.50), a Berthe Morisot (no.67), a Pissarro and a Renoir (nos.74 and 78). Under the terms of his Will, however, we are forbidden to lend any of his marvellous old master drawings, of which there are some 280, to exhibitions outside London. Seilern was a rare combination of scholar and connoisseur. We have been indeed fortunate in our benefactors.

Dennis Farr
Director,
Courtauld Institute Galleries

Notes

1. Douglas Cooper, *The Courtauld Collection. A Catalogue and Introduction* (University of London, The Athlone Press, 1954), pp.9-76. With a Memoir of Samuel Courtauld by Anthony Blunt. For a general discussion about patronage and the growth of the nation's collections, see Dennis Farr, *English Art 1870-1940* (Oxford, 1978), pp.327-66.
2. Henri Perruchot, *La Vie de Gauguin* (Paris, 1961), p.271; English ed. (1963), p.248.
3. Cooper, *op. cit.,* p.69, notes that of the sixty-five paintings bequeathed by Caillebotte, only forty were accepted by the French authorities after two years' bargaining with Caillebotte's executors. When the Moreau-Nélaton gift was accepted in 1906 the works were deposited in the Musée des Arts Décoratifs until transferred to the Louvre with the bequest in 1934 (see Françoise Cachin, *Manet* (Grand Palais, Paris, 1983), no.62, note on p.172).
4. Cooper, *op. cit.,* p.73. The Davies Collection is now in the National Museum of Wales, Cardiff.
5. Cooper, *op. cit.,* p.1, in the essay by Anthony Blunt, Samuel Courtauld as Collector and Benefactor. There is also a short personal memoir by his niece, Miss Jeanne Courtauld, in *Samuel Courtauld's Collection of French 19th Century Paintings and Drawings. A centenary exhibition to commemorate the birth of Samuel Courtauld* (1976). In preparing his own essay, the present compiler is much indebted to Cooper, Blunt and Miss Courtauld for the information they have published.
6. The Unitarians were unorthodox and the sect derived its name from the central belief of its members in the 'one-ness' (or unity) of God. They did not accept the traditional Christian belief of God as Three Persons (Father, Son, and Holy Ghost), the Doctrine of the Trinity.
7. Extracts from these unpublished autobiographical essays and other family papers, the originals of which can no longer be traced, were published by Blunt, *loc. cit.*
8. Blunt, *loc. cit.,* pp.3-4.
9. Cooper, *op. cit.,* pp.48-49; see also Frances Spalding, *Roger Fry: Art and Life* (1980). Although Fry's perceptive book, *Cézanne. A Study of His Development,* did not appear until 1927, he had championed him since 1906.
10. Denys Sutton, *Letters of Roger Fry,* II (1972), pp.399-400: Fry to Vanessa Bell, letter dated 3 July 1916: 'You know that de Bergen and I had both been trying to get at Seurat, buying reproductions and studying him, and now I've gradually come to think he was the great man we'd overlooked — well all the conversations in Paris ended in discussing Seurat . . .'

    In an essay, Retrospect, published in *Vision and Design* (1920; Bullen ed. 1981), p.202, Fry wrote: 'But my most serious lapse was the failure to discover the genius of Seurat, whose supreme merits as a designer I had every reason to acclaim.' Fry bought Seurat's *La Luzerne, Saint-Denis,* c.1884-85 (now National Gallery of Scotland) in about 1926, probably from the Seurat exhibition held at the Lefevre Gallery, London, in May 1926.
11. Blunt, *loc. cit.,* pp.6-7.
12. Helen Braham, *The Princes Gate Collection* (1981), in her introduction to this catalogue, gives a biographical sketch of Count Seilern and an account of the growth of his collection.

The Pictorial Language of Impressionism and Post-Impressionism

The Courtauld Collection contains many paintings of exceptional quality and importance. As a group, these pictures well illustrate the evolving patterns of avant-garde painting in France between 1870 and 1900: the painting now described as Impressionist and Post-Impressionist. The prime concern of the Impressionist painters in the 1870s was to recreate the effect of immediate visual experience. This involved questions of technique as well as subject matter, as the painters sought appropriate means of translating their experiences into paint, at the same time insisting that they should depict only their own surroundings, the scenes of modern life amid which they lived. They rejected out of hand the preoccupation with historical subjects and the forms of past art which characterized much of the most popular and commercially successful painting of the period.

During the 1880s, though, the Impressionist painters came to feel that painting should not be restricted to such direct depiction alone and sought ways of enlarging the scope of their art and enriching its methods. In the same years a younger generation of artists was emerging who challenged the Impressionist assumption that the everyday world should form the basis of painting, insisting instead on the artist's powers of imagination.

Pissarro's *Lordship Lane Station,* 1871 (no.72), shows a thoroughly contemporary scene: a train leaving a railway station recently built to serve the Crystal Palace of Sydenham in South London, with new suburban houses beyond punctuating the remnants of the countryside. Although the train is the central focus of the picture, the brushwork treats all the elements in it with simple touches of paint (*taches*) which vary according to the shape and texture of the objects depicted; none is marked out for special treatment. The scene is arranged, too, so that the elements in it are informally spread out beside each other, not fitted into any artificial compositional framework; all are equally part of the diverse scene, all equally worthy of the painter's attention.

The weather in Pissarro's picture is overcast and the colour correspondingly subdued, roughly following the observed local colours of the objects. During the same years, in their sunlit scenes, the Impressionists were nevertheless using an increasingly wide range of clear colour to depict what they saw; Monet's *The Seine at Argenteuil, Autumn,* 1873 (no.64), is an example. Black is banished from the palette (Pissarro still used it in *Lordship Lane Station*) and clear blues are the darkest tones in the picture. All the forms are suggested by variations of colour, the shadows in soft blues which contrast with the great mass of orange,

Claude Monet 1840-1926
The Seine at Argenteuil, autumn. *(detail)* **1873**
oil on canvas 55 x 74.5cm

Alfred Sisley 1839-1899
Snow at Louveciennes. 1874
oil on canvas 46.3 x 55.8cm

Alfred Sisley 1839-1899
Boats on the Seine. 1877
oil on canvas, on plywood 37.2 x 44.3cm

pink and yellow by the bank of sunlit trees on the left. The brushwork again echoes the natural textures: crisp individual accents in the foreground reflections are set off against the dense, almost encrusted layers in the foliage. Here, and more obviously in the tree on the right, Monet improvised late in the execution of the picture by scraping away some of the paint with the handle of the brush, presumably to enliven and variegate the surface. Throughout, he focused on the overall effect of the scene at the expense of the details of the parts that make it up. The subject is very unassuming, a view down a backwater of the river Seine outside Paris, with the village of Argenteuil in the background. The composition, with the image balanced by its reflection in the water, carefully denies the spectator direct access by a perspectival lead-in into the scene. Even in such simple subjects as these, painted largely out of doors, the composition is the result of careful planning expressed in the artist's choice of where to place the easel and how to frame the chosen scene.

The river in Monet's picture is still, the scene comparatively timeless, but he and his colleagues were much drawn to the river as a place of work and play often with recreational sail-boats or, as in Sisley's *Boats on the Seine* of around 1877 (no.90), with cargo-barges. Sisley's canvas shows the Impressionists' technique of the 1870s at its sketchiest. Though in its own terms it is a finished picture, the off-white canvas priming, slightly warm in key, shows through between the brushstrokes in many places and contributes much to its overall tonality; its colour is clear and varied. Another painting by Sisley, *Snow at Louveciennes, c.*1874 (no.89), shows that by the mid 1870s, even in overcast scenes, the Impressionists were coming to use nuances of atmospheric colour. Here muted blues are set against soft salmons and beiges to suggest the effect of melting snow.

The life of Paris was a crucial theme in Impressionist painting of the 1870s, particularly its new boulevards and places of entertainment. Three pictures in the collection, by Renoir, Degas and Manet, explore the world of the theatre, focusing on the audiences and the total spectacle rather than on the performers alone. Renoir's *La Loge*, 1874 (no.75), shows a box in a fashionable theatre; it is the interval, for the lights are up. The girl sits quietly while her companion looks out through his opera glasses, presumably looking at someone in another box just as we, the viewers of the painting, are looking at the girl as she sits on display, her glasses in her gloved hand. Her face, more delicately handled than the rest of the painting, acts as its focus, while her dress and adornments are treated with free sweeps and touches. Black is used in the costumes here: Renoir was only briefly to abandon black, in the later 1870s and early 1880s. Degas, in *Two Dancers on the Stage,* 1874 (no.23), is watching the performance rather than the audience, but tells us nothing of its subject or plot, focusing instead on the grouping of figures, seen from an unexpected viewpoint high in a box or gallery, and on the way the footlights illuminate them. The oddity of our angle of vision is stressed by the truncated fragment of a third figure, cut off by the left margin.

Both Renoir's and Degas's pictures explore the ways in which members of an audience relate to the perfomance and to each other. Renoir focuses on the self-conscious interplay of fashionable theatre-goers, Degas on the way in which a stage action is transformed by the way it is seen. Each uses the painter's artifice to construct a pictorial form which can express his theme. At first sight the contrivance, the viewpoints and the ways the forms are arranged, can seem so spontaneous, so natural; it reveals its complexity only as we explore the pictures further.

In Manet's *A Bar at the Folies-Bergère,* 1881-82 (no.49), we are made quickly aware of the artist's artifice, both in the discrepancies between the principal image and its reflection in the mirror beyond and in the disjunction between the barmaid's detachment from us and her apparent attentiveness, in the reflection, to the tophatted man. Whereas in Renoir's *La Loge* the relationships between the figures and between them and us seem relatively unambiguous, Manet's canvas is from the start a complex of uncertainties. These were fully intended: the preparatory study for the picture and the initial stages of the final work (as seen in x-rays) present a far more coherent set of physical and spatial relationships. These complexities, as well as the sumptuous richness of the painted surface, are integral to the view which Manet presents here of the Folies-Bergére, a café-concert where the fashionable world mixed freely with the demi-monde.

In one very important respect Manet's canvas differs from Renoir's and Degas's and from the landscapes by Pissarro, Monet and Sisley. It was painted for the annual Paris Salon exhibition, the principal outlet for modern painting in France at the time, where only sizeable and distinctive canvases were likely to attract notice. The other paintings, by contrast, are characteristic of a different type of painting which was becoming more common in this period and whose emergence is of central importance in understanding the historical position of Impressionism. This is the smaller, more informal canvas, of size suitable to be hung in an urban domestic interior. Canvases of this type were becoming the stock-in-trade of the specialist art dealers who were just emerging as an independent profession during these years. Such smaller paintings would have stood little chance of attracting attention on the crowded walls of the Salon and indeed would have been unlikely to be accepted by the selection jury. It was to gain a viewing and (it was hoped) a market for such paintings that the Impressionists organized their series of group exhibitions between 1874 and 1886, in smaller, more informal exhibition rooms, with more spacious hanging than the Salon. Renoir's *La Loge* was shown at the first of these shows, at which reviewers christened the painters 'Impressionists'. From the 1880s on, dealers began increasingly to mount their own exhibitions of such works in similar rooms; Monet's *Antibes* (no.66) was first shown in 1888 in an exhibition of this type. Renoir's *Portrait of Ambroise Vollard* (no.76) shows one of these dealers, who was the first to pioneer Cézanne's and then Picasso's art.

Though an increasing market was developing for smaller paintings, the Impressionists were urged during the 1870s, even by critics who supported their aims, to go beyond the sketchiness of works such as Sisley's *Boats on the Seine* and to produce more highly finished paintings. Dealers and collectors too were more willing to buy paintings which were more elaborately treated and showed more interesting subjects. At the same time the painters came to feel that paintings need not be restricted to capturing a scene in a fresh representational shorthand. The term Impressionist has some value as a stylistic label when applied to these rapidly executed, freshly coloured landscapes and scenes of modern life (though not to Degas's work, for example); but the term Post-Impressionism, coined by Roger Fry in 1910 to characterize the reactions against Impressionism, has no such stylistic coherence, since these reactions took many varied forms; what united them was a dissatisfaction with naturalist aims as the prime goal of painting.

Two landscapes in the collection, Monet's *Antibes,* 1888 (no.66), and Pissarro's *The Quays at Rouen,* 1883 (no.73), show the ways in which the Impressionist landscapists sought in the 1880s to go beyond the informality of their previous paintings. Monet's *Antibes* shows a more dramatic scene than his earlier landscapes, a tree beside the Mediterranean, silhouetted against distant mountains, and the brushwork is more accentuated and more rhythmic, crisp dashes and hooks of colour animate the paint surface. The colour is strong, and is organized into oppositions of warm

Paul Cézanne 1839-1906
L'Étang de Soeurs, Osny. 1877
oil on canvas 60 x 73.5cm

Paul Cézanne 1839-1906
Le Lac d'Annecy. 1896
oil on canvas 65 x 81cm

pinks and oranges against cool greens and blues in an attempt to translate into paint the dazzling light of the South. At the same time the whole is given a sense of atmospheric unity by the repetition of touches of related colours throughout the canvas. It was with paintings such as this that Monet first found a regular market among collectors in the late 1880s. In contrast to the dynamic handling of Monet's painting, the surface of Pissarro's *The Quays at Rouen* is very homogeneous. The scene is translated into soft, evenly weighted touches, often parallel to each other, which unite sky, distance and foreground. The same colours, too, recur all through the picture; but whereas in Monet's *Antibes* this liaison is subordinated to the dominant oppositions of warm and cool, in Pissarro's picture the related colours are interwoven throughout the canvas to suggest a delicate all-over effect of coloured atmosphere.

During the 1870s Pissarro had worked closely with Cézanne and introduced him to the practices of open air landscape painting and the attentive scrutiny of natural forms and effects. Cézanne, like Pissarro, began in the late 1870s to introduce a much greater order and regularity into his brushwork. In *Les Grands Arbres au Jas de Bouffan* (no.8), painted at about the same date as Pissarro's Rouen scene, the more thickly painted parts of the picture are organized into sequences of regular vertical or diagonal strokes, particularly in the foliage of the trees. These give the painting a surface which is structured in emphatically two-dimensional terms, but not at the expense of a sense of form and space. Cézanne always insisted that the painter should translate what he saw (his *sensations*) into planes of colour on the picture surface; by their graduations of colour and tone these planes had to suggest the effect of forms in space.

Even while Cézanne was working with Pissarro in the 1870s his paintings threw great emphasis on the two-dimensional paint surface, as in the palette-knife work in *L'Etang des Soeurs* (no.7). (Despite Pissarro's son's childhood memories that this was painted in 1877 it seems more likely to belong to 1875, when Pissarro was using the knife in a very similar way.) During the later 1880s, Cézanne's rather rigid parallel hatching, seen in *Les Grands Arbres au Jas de Bouffan,* gave way to the softer, more open handling seen in *La Montagne Sainte-Victoire, c.*1887 (no.9), and then in turn to the sequences of juxtaposed colour planes of *Lac d' Annecy,* 1896 (no.14). Here, from close to, these planes seem to be very evenly weighted on the picture surface, but as one stands back to look at the whole painting they fall into place to suggest the physical structure of the scene, with a valley leading back from the lake beyond the nearer, darker hillside.

In these paintings Cézanne found ways of giving his canvases an emphatic internal organization without sacrificing his basically naturalist intentions. By contrast, Gauguin during the 1880s drew on Cézanne's and Pissarro's experiments in surface organization, as seen in nos.8 and 73, to create a type of painting which rejected specific natural appearances.

In *Haymaking*, 1889 (no.30), there are clear echoes of Cézanne's and Pissarro's parallel brushstrokes, for instance in the central bush and on the bank to its right. But Gauguin's strokes, unlike theirs, remain resolutely flat in effect, rather than evoking three-dimensional form; indeed, we are left very uncertain how the various parts of the scene fit together spatially. Gauguin's aim was to capture what he felt to be the essential rhythms of a place rather than its passing appearance at a particular moment; this gave him the liberty to simplify and rearrange the objects in a scene. He spoke in Brittany of seeking to capture the primitive mood he found in that remote corner of France; in this picture he seems to evoke it by the simplified shapes of the women and the haystacks.

Gauguin's view of nature is a rejection of what Impressionism had stood for. Van Gogh and Seurat, in their landscapes, also sought to go beyond Impressionism, though without rejecting its basically naturalist premises. Van Gogh painted *Peach Blossom in the Crau* (no.98) in 1889 at Arles in southern France after he had discovered Impressionist painting in Paris. Its varied, emphatic touch reflects the effect of Impressionism, particularly of Monet, on Van Gogh's technique, but the painting combines dense paint layers with drawing in a way Monet never did. The drawing, executed with the brush, delineates many forms quite crisply and at times with considerable delicacy, as in the thread-like crimsony lines seen in the trees and the houses beyond them. Thematically, too, Van Gogh sought to give his landscapes a significance which went beyond the Impressionist preoccupation with light effects. He saw a landscape as essentially a social milieu, and his paintings as vehicles for expressing his personal response to his subject, concerns which he felt linked him more closely to his own Dutch heritage than to Impressionism.

If Van Gogh's painting extends the expressive potential of Impressionist techniques, Seurat, in *The Bridge at Courbevoie,* 1886 (no.82), pursues further their concern with analysis. He substituted his neutral dot-like brushmark for their more varied touch in an attempt to make his handling

Paul Gauguin 1848-1903
Haymaking. 1889
oil on canvas 92 x 73.3cm

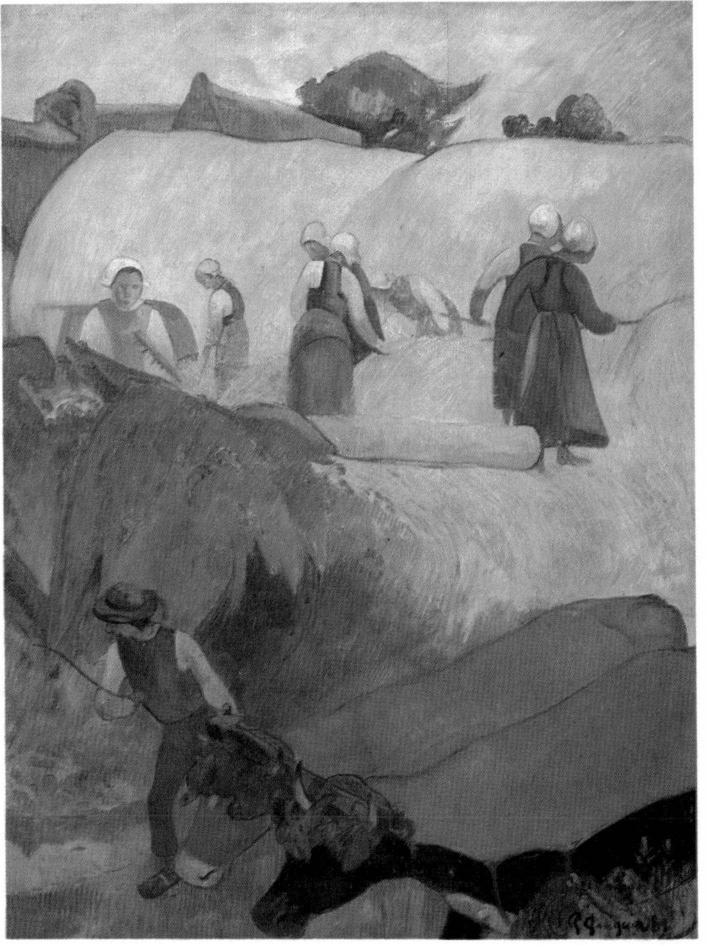

of light more scientific, to control more closely the quantities of each colour necessary to record the effects of direct and indirect lighting, reflections and shadows. It is often said that these dots and their varied colours fuse in the eye of the viewer to produce a more uniform colour. But this simply does not happen when one looks at the picture from a normal viewing distance (in this instance about two and a half metres); instead the particles of colour vibrate against each other to give a shimmer almost like the vibration of natural light, which is clearly the effect Seurat envisaged.

In his later paintings Seurat used the dot less to analyse light and colour than to create a mobile, decorative pictorial surface. In *A Young Woman Powdering Herself*, 1889 (no.84), the mood is one of playful irony rather than scientific analysis, as Seurat explores the contrast between his podgy mistress, wedged into her corset, and her tiny dressing table and mirror. The theme of cosmetics and self-adornment reflects the contrast between nature and artifice which fascinated Seurat and many of his contemporaries such as Toulouse-Lautrec. Here Seurat presented this contrast in the context of modern Paris and its fashions.

Gauguin's *Nevermore* (no.31), painted in Tahiti in 1897, used an image of life on an Oceanic island to explore a related theme. The naked girl listens anxiously, it seems, to the conversation of the two clothed figures beyond her; a contrast between innocence and knowledge, the title hinting that the state of nature can never be regained. Gauguin's image of Tahiti, in *Nevermore* and *Te Rerioa (The Dream),* 1897 (no.32), is in no way a realistic or documentary one. The settings are created out of a combination of Oceanic elements with reminiscences of ideas and images from many other cultures, both oriental and western. The broad, simplified technique of these late works further distances them from documentary depiction.

The Dream, as Gauguin described it in a letter, has at its core a deliberate uncertainty: whose dream is it? 'Everything is dream in the painting; is it the child, is it the mother, is it the rider on the path, or is it the dream of the painter? who knows?' The viewer is left to explore possible relationships within the picture, between the pensive women, the distant horseman, the sleeping child with the watchful carved figure on its cradle, and the stylized eroticism in the wall friezes. The picture is a work of the imagination, its subject is the imagination and its resonance is in the viewer's imagination; the whole is an archetypal statement of the Symbolist belief that art should concern itself with the inner vision, not with material appearances.

Cézanne's *Still Life with Plaster Cast, c.*1892-95 (no.13), is just as much concerned with the nature of art and asserts just as strongly the painter's control over the ingredients of the picture. Here these ingredients are objects; fruit and onions, a statuette and other paintings which the painter has physically brought together in his studio as he arranged his still-life subject; relationships between them are quite as complex as those in Gauguin's *The Dream.* Beyond the fruit and onions on the table appears more fruit, depicted in the picture leaning against the wall, a picture within a picture; and two statuettes appear, the Cupid and the cut-off figure at top right, the latter again in a picture within the picture. But the fruits are objects from nature, while the casts are works of art (or rather, since they are casts, reproductions of works of art) before the painter began his act of recreation. The space within the picture and the relative scale of the objects depicted create further complexities. However, all these forms, and the questions they raise about reality and illusion, about nature and art, are locked into a rich and calculated series of pictorial relationships; straight against curved, vertical against diagonal, warm against cool.

Cézanne's picture presents the artist as the architect of a pictorial world, built from natural objects and man's artefacts; Gauguin's presents the artist as dreamer, his world peopled by the fruits of the imagination. Both go far beyond the concerns of the Impressionist landscapists of the 1870s, stressing the artist's role as active creator rather than as recorder of the external world. Both Cézanne's and Gauguin's views of the role of the artist have had the greatest importance for the art of the twentieth century and much painting today is still centrally concerned with the arguments aroused by these rival points of view.

John House
Lecturer, Courtauld
Institute of Art

Constantin Guys 1802-1892
Two women with muffs. *c.*1863
pencil, pen and ink, brush and ink on paper
34.6 x 23.6cm

Honoré Daumier 1808-1879
The hypochondriac. *c*.1860-70
black chalk and watercolour on paper 20.7 x 27.1cm

Honoré Daumier 1808-1879
Don Quixote and Sancho Panza. ***c.*****1865**
oil on canvas 100 x 81cm

Édouard Manet 1832-1883
Le déjeuner sur l'herbe. 1862-63
oil on canvas 89.5 x 116.5cm

Édouard Manet 1832-1883
A bar at the Folies-Bergère. 1881-82
oil on canvas 96 x 130cm

Eugène Boudin 1824-1898
Deauville. 1893
oil on canvas 50.8 x 74.2cm

Claude Monet 1840-1926
The Seine at Argenteuil, autumn. 1873
oil on canvas 55 x 74.5cm

Camille Pissarro 1830-1903
Lordship Lane Station, Dulwich. 1871
oil on canvas 44.5 x 72.5cm

Claude Monet 1840-1926
Antibes. 1888
oil on canvas 65.5 x 92.4cm

Camille Pissarro 1830-1903
The quays at Rouen. 1883
oil on canvas 46.3 x 55.75cm

Claude Monet 1840-1926
Vase of flowers. c.1881-82
oil on canvas 100.4 x 81.8cm

Pierre-Auguste Renoir 1841-1919
Portrait of Ambroise Vollard. 1908
oil on canvas 81.6 x 65.2cm

Pierre-Auguste Renoir 1841-1919
La loge. 1874
oil on canvas 80 x 63.5cm

Pierre-Auguste Renoir 1841-1919
Woman tying her shoe. *c.*1918
oil on canvas 50.5 x 56.5cm

Pierre Bonnard 1867-1947
A young lady in an interior. 1906
oil on canvas 48.9 x 44.5cm

Henri de Toulouse-Lautrec 1864-1901
Jane Avril in the entrance of the Moulin Rouge, drawing on her gloves. 1892
pastel and oil on millboard, laid on panel 102 x 55.1cm

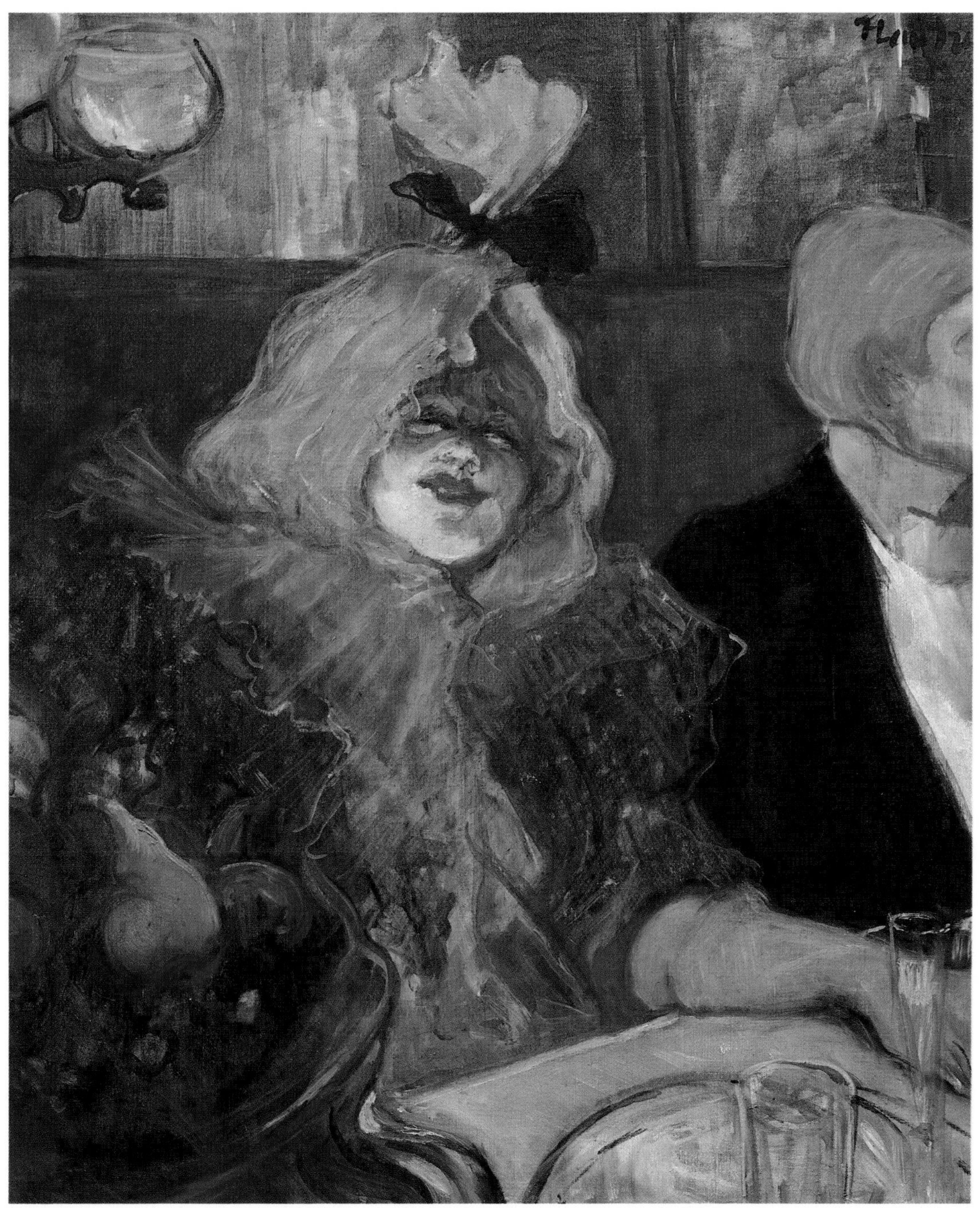

Henri de Toulouse-Lautrec 1864-1901
Tête-à-tête supper. 1899
oil on canvas 55.1 x 46cm

Edgar Degas 1834-1917
Two dancers on the stage. 1874
oil on canvas 61.5 x 46cm

Edgar Degas 1834-1917
After the bath; woman drying her chest. *c.*1889-90
pastel on paper, mounted on board 67.7 x 57.8

Georges Seurat 1859-1891
Man painting a boat. 1883
oil on panel 15.9 x 25cm

Georges Seurat 1859-1891
Beach at Gravelines. 1890
oil on panel 16 x 24.5cm

Georges Seurat 1859-1891
Study for the painting 'Le Chahut'. 1889
oil on panel 21.8 x 15.8cm

Georges Seurat 1859-1891
A young woman powdering herself. 1889-90
oil on canvas 95.5 x 79.5cm

Georges Seurat 1859-1891
The bridge at Courbevoie. 1886
oil on canvas 46.4 x 55.3cm

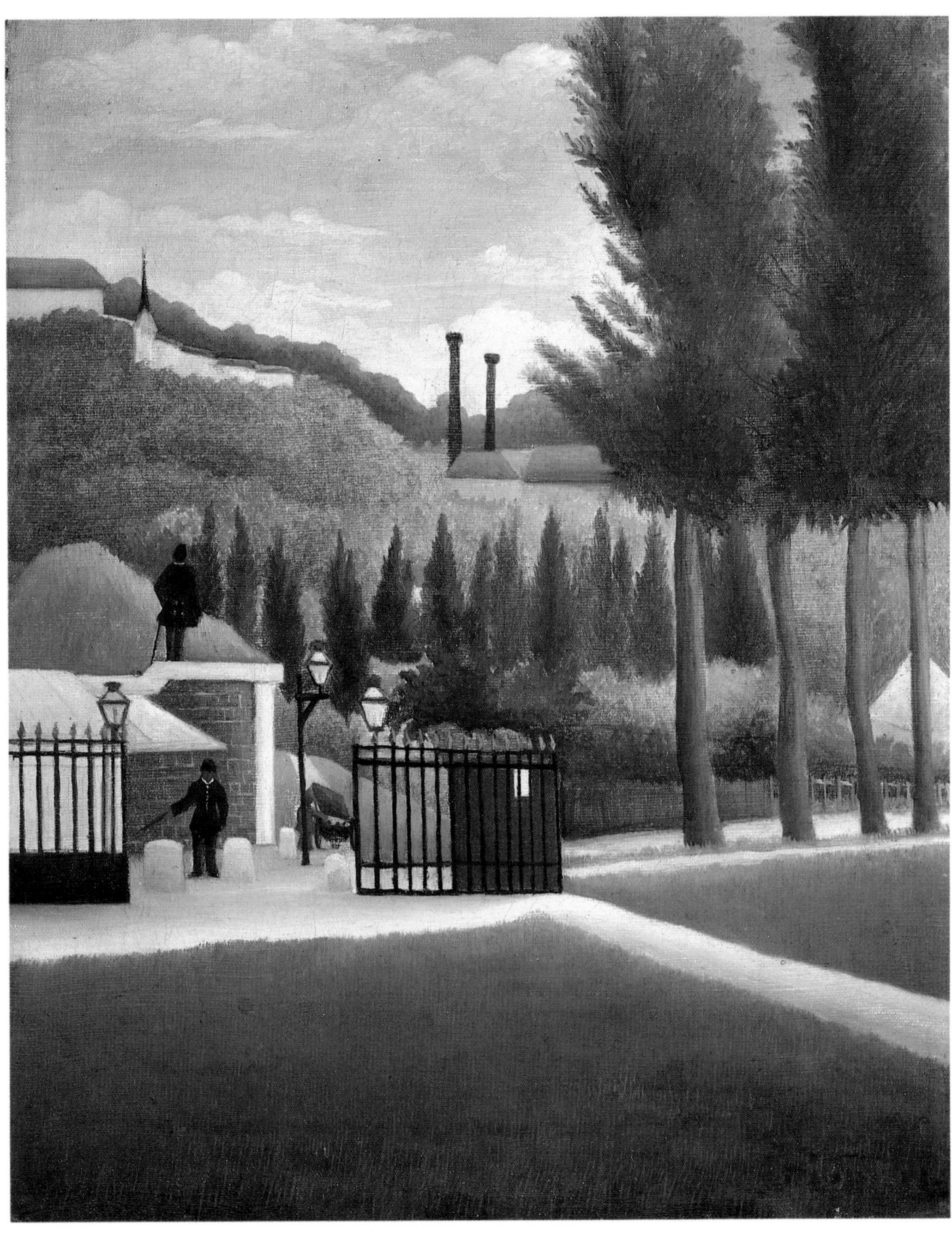

Henri Rousseau 1844-1910
The Customs Post. c.1900
oil on canvas 40.6 x 32.75cm

Paul Gauguin 1848-1903
Nevermore. 1897
oil on canvas 60.5 x 116cm

Paul Gauguin 1848-1903
Te Rerioa. 1897
oil on canvas 95.1 x 130.2cm

Paul Cézanne 1839-1906
Les grands arbres au Jas de Bouffan. c.1885-87
oil on canvas 65 x 81cm

Paul Cézanne 1839-1906
La montagne Sainte-Victoire. c.1886-88
oil on canvas 66.8 x 92.3cm

Paul Cézanne 1839-1906
The card-players. c.1892
oil on canvas 60 x 73cm

Paul Cézanne 1839-1906
The man with a pipe. c.1892
oil on canvas 73 x 60cm

Paul Cézanne 1839-1906
Still life with plaster cast. c.1895
oil on paper mounted on board 70.6 x 57.3cm

Paul Cézanne 1839-1906
Le lac d'Annecy. 1896
oil on canvas 65 x 81cm

Vincent Van Gogh 1853-1890
Peach blossom in the Crau. 1889
oil on canvas 65 x 81cm

Vincent Van Gogh 1853-1890
A tile factory. 1888
pencil and ink on wove paper 25.6 x 34.8cm

Paul Signac 1863-1935
Saint-Tropez. 1893
oil and pencil on panel 18.8 x 27.1cm

Édouard Vuillard 1868-1940
Interior with a screen. c.1909-10
oil over charcoal drawing on grey-buff card,
laid on panel 35.8 x 23.8cm

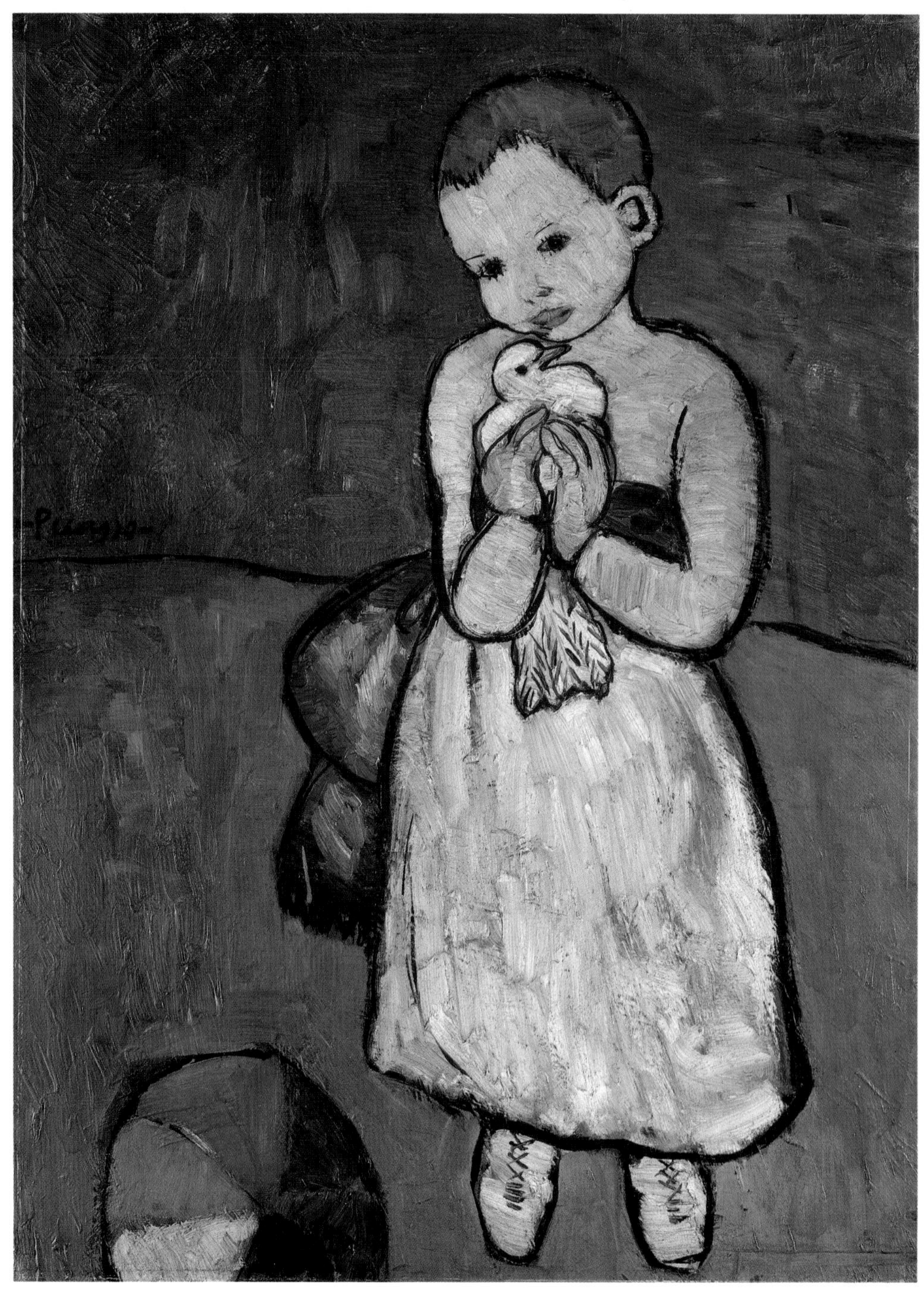

Pablo Picasso 1881-1973
Child with dove. 1901
oil on canvas 73 x 54cm

The Catalogue

It is thirty years since Douglas Cooper published his *The Courtauld Collection. A Catalogue and Introduction,* and just as he acknowledged the work of previous authors of catalogues of the Courtauld Collection published in 1934 and 1935, so we, too, must gratefully acknowledge our debt to him. Since 1954 much new research about the period covered by the Impressionist and Post-Impressionist part of the Courtauld Collection has been carried out and the compilers of the present catalogue have tried wherever possible to incorporate such new and relevant information about the paintings and drawings as has come to light.

Information about exhibitions has been restricted to those that shed light on the early history of a painting, and to the major retrospective exhibitions of a particular artist which have taken place since Mr Cooper's catalogue was published. Similarly, we have confined our references to the literature for each work to those standard books and catalogues raisonnés which contain essential information, referring the reader to Mr Cooper's catalogue for more extensive details. We have included within the text of the entries themselves references to books and articles which are the sources for particular information or opinions quoted therein. Where sources are quoted a number of times we have in some cases abbreviated the bibliographical references and provide a list of these abbreviations at the end of this catalogue. In the entries, the height of the support is given first, and measurements are in centimetres.

In the section dealing with provenance, 'with' or 'through' before a name indicates that a picture was handled by a dealer, either directly or as an intermediary.

Dennis Farr
William Bradford
Helen Braham

The Catalogue

BONNARD, Pierre 1867–1947
1 **The Blue Balcony** 1910
Oil on canvas, 52.5 x 76 cm
Signed, bottom left: "Bonnard"

PROVENANCE Bought from the artist by Bernheim-Jeune, Paris, 1910; Hugo Nattan; with Bernheim-Jeune 1912; Paul Vallotton, Lausanne; with Galerie Druet, Paris, 1928; Percy Moore Turner, London, from whom acquired by Samuel Courtauld *c.* 1928. Courtauld Gift 1932.
EXHIBITED *Oeuvres récentes (1910 et 1911) de Bonnard,* Bernheim-Jeune, Paris, May-June 1911 (14); Tate Gallery, 1948 (2); *Bonnard,* Kunsthaus, Zürich, June 1949 (90); Orangerie, Paris, 1955 (1); *Bonnard,* Royal Academy, London, January-March 1966 (92); Courtauld Centenary, 1976 (1); *Paintings from the Courtauld,* National Gallery, London, February-March 1983 (no cat.).
LITERATURE Home House Catalogue, no.50; Cooper, 1954, no.2; Jean et Henry Dauberville, *Bonnard. Catalogue raisonné de l'oeuvre peint,* II, 1906–19 (Eds. J. & H. Bernheim-Jeune, Paris 1968), p.209, no.625 (repr.).

Painted in 1910 (cf. Dauberville, *op.cit.),* the picture shows a view of the garden of the artist's house, "Ma roulotte", at Vernonnet, Eure. It is also known as *Le Balcon bleu* or *Jardin au printemps.* Photographs reproduced in Dauberville (*op.cit.,* p.22) show the wooden balcony at first floor level, which appears on the left of the painting. "Ma roulotte" literally means a gypsy caravan, and was used as a humorous name for Bonnard's country villa. The house appears to have been built on a slope, with the garden running down to a lower level beyond.

BONNARD, Pierre 1867–1947
2 **Landscape with Olive Trees and a Chapel** 1924
Oil on canvas, 48 x 61 cm
Signed, bottom right: "Bonnard"

PROVENANCE Bought from the artist by Bernheim-Jeune, Paris, 1924; Roger Fry. Fry Bequest 1934.
EXHIBITED *Bonnard,* Bernheim-Jeune, Paris, June-July 1924.
LITERATURE Home House Catalogue, no.94; J. et H. Dauberville, *Bonnard. Catalogue raisonné,* III, 1920–39 (Paris, 1973), p.185, no.1219 (repr.).

The landscape was painted at Cannet, near Cannes, in the Midi. Fry almost certainly acquired this painting from Bernheim-Jeune at, or soon after, the 1924 exhibition.

BONNARD, Pierre 1867–1947
3 **A Young Lady in an Interior** 1906
Oil on canvas, 48.9 x 44.5 cm
Signed, bottom right: "Bonnard"

colour plate, page 37

PROVENANCE Bought by Bernheim-Jeune, Paris, from Jos Hessel in 1919; Doctor Soubies; Roger Fry (after 1920). Fry Bequest 1934.
EXHIBITED *Artistes français des XIXe et XXe siècles,* Goupil Gallery, London, July 1920; *Bonnard,* Lyon 1954 (22), *Bonnard,* Royal Academy, London January-March 1966 (38); *Bonnard,* Haus der Kunst, Munich, October 1966–January 1967 (38); *Bonnard,* Orangerie, Paris, January-April 1967 (45).
LITERATURE *Bulletin de la Vie artistique,* 1re année, no.15 (1 July 1920), p.437, repr. no.16 (15 July 1920), p.467, and 6e année, no.21 (1 November 1925), repr. p.468; Home House Catalogue, no.95: J. et H. Dauberville, *Bonnard. Catalogue raisonné,* II (Paris 1968), p.48, no.405 (repr.).

Described variously as *Interior,* or *Woman on a Sofa,* or *Woman eating Grapes,* the sitter is the artist's mistress, Marthe, whose portrait he first painted in 1894 and whom he married in 1925. Another interior, also of 1906 and showing the same sitter, is recorded in Dauberville, *op.cit.,* no.406, *Femme devant le fenêtre (vue du pont Coulaincourt).*

BOUDIN, Eugène 1824–1898
4 **The Beach at Trouville** 1875
Oil on panel, 12.5 x 24.5 cm
Signed, bottom left: "E. Boudin" and inscribed, bottom right: "Trouville '75".

PROVENANCE Anon.; Louis de Wild, the Hague; sold Hotel Drouot, Paris, 29 May 1920 (lot 11); with Knoedler, London and New York, by 1925–26; Samuel Courtauld, July 1926. Courtauld Gift 1932.
EXHIBITED Tate Gallery, 1948 (3); Orangerie, Paris, 1955 (2); Courtauld Centenary, 1976 (2).
LITERATURE Jamot-Turner, no.2 (repr.), Home House Catalogue, no.20; Cooper, 1954, no.4 (repr.); Robert Schmit, *Eugène Boudin 1824–98,* I (Paris, 1973), p.363, no.1033 (repr.) as "Scène de Plage à Trouville".

One of many views of the beach at Trouville, a fashionable seaside resort in Normandy, France, painted by Boudin throughout his career. Robert Schmit *(op.cit.)* does not mention Louis de Wild as one of the early owners of this picture.

BOUDIN, Eugène 1824–1898
5 **Deauville** 1893
Oil on canvas, 50.8 x 74.2 cm
Signed, bottom left: "Deauville/E. Boudin 93". colour plate, page 28

PROVENANCE Dr. Delineau, Paris; Vente Dr. Delineau, Hotel Drouot, Paris, 1 February 1901 (lot 36); Devilder, Roubaix, France; with Wildenstein, Paris, London & New York; Samuel Courtauld, July 1936. Courtauld Bequest 1948 (on loan to Lord (R.A.) Butler until 1983).
EXHIBITED Tate Gallery, 1948 (4); Courtauld Centenary, 1976 (3).
LITERATURE Cooper, 1954, no.5 (where incorrectly dated 1883); Robert Schmit, *Eugène Boudin 1824–98,* III (Paris, 1973), p.210, no.3150 (repr.) as "Deauville. La Plage. Marée Basse" 1893.

Boudin painted a similar composition from the same viewpoint, but showing two horses and a cart with three figures in the left foreground, which is clearly dated 1893 (Schmit, *op.cit.,* p.210, no.3149 (repr.), same title as no.3150). There is another composition, taken further along the coast and showing part of the town of Deauville (Schmit, *op.cit.,* no.3152 (repr.) also of 1893). The painting, *Le Rivage de Deauville,* exhibited at the Salon de la Société Nationale des Beaux-Arts, 1894 (152, illus. cat.p.59) shows a totally different composition. The reference in Cooper (*loc.cit.)* to the Vente Atelier Boudin, 1899 (lot 102), refers to a *Deauville* composition 40 x 70 cm which is reproduced in Schmit *(op.cit.,* no.3356) and wrongly described as belonging to the Courtauld collection. This painting is not related to the *Deauville* described in this exhibition.

BOUDIN, Eugène 1824–1898

6 **Figures on a Beach, Trouville** 1866

Preliminary drawing with pencil; watercolour washes, with some drawing with the point of the brush; on blue wove paper. The sheet folded horizontally, twice, and unevenly trimmed at all sides.
10.3 x 16 cm
Unsigned.

Dated by the artist in pencil, top right: "1866", and bottom right: "66". Stamped in blue, bottom right: "E.B" (Lugt 828).
Verso: Slight sketch of three standing women, one with a parasol, in black chalk.
PROVENANCE Included in Boudin sale(?) date unknown; with Lefèvre Galleries, London, from whom purchased by Sir Robert Witt, late 1927 or early 1928. Witt Bequest, 1952 (no.2337).
EXHIBITED *300 Years of French Taste,* Batsford, London, 1932; *Drawings from the Witt Collection at the Courtauld Institute of Art,* Arts Council of Great Britain, 1953 (72); *Old Master Drawings from the Witt Collection,* Nottingham University, October-November 1966 (5); Nottingham University, 1969; Arts Council (2).
LITERATURE *Hand-list of the Drawings in the Witt Collection* (1956), no.2337.

The drawing is related in a general way to details of seated women with parasols in the Trouville oil compositions of 1866–67 (cf. Schmit, *op.cit.,* I, nos.397 *(Beach Scene,* 1866); 398 (*The Beach at Trouville,* 1866) and 410 (*The Beach at Trouville "The Conversation",* 1867).
The stamp of the artist's initials, bottom right (mistaken for a signature in the *Hand-list..., ibid.*) indicates that the watercolour was probably included in one of the sales of Boudin's work. Three such sales were held during the artist's lifetime (in 1878, 1879 and 1888) and there were two posthumous sales (in 1899 and 1900: Lugt, *op.cit.,* under 285, 286). As yet, it has not been possible to establish which sale included the Witt sheet.

CÉZANNE, Paul 1839–1906

7 **L'Étang des Soeurs, Osny** 1877

Oil on canvas, 60 x 73.5 cm
Unsigned.

PROVENANCE Camille Pissarro, Paris; Alphonse Kann, St. Germain-en-Laye; with Galerie Barbazanges, Paris; Reininghaus, Vienna; with Galerie Barbazanges, Paris; with Alex. Reid, Glasgow; with Agnew, London, from whom acquired by Courtauld in July 1923. Courtauld Gift 1932.
EXHIBITED *Französische Kunst des 19.u. 20 Jahrhunderts,* Kunsthaus, Zürich, November 1917 (19); *Masterpieces of French Art of the 19th Century,* Agnew, London, July 1923 (3); *Cézanne,* Leicester Galleries, London, June 1925 (15); Tate Gallery, 1948 (5); *Cézanne,* Edinburgh and London, 1954 (16); Orangerie, Paris, 1955 (3); Courtauld Centenary, 1976 (4).
LITERATURE Home House Catalogue, no.74; Venturi, *Cézanne,* no.174 (repr.); Cooper, 1954, no.6 (repr.); William Rubin (ed.), *Cézanne. The Late Work* (London and New York 1977–78) pp.5-6 (repr.).

Painted while Cézanne was staying with Camille Pissarro at Pontoise in 1877. Osny is not far from Pontoise. This painting has also been erroneously called *Bois des Soeurs*. it should be noted that Pissarro's *Festival at L'Hermitage,* also in this exhibition (cat.no.74), was once called *Festival at Osny* and is now dated to *c.* 1878, and that Cézanne also painted several views of the Hermitage at Pontoise in 1877.
Lawrence Gowing ('The Logic of Organized Sensations' in William Rubin (ed.), *Cézanne. The Late Work,* 1977–78) has noted that Cézanne has reverted in this picture to an earlier (i.e. 1866) technique, the use of the palette knife; but here colour is applied in "patches of colour with straight edges applied with the knife" and that "colour differentiation took its place as a chief medium of definition in Cézanne's art" in 1877, and this picture thus has a most crucial place in his development. Gowing also remarks that although this technique is "a last reminiscence of Courbet, who had lately died, and of the style that Cézanne had based on him", it also looks forward to the structure of parallel alignments of colour patches which was to be a feature of his work of the late 1890s up to his death.

CÉZANNE, Paul 1839–1906
8 **Les Grands Arbres au Jas de Bouffan** *c.*1885–87
Oil on canvas, 65 x 81 cm
Unsigned.

colour plate, page 50

PROVENANCE Ambroise Vollard, Paris; with Paul Rosenberg, Paris; Samuel Courtauld 1924. Courtauld Bequest 1948.
EXHIBITED *Grands Maîtres du 19me Siècle,* Paul Rosenberg, Paris, April 1922 (11); *Cézanne,* Leicester Galleries, London, June 1925 (16); Tate Gallery, 1948 (11); *Cézanne,* Edinburgh and London, 1954 (33); Orangerie, Paris, 1955 (8); Courtauld Centenary, 1976 (7).
LITERATURE Jamot-Turner, no.20 (repr.); Venturi, *Cézanne* no.475 (repr.); Cooper, 1954, no.11 (repr.).

The Jas de Bouffan was the name of the house and estate owned since 1859 by the artist's father, Louis-Auguste Cézanne, a wealthy banker. It lay some two kilometres to the west of Aix-en-Provence. After his father's death in 1886, the property and a sizeable income passed to Paul Cézanne; although in 1899, after his mother's death two years earlier, in order to settle his father's affairs, Cézanne was obliged to sell the Jas de Bouffan, greatly to his regret.
Cézanne was very fond of the house and garden of the Jas de Bouffan, and painted many views of them from 1866 to 1899. It was here that he found the solitude he needed to work, either in the garden or in the little studio beneath the roof with its views over the vineyards and the hills of Les Lauves.

CÉZANNE, Paul 1839–1906
9 **La Montagne Sainte-Victoire** *c.*1886–88
Oil on canvas, 66.8 x 92.3 cm (approx. 0.3 cm wide area of "made-up" paint on all four sides to edge of modern wooden slip).
Signed, bottom right: "P. Cezanne".

colour plate, page 51

PROVENANCE Given by the artist in 1896 to Joachim Gasquet, Aix-en-Provence; sold by Gasquet to Bernheim-Jeune, Paris, 1908; through Percy Moore Turner, London; acquired Samuel Courtauld, April 1925, Courtauld Gift 1934.
EXHIBITED Société des Amis des Arts, Aix, March-April 1896; *Französische Kunst des 19.u. 20. Jahrhunderts,* Kunsthaus, Zürich, November 1917 (35); *Grands Maîtres du 19me Siècle,* Paul Rosenberg, Paris, April 1922 (10); Centenary Exhibition, Norwich. October 1925 (63); *Cézanne,* Galerie Pigalle, Paris, 1929 (6); *French Art,* Royal Academy of Arts, London, 1932 (457); Tate Gallery, 1948 (10); *Cézanne,* Art Institute, Chicago, and Metropolitan Museum, New York, 1952 (52); *Cézanne,* Edinburgh and London, 1954 (39); Orangerie, Paris, 1955 (9); Courtauld Centenary, 1976 (8); National Gallery, London, Feb.-March 1983 (no cat.).
LITERATURE Home House Catalogue, no.75; Venturi, *Cézanne,* no.454 (repr.); J. Gasquet, *Cézanne* (Paris 1921), 79; Cooper, 1954, no.12 (repr.); Henri Perruchot, *Cézanne,* 1961) pp.263-64; John Rewald, *Cézanne, Geffroy et Gasquet; suivi de souvenirs, sur Cézanne de Louis Aurenche et de lettres inédites* (Paris, 1960), 20, 29, 39, 49, 50.

This is one of the few signed works by Cézanne, and shows the mountain which lies a few miles to the north-east of the artist's birthplace, Aix-en-Provence. It was one of his favourite motifs, which he painted from several viewpoints. A variant of this composition, also taken from the same vantage-point, but including the trunk of a pine-tree on the right, and of slightly later date, is in the Phillips Memorial Gallery, Washington DC. A watercolour, very similar in composition to the Courtauld picture, is listed by Venturi (no.914), and once belonged to the artist's son, Paul.
When this painting, along with a *Champ de blé,* was shown by invitation of the Société des Amis des Arts at Aix (a society of amateur artists) in 1896, it was received with incomprehension and dislike.
Comparisons between photographs of Mont Sainte-Victoire taken from approximately the same position as that used by Cézanne, and the finished composition, show interesting differences in perspective. The middle-distance, that is the valley lying between the spectator and the mountain, appears compressed and the height of the mountain is increased in the painting, so as to suggest that it is closer to the viewer than in reality (cf. Erle Loran, *Cézanne's Compositions,* (1st ed. 1943), Berkeley, Univ. of California Press, 3rd ed. 1963, p.60; Rewald, *The Ordeal of Paul Cézanne* (London 1950), pls.84, 85).
Joachim Gasquet, the first owner of the picture, was a poet, son of Cézanne's contemporary, Henri Gasquet, and one of a group of young admirers of Cézanne's work in the 1890s. They met in 1896, but the friendship, at first very cordial, soon began to cool and by 1904 the break was complete (cf. John Rewald, *The Ordeal of Paul Cézanne,* 1950, 153-55; and Rewald, *Cézanne, Geffroy, et Gasquet,* 1960, 20ff.). In 1908, Gasquet sold this painting for the very high price of 12,000 francs to Bernheim-Jeune, two years after Cézanne's death.

CÉZANNE, Paul 1839–1906
10 **Pot of Flowers and Pears** *c.*1888–90
Oil on canvas, 46 x 56.25 cm
Unsigned.

PROVENANCE C. Hoogendijk, Amsterdam; with Paul Rosenberg, Paris; Marquis de Rochecouste, Paris; with Galerie Barbazanges, Paris; with Bignou, Paris; with Alex. Reid and Lefevre, London; acquired by Samuel Courtauld, January 1928. Courtauld Bequest 1948 (H.H. 209).
EXHIBITED *Cézanne,* Bernheim-Jeune, Paris, June 1926; *19th Century French Painters,* Knoedler, London, 1926 (21); de Hauke Gallery, New York, April 1927; Tate Gallery, 1948 (12); *Cézanne,* Edinburgh and London, 1954 (40); Orangerie, Paris, 1955 (10); Courtauld Centenary, 1976 (9).
LITERATURE Jamot-Turner, no.25 (repr. as *La Primule*); Venturi, *Cézanne,* no.623 (repr.); Cooper, 1954, no.13 (repr.).

Cooper considers the Venturi dating of this painting, to 1890–94, to be too late and proposes 1888–90 on the basis of its brushwork and tonality.
The painting shows a table, and a white plate with two pears; to the right a pot containing a large leafy plant (? primula), and in front another pear; behind is seen a chassis of a canvas, and the indication of another canvas leaning against the wall to the left.

CÉZANNE, Paul 1839–1906
11 **The Card-Players** *c.*1892
Oil on canvas, 60 x 73 cm
Unsigned.

colour plate, page 52

PROVENANCE With Paul Cassirer, Berlin; Dr. Julius Elias, Berlin; J.B. Stang, Oslo; with Alfred Gold, Berlin; acquired by Samuel Courtauld, April 1929. Courtauld Gift 1932.
EXHIBITED *Cézanne,* Galerie Pigalle, Paris 1929 (8); *French Art,* Royal Academy, London, 1932 (392); Royal Scottish Academy, Edinburgh, March 1933 (142); *Chefs d'Oeuvres de l'Art Français,* Paris 1937 (256); Tate Gallery, 1948 (13); *Cézanne,* Edinburgh and London, 1954 (52); Orangerie, Paris 1955 (11); Courtauld Centenary, 1976 (10).
LITERATURE Jamot-Turner, no.23 (repr.); Home House Catalogue, no.1 (repr.); Venturi, *Cézanne,* p.59, no.557 (repr.); Cooper, 1954, no.14 (repr.); Bernard Dorival, *Cézanne* (Paris 1948), pp.62-65; Kurt Badt, *Die Kunst Cézannes* (Munich, 1956) pp.64-98 (repr. fig.11).

There are five versions of this subject, which greatly preoccupied Cézanne during the 1890s. Three of these pictures (Venturi nos.556-58), although differing in size, are more or less identical and contain only two figures: the present picture, another in the J.V. Pellerin Collection (identical with the Courtauld painting except for a highlight on the front of the bottle), and a third in the Louvre (Legs Camondo). The remaining two versions (Venturi nos.559 and 560) are larger and contain three card-players, as well as spectators. Both paintings are in the United States of America (Stephen C. Clark, New York, and Barnes Foundation, Merion, Pa.).
Cézanne also painted and drew a number of studies for the individual figures in different poses, all of which are more or less complete in themselves. Venturi reproduced four studies for the figure on the left, and seven for the right-hand figure. (cf. Adrien Chappuis, *The Drawings of Paul Cézanne. A Catalogue Raisonné,* 1973, I, p.250, nos.1092-95).
One of the oil studies (Venturi no.564), *Man with a Pipe,* is also in the Courtauld Collection and is catalogued below.
The theme of card-players is rare in 18th and 19th century French art and it may have been suggested to Cézanne by the *Soldiers playing at Cards,* attributed to the School of Louis Le Nain, which has hung in the Musée Granet at Aix since 1855. Kurt Badt (*op.cit.*) not only postulates a later date (*c.*1899) for this and the two related versions, a view not shared by most authorities, but also sees in them an elaborate symbolism which does not seem to be supported by the facts. The exact sequence in which the five were painted within the generally accepted span, 1890–92, is also debated: the two larger versions (with five figures) are sometimes regarded as earlier than the three smaller (i.e. two figure) compositions (Lawrence Gowing, 'Notes on the Development of Cézanne', *Burlington Magazine,* vol.98, 1956, 191); or the other way round (Douglas Cooper, "Two Cézanne Exhibitions", *Burlington Magazine,* vol.96, 1954, 380). Theodore Reff ("Painting and Theory in the Final Decade", *Cézanne. The Late Work,* ed. William Rubin (New York 1977, pp.17-21), prefers to see the smaller compositions as a later development, in which Cézanne simplifies and concentrates on the essentials, a view shared by this compiler.

CÉZANNE, Paul 1839–1906
12 **The Man with a Pipe** *c.*1892
Oil on canvas, 73 x 60 cm
Unsigned.

colour plate, page 53

PROVENANCE Ambroise Vollard, Paris; Paul Gallimard, Paris; with Galerie Barbazanges, Paris; with Bignou, Paris; with Alex. Reid and Lefevre, London, from whom acquired by Samuel Courtauld 10 October 1927. Courtauld Gift 1932.
EXHIBITED *La Libre Esthétique, Brussels,* 1904 (no number); *Cézanne,* Galerie Pigalle, Paris 1929 (9); Tate Gallery, 1948 (14); *Cézanne,* Edinburgh and London 1954 (51); Orangerie, Paris 1955 (12); Courtauld Centenary, 1976, (11); National Gallery, London, February-March 1983 (no catalogue).
LITERATURE Jamot-Turner, no.22 (repr.); Home House Catalogue, no.9; Venturi, *Cézanne,* no.564 (repr.); Cooper, 1954, no.15 (repr.).

The model is the same as that for the left hand figure in *The Card-Players* (see above, cat.no. 11). He was a peasant gardener who posed for Cézanne and is referred to by Gustave Coquiot (*Paul Cézanne,* Paris 1919, p.97) as "le sieur Paulet", but by Georges Rivière (*Le Maître Paul Cézanne,* Paris 1923, p.217), as "le père Alexandre". Rivière had been introduced to Cézanne by Renoir in 1877 (cf. Rewald, *The Ordeal of Paul Cézanne,* London 1950, p.83), and became the artist's friend and champion, filling the place occupied by Emile Zola, who had by then abandoned art criticism. Zola's break with Cézanne, whom he had known since childhood, took place in March 1886, after the publication of *L'Oeuvre,* in which the painter recognised a portrait of himself in the fictional artist-hero, Claude Lantier, described by Zola as the "abortive genius".
This painting has been dated to 1893 by Lawrence Gowing in the Tate Gallery exhibition catalogue, in line with his views about the dating of the smaller versions of *The Card-Players* quoted for cat.no.11 of this exhibition.

CÉZANNE, Paul 1839–1906
13 **Still Life with Plaster Cast** *c.*1895
Oil; on a warm-white wove paper. The sheet unevenly trimmed, apparently to a ruled line in pencil, at the top, left and right sides. The bottom left corner of the sheet torn away (backing tinted, to make it up). Pin holes visible bottom left, right, and centre. Laid on board. 70.6 x 57.3 cm
Unsigned.

colour plate, page 54

PROVENANCE With Bernheim-Jeune, Paris; Dr. G. Jebsen, Oslo; with Paul Rosenberg, Paris; with Alex. Reid, Glasgow; with Agnew, London, from whom acquired by Samuel Courtauld in 1923. Courtauld Bequest 1948 (H.H. 183).

EXHIBITED *Fransk Malerkonst d. 19 Jaarhonderts,* Copenhagen, May 1914 (20); *Cézanne,* Montross Gallery, New York, January 1916 (16); *Masterpieces of French Art of the 19th Century,* Agnew, Manchester, October 1923 (5); Tate Gallery, 1948 (15); *Cézanne,* Edinburgh and London 1954 (50); Orangerie, Paris 1955 (13); Courtauld Centenary, 1976 (12); *Cézanne. The Late Work,* Museum of Modern Art, New York, 1977 (23) and toured to Houston, Tex., and Paris 1977–78; National Gallery, London, February-March 1983 (no cat.).
LITERATURE Jamot-Turner, no.24 (repr.); Venturi, *Cézanne,* no.706 (repr.); Cooper, 1954, no.16 (repr.); William Rubin (ed.), *Cézanne. The Late Work* (New York and London, 1977–78), pp.30-32 (repr.).

The dating of this work is traditionally ascribed to *c.*1895 (Venturi, Cooper and Rewald), but Lawrence Gowing (in 1954 Tate Gallery exhibition catalogue) and Theodore Reff (Rubin (ed.), *Cézanne. The Late Work,* pp.30-32) argue for an earlier date. Reff asserts that the painting was one of two still-lifes that, according to Paul Signac, Paul Alexis brought back from Aix in 1892 (see also: J. Rewald, *Cézanne: sa vie, son oeuvre, son amitié pour Zola* (Paris, 1939), p.336, where the date 1891 is given). If so, an earlier dating might be sustainable on circumstancial evidence alone. However Reff misread Rewald's text and stated 1892 when, in fact, the event recorded by Rewald took place in 1891. There is no proof that the *Still Life with Plaster Cast* was one of the two still-lifes brought back by Alexis, and stylistically the arguments for an earlier dating (i.e. to 1891) are not conclusive. Rewald, in his note for this picture in the catalogue to the *Cézanne. The Late Work* exhibition (see above), states that it is a "moot question whether this still-life was painted in Paris or in Aix". He also notes that the intensely blue drapery appears in a number of still-life arrangements which cannot be identified with any particular period or place, "except that it does not show up in compositions dating after 1895 . . ." Rewald, in the same catalogue, retains the date *c.*1895 for this painting,

while acknowledging that Gowing and Reff prefer *c.*1892.
Some of the elements in this still-life, such as the plaster cast of a Cupid, once attributed to Pierre Puget, and now identified as by Francois Duquesnoy (*c.*1630–40), and the cast of a flayed man (the so-called *Anatomy* formerly attributed to Michelangelo), which here appears as a painted copy (Venturi 709) at the top right-hand corner of the composition, are still preserved in Cézanne's former studio at Les Lauves, Aix.
Cooper lists another still-life in which the plaster cupid appears (Venturi no.707; Nationalmuseum, Stockholm) as well as numerous drawings and watercolours which are related to this motiff.
The composition is one of the most complex and intriguing of the late still-lifes. The plaster cast is seen "close-up" and appears larger than life-size; the artist has also attempted to extend his angle of vision so as to bring in as much of the studio surroundings as possible. Thus objects such as the apple on the steeply-tilted floor near to the copy of the *Anatomy,* are shown as large as, if not larger than, the apples on the table in the foreground. The "real" blue drapery in the left foreground merges with the painted blue drapery on the canvas of the still-life which leans against the studio wall on the left; similarly the foliage of the "real" onion fuses with the table leg in the same still-life. Cézanne has also contrasted the "real" plaster cupid with the painted plaster figure of the flayed man which appears on the canvas leaning against the back wall of the studio, and has framed the cupid by the inclined plane of a canvas occupying the middle-distance of the composition.
The deliberate use of paradox, and the highly contrived spatial relationships between the various elements in this composition, anticipate the innovations of the Cubists a decade later.

CÉZANNE, Paul 1839–1906
14 **Le Lac d'Annecy** 1896
Oil on canvas, 65 x 81 cm colour plate, page 55
Unsigned.

PROVENANCE Purchased from the artist by Ambroise Vollard, Paris (1897); C. Hoogendijk, Amsterdam; with Paul Rosenberg, Paris; Marcel Kapferer, Paris; with Bernheim-Jeune, Paris; acquired through Percy Moore Turner by Samuel Courtauld, January 1926. Courtauld Gift 1932.
EXHIBITED *Grands Maîtres du 19me Siècle,* Paul Rosenberg, Paris, April 1922 (14); *Les Grandes Influences,* Paul Rosenberg, Paris, January 1925 (14); *Cézanne,* Galerie Pigalle, Paris, 1929 (7); *French Art,* Royal Academy, London, 1932 (505); Tate Gallery, 1948 (16); *Cézanne,* Edinburgh and London, 1954 (55); Orangerie, Paris, 1955 (14); Courtauld Centenary, 1976 (13).
LITERATURE Jamot-Turner, no.27 (repr.); Home House Catalogue, no.8; Venturi, *Cézanne,* no.762 (repr.); Cooper, 1954, no.17 (repr.); J. Rewald, *Cézanne, Geffroy et Gasquet . . .* (Paris 1960), 27, 28, repr. pl.8; William Rubin (ed.), *Cézanne. The Late Work* (New York and London 1977–78), pp.26, 64 (repr. col.pl.68).

Painted while Cézanne was on holiday at Talloires on the shores of Lake Annecy (Haute Savoie) in July 1896. The view is taken from Talloires and on the far side of the lake is the Château de Duingt, half-hidden by trees.
The picture is notable for the intensity of the blues and greens by which the artist suggests an effect of limited atmospheric recession; this effect is counterbalanced by the strong horizontals of the far shore of the lake and the verticals of the reflections in the water of the Château, reflections which are elongated far beyond their actual appearance in nature. Cézanne is here beginning to move towards the complex web and infinitely subtle gradations of colour, especially blue, which characterize his work after 1900, and of which *'Route Tournante'* (cat.no.15) is an excellent example.
In a letter to Gasquet of 21 July 1896 written from Talloires (quoted by Rewald, *op.cit.*), Cézanne describes the view of Lake Annecy shown here, and comments that it "seems to lend itself to the linear exercises of young lady tourists". This was an allusion to the superficial picturesqueness of the location which, by implication, Cézanne was determined to avoid in his rendering of the subject.

CÉZANNE, Paul 1839–1906
15 **'Route Tournante'** after 1900
Oil on canvas, 73 x 92 cm
Unsigned.

PROVENANCE Ambroise Vollard, Paris (until 1937); Sir Kenneth Clark, London, from whom acquired by Count Antoine Seilern in August 1941. Seilern Bequest (Princes Gate Collection, no.209) 1978.
EXHIBITED *The Princes Gate Collection,* Courtauld Institute Galleries, London, from 17 July 1981 (10).
LITERATURE Venturi, *Cézanne,* no.1532 (repr.); A.S. [Antoine Seilern], *Paintings and Drawings of Continental Schools other than Flemish and Italian at 56 Princes Gate, London SW7,* III (London, 1961), p.58 (repr.); Kenneth Clark, *Another Part of the Wood* (1974), pp.240-41.

Presumably acquired by Vollard from the artist, or from the artist's son soon after Cézanne's death, the picture remained in Vollard's possession until Kenneth Clark bought it from him in about 1937 (cf. Clark's autobiography, *Another Part of the Wood;* and French packer's label, "Ch. Pottier/ Emballeur", inscribed with Clark's name and the date "14.10.37"). The

stretcher bears a pencil inscription "Village et Eglise", possibly in Vollard's hand, but Venturi published this painting as *'Route Tournante'*.
Although it has not been possible to identify the location with any precision, comparsion with other late works such as the *Garden of Les Lauves* (Venturi no.1610), where a similar broad expanse of horizontal bands of terrain appears, suggests that this painting may be a view from Cézanne's studio at Les Lauves which stood on high ground to the north of Aix, and which he occupied from September 1902. On the eastern side, in Cézanne's day, a view of Montagne Sainte-Victoire could be seen; to the south lay Aix, and it is possible this is a view to the north. The church steeple does not appear to resemble that of St. Jean de Malte, which lay to the west of Aix and in any case, more of the town itself would have been visible. In recent years all the area around Les Lauves has been intensively developed and the views once enjoyed by Cézanne are now hidden by high-rise buildings.
The colourman and dealer, Père Tanguy, noted Cézanne's habit in his later years of apparently leaving canvases unfinished (cf. Rewald, *The Ordeal of Paul Cézanne*, p.143), but it can also be argued that, in works like *'Route Tournante'*, Cézanne uses the colour of the primed canvas as part of the overall matrix of tonal construction. His late watercolours such as cat.no.18 show a similar preoccupation, where the white paper is allowed to appear as an integral part of the composition.
There is no discernible varnish on the painting and much of the ground, originally white, is exposed, and has in places a mottled appearance which is apparently common in Cézanne's late works. This effect is probably caused by the discoloration of some constituent in the ground.

CÉZANNE, Paul 1839–1906
16 **A Garden Shed** *c.*1880
Extensive preliminary drawing in soft pencil; restricted watercolour washes, with extensive drawing with the point of the brush (particularly with black and grey washes), and some use of the dry brush; on off-white (now stained) wove paper. The sheet unevenly trimmed at the bottom. A tear repaired, top, right of centre.
31.4 x 47.5 cm
Unsigned.

Inscribed in pencil, *verso:* "X Vold" (? the last letter doubtful), and numbered in blue crayon. "66". Traces of pencil and pale blue-grey wash on the *verso* of the sheet, apparently transferred from another drawing.
PROVENANCE With Paul Rosenberg, Paris; Samuel Courtauld (no details of acquisition). Courtauld Gift 1932 (H.H. 23).
EXHIBITED City Art Gallery, Leicester, 1936; *Cézanne Watercolours,* Tate Gallery, London, 1946 (3); Tate Gallery, 1948 (84); *Landscape in French Art,* Royal Academy, London, 1949–50 (546); Orangerie, Paris, 1955 (70); *Paul Cézanne,* Österreichische Galerie, Vienna, 14 April-18 June 1961 (47); *Watercolour and Pencil Drawings by Cézanne,* Laing Art Gallery, Newcastle-on-Tyne, and Hayward Gallery, London, September-December 1973 (42); Courtauld Centenary, 1976 (62); British Museum, 1983 (98).
LITERATURE *L'Amour de l'Art, 1924,* p.36; *Home House Catalogue,* no.23; Venturi, no.837; Cooper, 1954, no.109; Alfred Neumeyer, *Cézanne Drawings* (New York, 1958) p.27 and no.67; Robert Ratcliffe, *Watercolour and Pencil Drawings by Cézanne* (1973), no.42.

The drawing, dated by Venturi to 1872–77 (*ibid.*) was assigned a revised date of *c.*1880 by Alfred Neumeyer (*ibid.*), which was confirmed by Robert Ratcliffe (*ibid.*).

This comparatively early watercolour — Cézanne took up the medium seriously only in *c.*1885, although he had experimented with it since *c.*1866 (Lionello Venturi, *Paul Cézanne Water Colours,* 1943, pp.4-7) — shares with two versions of the *Entrance to a Garden* of 1872–77 (ex. coll. Hans Purrmann, Berlin; and coll. W. Weinberg, Stephen Higgins, Paris: Venturi nos.840 and 842, respectively) an interest in domestic subject matter (Neumeyer, *ibid.*)
Unlike these drawings, however, the *Garden Shed* sacrifices the notation of incidentals of line and colour in favour of a more searching exploration of the structure of the motif. In so doing it is related to the architectural sketches on pp.VI, VII of sketchbook V of 1875–85 (coll. Mr. and Mrs. Leigh B. Block, Chicago: *Cézanne Carnets de Dessin,* edited, and with a catalogue raisonné by John Rewald (Paris, 1951) and to the drawing of *Little Houses* of 1879–82 (ex. coll. Paul Cézanne fils: Venturi, no.836) although the spare and rigorously linear handling of these works suggests that they are of a later date than the Courtauld sheet.
The watercolour whose handling and subject matter appears to be most closely related to the Courtauld work is the *Roofs, Houses and Garden Walls,* dated by Venturi to 1879–82 (coll. Flechtheim, Berlin: Venturi, no.1247): in this sheet both linear and modelled manners of drawing are united with glides of watercolour to describe an intimate subject in which geometrical forms are relieved by undulating areas of foliage.
The restricted colour, evenly distributed over the Courtauld sheet, has only a limited life of its own divorced from the armature of detailed underdrawing: its main function is to accent the edges of forms by tinting contiguous areas — a sort of 'carving back' into the picture surface (cf. Kurt Badt, "Cézanne's Watercolour Technique", *Burlington Magazine,* LXXXIII (October 1943, p.246). In the grass at the edge of the composition, and in the foliage at the right, are the beginnings of alignments of vertical brushstrokes, which in the oil paintings and watercolours of the next decade will describe the extent of planes.

CÉZANNE, Paul 1839–1906

17 **La Montagne Sainte-Victoire** 1885–87

Drawing with soft pencil; watercolour or very dilute gouache, with extensive drawing with the point and flat of the brush (pencil apparently mixing slightly with this medium in certain areas); an off-white (now stained) laid paper, watermarked: "VIDALON". The sheet unevenly torn along the bottom, and in part torn away at the left side. All other sides uneven.
Tears repaired at the left and right sides.
32.8 x 50.5 cm
Unsigned.

PROVENANCE Bernheim-Jeune, Paris (purchased from the artist, 1904); Percy Moore Turner, from whom purchased by Samuel Courtauld (1929). Courtauld Gift 1932 (H.H.22).
EXHIBITED *Cézanne,* Leicester Galleries, London, 1925 (4); *French Art, 1200–1900,* Royal Academy, London, 1932 (989); City Art Gallery, Leicester, April 1936; *Modern French Paintings.* Art Gallery, Melbourne, 1939 (24a); Tate Gallery, 1948 (85); *Landscape in French Art,* Royal Academy, London, 1949–50 (554); *Het Franse Landschap,* Rijksmuseum, Amsterdam, 1951 (151); *French Drawings,* Arts Council, 1952 (15); Orangerie, Paris, 1955 (71), *Paul Cézanne,* Österreichische Galerie, Vienna, 14 April-18 June 1961 (65); Manchester, 1962 (55); *Cézanne Watercolours,* Columbia University, New York, Benefit Exhibition, Knoedler Galleries, New York 2-20 April 1963 (27); *Watercolour and Pencil Drawings by Cézanne,* Laing Art Galley, Newcastle-on-Tyne, and Hayward Gallery, London, September-December 1973 (98); Courtauld Centenary, 1976 (63); British Museum, 1983 (100).
LITERATURE Home House Catalogue, no.22; Venturi, no.1023; *R.A. Commemorative Catalogue* (1933), no.795; Erle Loran, *Cézanne's Composition* (Berkeley and Los Angeles, 1946 and 1959), p.101; René Huyghe, *Le Dessin Français au XIX Siècle* (Lausanne, 1948), pl.105; Cooper, 1954, no.110; Robert Ratcliffe, in *Watercolour and Pencil Drawings by Cézanne* (1976), no.55; Lawrence Gowing, "The Logic of Organized Sensations", p.58 *Cézanne. The Late Work* (New York, 1977).

The watercolour was initially dated by Venturi (*ibid.*) to 1890–1900, although Robert Ratcliffe (*ibid.*) has assigned to it the earlier date of 1885–87, a period during which Cézanne painted a similar view of the mountain in oil, from Bellevue looking west (Barnes Foundation, Merion, USA: Venturi, no.457). The viewpoint adopted for the Courtauld oil of this subject, which similarly dates from 1885–87, is also related to that of the present work (see cat.no.9).
The drawing, which is in soft pencil and lies both under and over the painted areas, is of two types: in the mountain it is purely linear, describing only the contour, with frequent *pentimenti,* while lower down the composition the linear manner is mixed with restricted areas of modelling composed of diagonally hatched strokes.
The watercolour or dilute gouache is evenly applied in patches; these are either long and thin to indicate the edge of an object (as in the contour of the mountain, left), or are broad glides of colour, or wide, generally oblong or lozenge-shaped strips formed by aligning short, diagonal brushstrokes, which describe planes. Such groups of directional brushstrokes, analogous to the drawn areas of hatching, are similarly employed to describe planes in the oil painting of this subject (see above).
The application of the watercolour, more dense in the foreground than in the mountain itself, suggests the receding space of the landscape, complementing the atmospheric blue which becomes increasingly predominant towards the top of the composition.
The colours can be seen to be grouped on the sheet in three fluid lateral zones, set one on top of the other. In the lowest the foreground third of the composition — the sequence of colours, which follows that of the spectrum, is the most strongly contrasted: a deep pink moves through an orange-ochre to yellow, and is opposed to greens ranging from yellow to emerald, blues and a cool grey-violet. Across the centre of the composition, encompassing the foliage and the foothills, greens, blues and grey-violet predominate: in the upper third of the sheet the palette is restricted to blues and grey-violets contrasted with subtle washes of pink and a patch of startling yellow (located near the mountain's summit), which echo similar colour juxtapositions lower down the composition.
Variations of clusters of colour patches, grouped according to a consistently logical principle, thus reverberate over the entire pictorial area, constructing the mass of trees and linking it with the form of the mountain (Gowing, *ibid.*) in an emergent and rigorous composition in which background and foreground are united on the surface of the sheet.

CÉZANNE, Paul 1839–1906

18 **Still Life with Apples, Bottle and Chairback** 1902–06

Extensive drawing with pencil, both under and over painted areas; gouache of varying strengths, with extensive drawing with the point and flat of the brush, and apparently slight addition of gum or varnish (?) (in the red of the second apple on the right, the blacks on the shoulder of the bottle and the stem of the glass); on white wove paper, watermarked: "ANC$^{\underline{NE}}$ MANUF$^{\underline{RE}}$ CANSON Et MONTGOLFIER VIDALON LES ANNONAY". The sheet unevenly torn, right, apparently to ruled pencil lines, and torn, bottom.

Tears repaired, lower right and upper left.

45.8 x 60.4 cm

Unsigned.

Numbered in blue crayon, *verso:* "13."

PROVENANCE Paul Cézanne fils, Paris; with Galerie Thannhauser, Berlin and Lucerne; with Wildenstein, New York and London; Samuel Courtauld (purchased 1937). Courtauld Bequest 1948 (H.H.184).

EXHIBITED *Eighth Exhibition of Watercolours and Pastels,* Cleveland Museum of Art, 1930; *Works of Cézanne,* Philadelphia Museum of Art, 1934 (55); *Hommage to Paul Cézanne,* Wildenstein, London, 1939 (73); *Cézanne Watercolours,* Tate Gallery, London, 1946 (56); Tate Gallery 1948 (86), Orangerie, Paris, 1955 (72); *Paul Cézanne,* Österreichische Galerie, Vienna, 14 April-18 June 1961 (81); *Watercolour and Pencil Drawings by Cézanne,* Laing Art Gallery, Newcastle-on-Tyne, and Hayward Gallery London, September-December 1973 (98); *French Paintings from the Courtauld Collection,* Graves Art Gallery, Sheffield, 10 January-15 February 1976 (64); Courtauld Centenary, 1976 (64); *Cézanne. The Late Work,* Museum of Modern Art, New York, and the Museum of Fine Arts, Houston, October 1977-March 1978 (77); *Cézanne Aquarelle,* Kunsthalle, Tübingen, and Kunsthaus Zurich, January-May 1982 (93, with erroneous provenance); British Museum, 1983 (102).

LITERATURE *Eugenio d'Ors, Paul Cézanne* (Paris, 1930), pl.20; Venturi, no.1155; Cooper, 1954, no.111; Frank Elgar, *Cézanne* (1969), p.249; Lawrence Gowing and Robert Ratcliffe, *Watercolour and Pencil Drawings by Paul Cézanne* (1973), p.21, and p.170, no.98, respectively. Theodore Reff, "Paintings and Theory in the Final Decade", p.36, and John Rewald, no.77, in *Cézanne. The Late Work* (New York, 1977).

Cézanne's ultimate conception of still-life may be seen in the late watercolours only, since the oil paintings are of different subjects (Reff, *ibid.*). The present example, whose composition is reminiscent of the watercolour *Apples and Inkwell* (coll. Mr. and Mrs. Paul Hirschland, Great Neck, New York: not in Venturi, but illustrated in *Cézanne. The Late Work,* pl.182), has been dated by Venturi (*ibid.*) to 1904–06, and reassigned a wider dating of 1902–06 by Robert Ratcliffe (*ibid.*), endorsed by Lawrence Gowing and John Rewald (*ibid.*).

Ratcliffe (*ibid.*) has observed that the boldly brushed in chairback of the present sheet has close affinities with the drawing *The Rococo Clock* (Adrien Chappuis, *The Drawings of Paul Cézanne* (Greenwich Conn., 1973) no.1233), possibly one of Cézanne's final works in pencil. The chairback is also reminiscent of that in the watercolour formerly in the collection of Lord Clark of Saltwood (Venturi, no.850), while the forms of similar, although less curvilinear chairbacks had been the subject of sketches by Cézanne on pp.VIII and XLVI *recto* in a notebook datable to 1875–85 (coll. M. and Mrs Leigh B. Block, Chicago: *Cézanne Carnets de Dessin,* op.cit.). The tall glass with twisting stem, and striped wallpaper, in the present sheet also appear in the watercolour *The Dessert* (coll. Gaston Bernheim de Villiers, Paris: Venturi, 1153)

Lawrence Gowing has observed (*ibid.*) that the areas of paper left blank near the centre of objects in the late watercolours represent the 'culminating points' of forms, mentioned by Cézanne in a letter of 25 July 1904 to Émile Bernard (1868–1941) (John Rewald (ed.), *Paul Cézanne Letters,* Oxford, 1976, pp.305–06). The 'culminating point' is that area of the object closest to the eye: although it is the palest area of a form, it is not to be confused with the highlight. Gowing also noted (*ibid.*) that in Cézanne's late work, colours fan out from this point in the logical sequence of the spectrum: towards the end of 1900, areas of individual colour become increasingly clearly differentiated.

Such is the case with the motif of apples in the present sheet: here, the colours are at their most intense, following the sequence from the 'culmination point' through yellow, red and blue. Intermediate hues, such as orange, are applied sparingly and always between yellow and red, while a green is normally juxtaposed with blue, although touches of it are introduced on to the surface of the table and in the chairback to activate the reds and browns of these areas and control the placing of fruit and dish.

The colour intensity of the fruit is complemented by the density and opacity of the gouache which describes them: the paint in this motif is sufficiently thick to form a ridge at the edge of brushstrokes (visible in the blue contour of the apple to the right of the dish, in the right edge of the penultimate apple, right, and in the leaves, far right), which accentuates the weight of the fruit. Reff's description (*op.cit.,* p.184) of the objects in the final watercolours as being "dissolved into weightless floating shapes" is thus inapplicable to the apples in the Courtauld picture.

Gowing (1973, *ibid.*) has noted how the pile of fruit is constructed by arcs of colour interlocking with the white of the paper: although these arcs are contained by the curving crosspiece of the chairback, similar forms, supported by a free pencil drawing of curves, fill the kidney-shaped space above it. Much diluted, the colours of these smaller arcs clearly repeat those of the bowl of fruit, and it is possible that these forms represent the reflection of that motif in a mirror located on the wall behind the chair.

The present watercolour is made up of distinct zones composed of brushstrokes of similar type. The extreme left and right of the table top is formed by a series of multidirectional, overlapping patches of irregular shape, which metamorphose into definite brushstrokes whose length and thinness increase as they approach the centre of the composition: here, they curve around the base of the fruit dish, suggesting the reflection of the underside of its lip in the table top. The lateral edges of the walls are described with broad vertical strokes, which become shorter, bending inwards as they approach the edges of the chairback. The concentration of arched forms of the bowl of fruit, chairback and reflection is thus simultaneously anticipated and contained by the brushstrokes of the wall and table, which become increasingly curved as they advance towards the centre of the composition.

Although the horizontal edge of the table upon which the still-life is composed is not sharply defined — a characteristic of Cézanne's still-life watercolours after *c.*1895 observed by Geneviève Monnier ('The Late Watercolours', p.114, in *Cézanne. The Late Work*) it is nonetheless indicated by a massing of horizontal brushstrokes of different lengths and thicknesses above an area of very dilute gouache applied with balayé strokes. The indications of the table's edge become noticeably stronger at the centre of the sheet, stabilising the motifs above.

In contrast with the density of paint at the centre and right of the composition, that employed throughout the remainder of the sheet is both fluid and transparent — properties which Cézanne exploits not only to maintain the status of each patch of colour as a separate statement, but also to add an edge or direction to all contours (other than those in blue). These are clearly accented, either at the lateral edges (by drawing partly into an area of wet paint, or by turning the brush slightly while drawing), or at the tops and bottoms (by momentarily resting the brush). It would seem that the sheet was also tilted to encourage the flow of paint to one area of the contour: such 'directional' contours appear both along the crosspiece of the chairback and at the right side of the bottle.

By contrast, the blue contours at the centre of the composition are generally less modified, either in terms of opacity or hue, than those described above. The suggestion of atmosphere inherent in that colour, combined with the dense nature of the paint itself, simultaneously creates space between the apples while uniting them in a solid compositional wedge. Although the blue is echoed in both foreground and background, it is a pale resonance of that running across the centre of the sheet.

It is tempting to interpret the curves of blue below the apples, right, as *pentimenti* — an indication that the artist has relocated the fruit approximately 6 cm higher in the sheet. That the line of the apples remains in its original position is confirmed by the underlying pencil drawing: the blue strokes may therefore be interpreted as the reflection in the wood of the space between the apples, and as such demonstrate a facet of Cézanne's rich imaginative and interpretative vision, which Emile Bernard (*Souvenirs sur Paul Cézanne* (Paris 1921), p.30) had noted.

DAUMIER, Honoré 1808–1879

19 **Don Quixote and Sancho Panza** *c.*1865

Oil on canvas, 100 x 81 cm

Unsigned.

colour plate, page 25

PROVENANCE Ambroise Vollard, Paris; with Paul Rosenberg, Paris; with Bignou, Paris; with Lefèvre and Son, London, from whom acquired by Samuel Courtauld in May 1923. Courtauld Gift 1932.

EXHIBITED *Daumier,* École des Beaux-Arts, Paris, May 1901 (89); *Daumier,* Galerie Rosenberg, Paris, April 1907 (32); *Art Français au 19me Siècle,* Paul Rosenberg, Paris, June 1917 (20); *L'Art Français,* Basel, May 1921 (52); *Grands Maîtres du 19me Siècle,* Paul Rosenberg, Paris, April 1922 (34); *Impressionist School,* Lefèvre Gallery, London, May 1923 (17, repr.); *French Art,* Royal Academy, London, 1932 (376); Tate Gallery, 1948 (20); Orangerie, Paris, 1955 (17); *Daumier: Paintings and Drawings,* Arts Council at Tate Gallery, June-July 1961 (97, repr.); Courtauld Centenary, 1976 (15).

LITERATURE Jamot-Turner, no.3 (repr.); Home House Catalogue, no.2 (repr.); Cooper, 1954, no.20 (repr.); Roger Fry, 'French Art of the Nineteenth Century', *Burlington Magazine,* XL (June 1922), p.277-78 (repr.pl.IIID); Erich Klossowski, *Honoré Daumier* (2nd rev. ed., Munich, 1923), cat.no.51 (repr.pl.43); Eduard Fuchs *Der Maler Daumier* (2nd ed., Supplement; Munich, 1930), no.165; Jacques Lassaigne, *Daumier* (Paris, 1938), pl.155.

Dated variously between 1865, 1868, and even 1875, this sketch is of a theme from the book by Cervantes which was a favourite of Daumier's. He is known to have done at least thirty paintings from *Don Quixote*. The first of these to be exhibited was *Don Quixote and Sancho Panza going to the Wedding of Gamache,* at the Salon of 1851. The earliest known of his oil paintings date from 1850.

Roger Fry (*loc.cit.*) speaks of the tragic overtones of this painting, which he likened to a work by Rembrandt, and regretted that Daumier was forced to spend so much of his creative activity in producing caricatures for the Parisian humorous journals like *Le Charivari,* instead of being able to devote himself to painting.

DAUMIER, Honoré 1808–1879

20 **The Defence** c.1860–70?

Slight preliminary drawing in soft pencil; pen and grey ink; drawing with the point of the brush and use of the dry brush, in pale grey ink wash; pen and black (Indian?) ink to strengthen some of the contours (particularly those of lawyer and defendant); some re-drawing of the lawyer's desk in pencil; on white (now unevenly discoloured) wove paper. The left side of the sheet unevenly torn (? a page from a sketchbook) and all other sides unevenly trimmed. Vestiges of lines in pen and black ink at all edges of the sheet (from a previous mount).

23.7 x 31.5 cm

Signed in pencil, lower right: "h.D"

Numbered in a different hand in pencil; *verso:*"29-81"

PROVENANCE Georges Lecomte; Percy Moore Turner, from whom purchased by Samuel Courtauld 1928. Courtauld Bequest 1948 (H.H.192).

EXHIBITED *Daumier,* École des Beaux-Arts, Paris, 1901, (217); *Daumier — Gavarni,* Maison Victor Hugo, Paris, 1923 (80); *Daumier,* Galerie Dru, Paris, 1927 (4); *French Art 1200–1900,* Royal Academy, London, 1932 (949); Tate Gallery, 1948 (89); Orangerie, Paris, 1955 (73); *Honoré Daumier,* Tate Gallery, 1961 (220); Manchester, 1962 (57); Courtauld Centenary, 1976 (65); Arts Council (6); British Museum, 1983 (104).

LITERATURE Erich Klossowski, *Honoré Daumier* (Munich, 1908, 2nd ed. 1923), no.152; Léon Marotte and Charles Martine, *Dessins de Maîtres français IV: Honoré Daumier* (Paris, 1924), no.31; Eduard Fuchs, *Der Maler Daumier* (Munich, 1927), no.184a; Royal Academy Commemorative Catalogue, (1933) no.814; Cooper, 1954, no.112; K.E. Maison, *Honoré Daumier catalogue raisonné of the paintings, watercolours and drawings* (2 vols.), 1968, no.II, 657.

K.E. Maison (*op.cit.,* pp.8, 9) has noted the impossibility of establishing a correct chronology, based on style, for Daumier's drawings, none of which were dated by the artist. Daumier's facility as a draughtsman was such that he was capable of drawing in a variety of manners with equal ease, when the occasion suggested, as examination of the lithographs (executed for newspapers and therefore datable) clearly shows (cf. Loys Delteil, *Le peintre — graveur illustré: Honoré Daumier* (Paris, 1925)). The sheet upon which the Courtauld drawing is executed bears no watermark, precluding even this unsatisfactory method of dating.

A slightly smaller, unsigned version of this subject (private coll., Germany: Maison, *op.cit.,* II, 656) is practically identical to the Courtauld drawing, except that the latter has a deeper-toned wash lending more substance to the forms of table and lawyer, while that figure's pointing hand is rendered in a more agitated manner which is heightened by the *pentimenti* above it. No reason can be suggested for the replicas: that one version was executed from a tracing of the other is denied by the equally nervous vitality of line in both drawings.

The motif of the lawyer who plays upon the emotions of either the judges or his client by pointing towards a painting of an obviously symbolic and moralizing nature also appears in Daumier's oil composition *The Pardon* of 1865–67 (Boymans-van Beuningen Museum, Rotterdam: Maison, *op.cit.,* I, 119) and in its preparatory drawings (coll. Claude Roger-Marx, Paris; and private coll., Paris: Maison, *op.cit.,* II, 686, 687, respectively). In this oil, the lawyer points towards a painting of the Crucifixion. In the Courtauld drawing, the lawyer gesticulates towards a painting whose subject is, ironically, *Divine Justice and Vengeance pursuing Crime.* This picture (now in the Musée du Louvre), was initially commissioned from the artist Louis Prud'hon (1758–1832) by the French Supreme Court of Appeal.

DAUMIER, Honoré 1808–1879

21 **The Hypochondriac** c.1860–70?

Faint preliminary drawing in black chalk; black (Indian?) ink washes, and blue, yellow, pink and brown watercolour washes (all of varying strengths and combinations), with extensive drawing with the pen (for the background hatching), and with drawing with the point of the brush; extensive re-drawing of the figures with black (lithographic?) crayon; on off-white (now stained) laid paper (the watermark cut away at the top and illegible).

20.7 x 27.1 cm

Signed in pen and black (Indian?) ink wash, lower left: "h.", and in pen and black (Indian?) ink, below: "h. Daumier" (over an earlier signature in black ink wash).

Numbered by a different hand in pencil, *verso:* "57.47"

colour plate, page 24

PROVENANCE Lemaire, Paris; with Bignou, Paris; with Reid and Lefèvre, London, from whom purchased by Samuel Courtauld 1928. Courtauld Gift 1934.

EXHIBITED *Works by Corot, Daumier,* Museum of Modern Art, New York, October 1930 (98); *French Art, 1200–1900,* Royal Academy, London, 1932 (904); British Institute of Adult Education, Silver End, Essex, March 1935 (13); Tate Gallery, 1948 (90); *Daumier, le peinture,* Bibliothéque Nationale, Paris, 1958 (211); *Honoré Daumier,* Tate Gallery, 1961 (165); *Daumier,* Ingelheim-am-Rhein, 24 April–31 May 1971 (38); Courtauld Centenary, 1976 (66); Arts Council (5); *Daumier et ses amis républicains,* Musée Cantini, Marseille, 1 June–31 August, 1979 (65); British Museum, 1983 (103).

LITERATURE Cahiers d'Art III (1928), p.49; Eduard Fuchs, *Der Maler Daumier* (Munich, 1927), no.337; Royal Academy Commemorative Catalogue (1933), no.805; Home House Catalogue, no.76; Cooper, 1954, no.113 *Revue Municipale* no.29 (Marseille, 1956), p.39; K.E. Maison, *Daumier Drawings* (New York, 1960), no.98; K.E. Maison, *Honoré Daumier catalogue raisonné of the paintings, watercolours and drawings.* (2 vols.) 1968, no.II, 486.

The drawing is related to the group of works which Daumier executed illustrating Molière's satire *Le Malade Imaginaire,* although neither it, nor other drawings of the group can be dated with any certainty (the problems of dating are discussed in the preceding catalogue entry).

The two paintings which clearly form part of the same group, *The Hypochondriac* (Philadelphia Museum of Art: Maison I, 154) and *Dr. Diafoirus* (coll., Dr. and Mrs. Harry Bakwin, New York: Maison I, 223) are dated to 1860–63 and 1870, respectively. The same author also suggests that Daumier may have executed many of the watercolours and wash drawings during the period of the early 1860s, when his contract with the paper *Le Charivari* was broken (K.E. Maison, *Daumier Studies,* 1954, unpaginated but p.1).

The Courtauld drawing is clearly related in theme to the Philadelphia painting, in which the hypochondriac, Argan (also wearing a night-cap with a bow) is seen in profile, cowering before a doctor whose assistant stands at the rear holding a large syringe. Unlike the present work, however, the interest in the painting is centred more closely upon the figure of the hypochondriac, who is situated in the foreground, facing left.

The work whose composition approaches most nearly that of the Courtauld sheet is the charcoal and crayon study of *The Sick Man and Death* (Private coll., Paris: Maison II, 402), a drawing outside the *Malade Imaginaire* group. Here the patient, whose pinched features recall those of the hypochondriac, lies in profile facing the right, the subject of the contesting wills of a doctor (right) and Death (left).

The doctors in the present drawing are variants of the couple who feel the dying man's pulse in the drawing in Yale University Art Gallery (Maison II, 835) and these in turn are related to the charlatan who appears in the lost (presumed destroyed) drawing of *The Hypochondriac* (Maison II, 476) and its preliminary study (location unknown: Maison II, 473). Similar figures of doctors, one of whom carries an enormous syringe, appear in force in a lithograph published in *Actualités* of 28 May 1867, *Yesterday the breech-loading gun, tomorrow these fellows . . .* (Delteil, *Daumier, op.cit.,* no.3577), while the figure of Æsculapius, armed with a similar syringe, had appeared in a caricature published in the same paper on 16 March 1859 (Delteil, *Daumier,* no.3133).

Jean Adhémar's suggestion (*Honoré Daumier, Drawings and Watercolours,* Basle, 1954, no.35) that the figure of the hypochondriac in the lost drawings, mentioned above (Maison II, 475, 476), is comparable to that of the perspiring Parisian in the 1857 lithograph *Thirty two degrees* (Delteil, *Daumier,* no.2856) may be discounted: it is more exactly similar to the dental patient in the lithograph *Let's see . . . open your mouth . . .* of 1864 (Delteil, *Daumier,* no.3272).

It can thus be seen that the figures of doctor and patient/hypochondriac, either separately or related, appear in painted and lithographed compositions which can be reliably dated to the decade of the 1860s: the thematic and formal links which exist between these works and the drawings of the *Malade Imaginaire* group, including the Courtauld sheet, suggest that it, too, may be tentatively dated to the same period.

DEGAS, Edgar 1834–1917

22 **Woman at a Window** *c.*1871–72

Oil on paper, mounted on linen, 61.3 x 45.9 cm

Signed, bottom right: "Degas" and stamped, in red, bottom right "Degas"

PROVENANCE Read [i.e. Alexander Reid], Glasgow; Read [Reid] Sale (Vente de M.A. ...), Paris 10 June 1898 (lot 26;2,900 Frs); with Durand-Ruel, Paris; Mrs. Walter Sickert, London; Mrs. Cobden-Sanderson, London; Miss M.F.C. Knox, London, 1917; Mrs. Cobden-Sanderson, 1917; Miss Stella Cobden-Sanderson, London, 1926; with the Leicester Galleries, London, from whom acquired by Samuel Courtauld 1927. Courtauld Gift 1932.

EXHIBITED International Society, The New Gallery, London, 1908 (86, wrongly described as 'watercolour'); Goupil Gallery Salon, London, 1923 (72); *Degas,* Musée de l'Orangerie, Paris, April 1937 (not catalogued); Tate Gallery, 1948 (22); *Degas,* Edinburgh and London, 1952 (13); Orangerie, Paris, 1955 (19); Courtauld Centenary, 1976 (16).

LITERATURE Home House Catalogue, no.14; Paul Jamot, *Degas* (Paris 1924), pp.56, 140 (repr.pl.29); P.A. Lemoisne, *Degas et son oeuvre,* II (Paris 1946), p.206, no.385 (repr.); Walter Sickert, in "Monthly Chronicle: Degas", *Burlington Magazine,* XLIII (December 1923), p.308 (repr.); Jamot-Turner, no.12 (repr.); Cooper, 1954, no.22 (repr.); Denys Sutton, *Walter Sickert. A Biography* (1976), pp.111-12.

The dating of this picture has been variously given as 1872–74 (Jamot), 1875 (Jamot-Turner), and by Lemoisne as 1875–78. However, the painter Walter Sickert, who knew Degas well, has recorded (*loc.cit.*) that Degas told him this work belonged to the period either "during or soon after" the Seige of Paris (1871) and before the affliction of a blind spot in his right eye made painting difficult for him. This would suggest a date of 1871–72, and there is additional evidence for this dating. Sickert apparently bought this painting from Durand-Ruel for £400 in about 1901–02 for Mrs. Sickert (Ellen Cobden). Although Sickert was divorced from Ellen Sickert in 1899, they remained on friendly terms and saw each other quite often until her death in 1914. Sickert wrote to his friend and patron, Sir William Eden, to announce "I have just bought Degas's *finest* work, had my eye on it for 12 years or so!, for £400! for Mrs. Sickert, and sold the one I bought for £74 or so to an American for £3000, he paying dealer's percentage — say 10 p.c. — and duty into America . . ." (quoted by Sutton, *Sickert,* p.111). The

painting Sickert sold was the *Répétition d'un Ballet sur la Scéne,* which passed with the H.O. Havemeyer collection to the Metropolitan Museum, New York (see also ca.no.23).
Sutton (*op.cit.,* p.112) also records that according to an annotation on Sickert's own copy of Jamot's life on Degas, the artist told him that the sitter was a cocotte and that during the Seige of Paris he had bought her a piece of raw meat "which she fell upon, so hungry was she, & devoured whole". Sickert, on enquiring why he was able to buy this picture for less than a pastel, was told by Durand-Ruel, "because the amateur of Degas always wanted ballet girls".
Stylistically, the painting is close to *Madame Olivier Villette* of 1872 (Fogg Art Museum, Cambridge, Mass.; Lemoisne no.314). The technique Degas used here is peinture à l'essence, that is to say oil paint which has been thinned and dried out with white spirit.

DEGAS, Edgar 1834–1917
23 **Two Dancers on the Stage** 1874
Oil on canvas, 61.5 x 46 cm
Signed, bottom left: "Degas"

colour plate, page 40

PROVENANCE Captain Henry Hill, Brighton (by 1874); Hill Sale, Christie's, 25 May 1889 (lot 31, £64.05), bought Goupil (i.e. Theo Van Gogh); Victor Desfossés; sold by Desfossés 4 November 1889 to Goupil-Boussod Valadon successeurs (5000 Frs.); Goupil-Boussod Valadon successeurs, sold 13 November 1889 (6000 Frs.) to Paul Gallimard, Paris; with Alex. Reid, Glasgow; Sir James Murray, Aberdeen, sold Christie's 29 April 1927 (lot 41, repr. £7,200); with Knoedler, London; Samuel Courtauld, June 1927. Courtauld Gift 1932.
EXHIBITED Ninth Exhibition of Society of French Artists, Paul Durand-Ruel, London, November 1874 (9) as "Scène de Ballet"; Galerie 'Les Arts', Paris, June 1912 (16); *French Impressionists,* Lefèvre Gallery, London, May 1920 (8); Opening Exhibition, Modern Foreign Gallery, Tate Gallery, June 1926; *Degas,* Musée de l'Orangerie, Paris, April 1937 (26); Tate Gallery 1948 (24); *Degas,* Edinburgh and London, 1952 (16); Orangerie, Paris, 1955 (21); *Impressionism,* Royal Academy, London, February-April 1974 (56); Courtauld Centenary, 1976 (17).
LITERATURE Home House Catalogue, no.25; Jamot-Turner, no.11 (repr.); Lemoisne, *Degas,* II, p.234, no.425 (repr.); Cooper, 1954, no.24 (as "c.1877"); R. Pickvance, "Degas's Dancers: 1872–6", *Burlington Magazine,* CV (June 1963), pp.263-66; John Rewald, "Theo Van Gogh, Goupil, and the Impressionists — Part II"; *Gazette des Beaux-Arts, LXXXI (February 1973), p.90.*

Douglas Cooper *(op.cit.)* summarises the use Degas made of these two figures in three other compositions, two in the Metropolitan Museum of Art, New York (Havemeyer Collection), and a third in the Musée du Louvre (Legs Camondo). Each shows a ballet rehearsal in progress, and takes in the whole stage. Lemoisne also lists and reproduces a number of preparatory sketches. Pickvance (*loc.cit.*) produces evidence which seems to prove quite conclusively that this painting was completed in 1874, not *c.*1877 as Lemoisne and Cooper had thought. He identifies the Courtauld picture from descriptions in contemporary press reports with one that Durand-Ruel included in his ninth London exhibition of Impressionist painting in November 1874, where it was bought by Captain Henry Hill (1812–82), of Marine Parade, Brighton. This was also the first Degas to be bought by Hill, who was one of the very first English collectors of this date to be interested in French Impressionist art and eventually owned six ballet subjects by Degas. The painter Walter Sickert was another (see cat.no.22), but all the Degas paintings owned by him and his first wife, Ellen Cobden, from 1889–95, were either sold or reverted to his wife, following his divorce from her in 1899.
Pickvance also modifies our view of Degas' working methods at this time. He observes that the Courtauld painting was not a later reworking of an earlier theme, but followed very soon after the Louvre picture, which served as the starting point for a series of four closely-related variant designs, executed in fairly rapid succession, and not, as previously believed, spread over four or five years. Degas also used them to carry out technical experiments, and their evolution can be followed by a study of the many preparatory drawings for them which still exist. That this was an intensive and continuous process of development is borne out by the number of *pentimenti* which have been observed in the Courtauld picture, and which are discussed below.
Lillian Browse (*Degas Dancers,* London 1949, p.355) describes in technical terms the positions of these two dancers: one is *sur les pointes,* the other is "standing next to her in fourth position with arms in *demi-seconde*". The ballet has not been identified.
A detailed examination of the painting shows a number of *pentimenti.* The dancer on the extreme left, downstage and almost hidden by scenery, has been extensively reduced in scale and her position moved by approximately 1.5 cm to the left edge of the canvas. It may be that the *pentimenti* here cover two figures, since there are indications of two sets of legs. The centre dancer has extensive *pentimenti* to left of feet, and there are minor adjustments to the positioning of the right leg and foot, as well as a slight *pentimento* in the upper right arm. The left foot of the dancer on the far right of the composition has been lengthened and points more forward, while the leg itself has been shortened.
Although Degas had painted several theatre scenes in the late 1860s, his preoccupation with the ballet really begins in 1872 with a scene from *Robert le Diable* (Lemoisne no.294), and continues throughout his working life. It was part of his fascination with the problems presented by attempting to record the fleeting movements of a wide variety of subjects, from racehorses to ballet dancers, and laundresses at work at their ironing boards. His observation may have seemed detached or aloof, but his portrayals of ballet dancers at rehearsal, or at rest during an interlude, show him fully aware of the physical demands made upon them by their vocation.

DEGAS, Edgar 1834–1917
24 **After the Bath, Woman Drying her Chest** *c.*1889–90
Pastel, both dry and with use of the (?) damp brush; on very thin buff wove paper. The drawing made up of two sheets (the second sheet added at the bottom of the drawing, apparently quite early during its execution), both laid down on thin buff wove paper and laid down again on millboard faced with cardboard. 67.7 x 57.8 cm (including the additional lower sheet, 7.9 x 57.8 cm)
Unsigned.
Stamped in red oval, on original backing: ATELIER/ED. DEGAS"

colour plate, page 41

PROVENANCE 1re Vente Degas, Paris, 6 May 1918 (lot no.281, repr.; 25,000 Frs.); Trotti, Paris; with Winkel and Magnussen, Copenhagen; with Galerie Barbazanges, Paris; through Percy Moore Turner, London; Lord Ivor Spencer-Churchill, London; through Percy Moore Turner, London; Samuel Courtauld by 1929. Courtauld Gift 1932.
EXHIBITED *Degas-Utställning,* Nationalmuseum, Stockholm, January 1920 (30, repr.); *Degas Udstilling,* Ny Carlsberg Glyptothek, Copenhagen, March 1920 (30, repr.); Tate Gallery, 1948 (93); Courtauld Centenary, 1976 (18).
LITERATURE Home House Catalogue, no.26 (repr.); Jamot-Turner, no.14 (repr.); Lemoisne, *Degas,* III, p.558, no.1011 (repr.); Cooper, 1954, no.27 (repr.).

Lemoisne lists four studies for this picture (*op.cit.,* nos.1340-43). Several *pentimenti* are visible in the raised left arm, the right arm, both knees and thighs, and there is the trace of a diagonal line leading from the right knee towards the top left of the sheet.
This line may have been intended to denote the base of the tub, or, more likely, the line of the floor or skirting board. There are anatomical inconsistencies in the position of the right arm and hand in relation to the woman's body and the placing of the towel. The structure of the right hand and wrist appears to have been deliberately obscured.
The blind spot in Degas' right eye, from which he suffered increasingly from 1872 onwards, meant that he could not focus directly on a subject but was forced to observe it from an angle. He also turned to working with pastel since this was a medium in which he could record his ideas more rapidly than in oil painting and with less continuous strain on his eyes.
It is tempting to suggest that Degas, in attempting to catch the movements of the woman drying herself, has in this work constantly re-adjusted her pose until he has reached an approximation which more or less satisfied him.

DEGAS, Edgar 1834–1917
25 **Seated Woman Adjusting her Hair** *c.*1884
Chalk and pastel, with extensive rubbing and effacing; on buff hand-made laid paper. The drawing made up of two sheets placed edge to edge (the artist's registration marks in pencil, upper left and right) and laid down on white wove paper (apparently previously "tipped" at the edges on to millboard).
63 x 59.9 cm
Unsigned.
Stamped in red, bottom right: "Degas" (Lugt 658)

PROVENANCE IIeme Vente Degas, Paris, 11 December 1918 (lot 94); with Nunès and Fiquet, Paris; with the Leicester Galleries, London, by January 1922, from whom purchased by Samuel Courtauld 1923. Courtauld Bequest 1948 (H.H. 232).
EXHIBITED Degas Exhibition, Leicester Galleries, London, January 1922 (42); Tate Gallery, 1948 (92); Orangerie Paris, 1955 (75); Manchester, 1962 (58); *Degas: Pastels and Drawings,* Nottingham University, 1969 (20); Courtauld Centenary, 1976 (19); British Museum, 1983 (105).
LITERATURE Lemoisne, *Degas,* III, no.781; D. Cooper, "The Courtaulo Collection", *Burlington Magazine,* CX (June 1948), p.170; Jamot Turner, no.13; Cooper, 154, no.115; Franco Russoli and Fiorella Minervino, *L'opera completa di Degas* (Milan, 1970), no.620.

This pastel, dated by Lemoisne *(ibid.)* to 1884, is considered by that author to be a preparatory study for the oil painting *Woman doing her Hair* (formerly coll. Georges Viau: Lemoisne, 780): by contrast, Russoli and Minervino *(ibid.)* suggest that the oil composition is a study for the pastel! Such contrary claims need investigation, since the pose of the figure in the painting and pastel vary considerably.
Examination of the pastel indicates that the entire figure was initially stated in brown and black on the lower of the two sheets which make up the drawing: the head, originally placed further to the right, was also turned more to the right (confirmed by *pentimenti* to the right of the collar), its form slightly cropped at the top of the sheet. Extensive *pentimenti* below the arms, at the left hip, and by the breast (in brown pastel in the latter area, now largely effaced) indicates that the torso was similarly placed

lower on the sheet, in a more erect pose, and was described by comfortably rounded contours.

This is the form and pose of the model as she appears in the Viau work: added confirmation that the initial drawing on the Courtauld sheet represents the Viau figure is derived from the similar details of costume. In the painting, the model wears a dress fastened at the back by a row of large buttons: in the pastel, the forms of the same buttons, although largely effaced, are still visible between the figure's shoulder-blades.

It would seem that Degas's extensive effacing and re-drawing of the Courtauld sheet was prompted by his dissatisfaction with the model's final form in the oil composition: the body appears rather weak and flaccid, while the pose, a conflation of those of the women in the pastel *At the Milliners* of 1883 (coll. M[me] E. Rouart, Paris: Lemoisne no.729) is curiously stilted.

In the Courtauld work, a second sheet was added end to end with the top of the original sheet, in order to enlarge and re-state a more angular and dynamic silhouette, whose continuity over both sheets is stressed by the unbroken contours at the left side. The front of the skirt, a diagonal line meeting the corner of the oil composition, is re-stated in the drawing as an angular form, the limits of which are indicated by a faint ruled line at the knee. The folds of shot material at the back of the skirt are, by contrast, freshly and crisply handled in a detailed manner reminiscent of that of earlier northern masters, such as Holbein, Cranach or Dürer, copies after whose work Degas had made between 1859–64 (Theodore Reff, *Degas: The Artist's Mind* (1976) p.104, note 46). Since a similar depiction of drapery is not evident in the painting, it may be assumed to be a later addition to the drawing. That Degas should strive for such a high degree of finish in this area suggests that he regarded the pastel as a work of art independent of the oil painting: the Courtauld sheet had superseded the oil for which it was a preliminary work.

DEGAS, Edgar 1834–1917

26 **Lady with a Parasol** *c.*1870–72

Oil (?) on canvas, 75.3 x 85 cm

Atelier sale stamp, bottom right: "Degas"

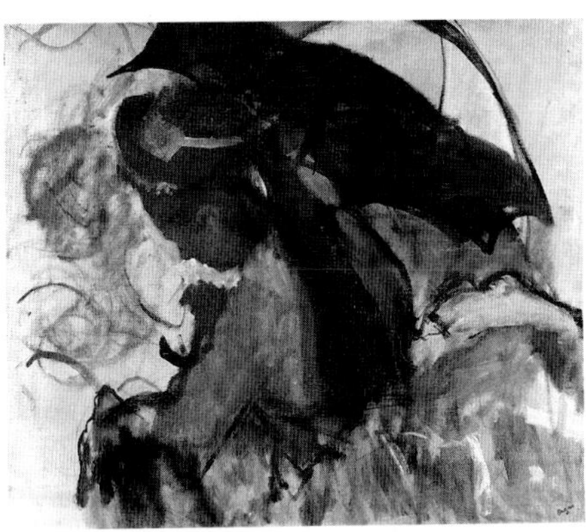

PROVENANCE Sale of contents of Degas' studio (second sale), Georges Petit, Paris, 11-13 December 1918 (lot 36); Marcel Guérin, Paris, by 1923; acquired by Count Seilern, Paris, 1954. Seilern Bequest (Princes Gate Collection, no.207) 1978.

EXHIBITED *Paris,* Galerie Charpentier, Paris, 1944–45 (45); *The Princes Gate Collection,* Courtauld Institute Galleries, London, from 17 July 1981 (16).

LITERATURE Henri Rivière, *Les Dessins de Degas,* II (Paris, 1923), no.81 (repr.), English edition (New York, 1973), no.57 (repr.); P.A. Lemoisne, in *L'Amour de l'Art,* XII, July 1931, pp.289, 291 (repr.); P.A. Lemoisne, *Degas,* II, no.414 (repr.); A.S. [Antoine Seilern], *Paintings and Drawings of Continental Schools other than Flemish and Italian at 56 Princes Gate London SW7,* III (1961), pp.55f., no.207 (repr.); R. Pickvance and J. Pečírka, *Drawings. Degas* (London etc., 1969, 2nd ed.), p.25, no.32 (repr.).

Although painted on canvas this work has, on a number of occasions, been published as a drawing *à l'essence,* a term which indicates the drying out of the oil medium and dilution with turpentine. There is evidently little medium in the ground, which is in a very friable state and, being unvarnished, is discoloured by a quantity of accumulated dirt. It is unpainted in the background and visible through the thin dry brushstrokes of the "drawing".

This rapidly executed painting is clearly of a boldly experimental nature which could not, to the artist's satisfaction, become a "finished" painting. It seems to belong to a period around 1870 when Degas was particularly interested in exploring the effects of light, a period to which also belongs the *Woman at a Window* (no.22 in this exhibition), with its comparable effect of *contre-jour* lighting. Degas' written notes on projected pictures of this period confirm this interest: ". . . pas de montrer toujours la source de la lumière, mais l'effet de la lumière . . ." and (this fairly describes the present work): "faire en grand de groupes en pure silhouette au crépuscule" (T. Reff, *The Notebooks of Edgar Degas* (Oxford, 1976), I, Notebook 23, p.117 (45); p.118 (60) – notebook datable to c.1868–72).

The subject appears to be a spectator at the races; indeed, although known in the literature by the present title, following the atelier sale description as *Femme à l'ombrelle,* an old label formerly on the back of the stretcher is inscribed: "Aux Courses". It is close in subject and composition to a small painting also known as *Aux Courses* (19 x 24 cm; Mr. and Mrs. Eugene Victor Thaw Collection, New York; Lemoisne, no.495), and may also be compared with the perhaps slightly earlier race-course scenes: *False Start* (John Hay Witney Collection, New York; Lemoisne, no.258) and *Racehorses passing the Stands* (Musée du Jeu de Paume, Paris; Lemoisne, no.262) – both displaying *contre-jour* light effects. In *Carriages at the Races* (Museum of Fine Arts, Boston; Lemoisne, no.281) the central group shelters, similarly, under a parasol, as do a number of female spectators in the two former scenes. Studies thought to be for these women are to be found in Degas' Notebook 22 (pp.109-17; Reff, *op.cit.,* II) and in further drawings (Lemoisne, nos.259-61).

Rivière *(loc.cit)* and Lemoisne *(loc.cit.)* dated the present work to the second half of the 1870s; Count Seilern *(loc.cit.),* following Anthony Blunt's suggestion, is evidently justified in considering it to have been executed just before Degas left for New Orleans in 1872.

DERAIN, André 1880–1954

27 **Trees by a Lake, Le Parc de Carrières-Saint-Denis** 1909

Oil on canvas, 54.1 x 65 cm

Unsigned.

PROVENANCE With Galerie Kahnweiler, Paris; bought by Roger Fry from the *Manet and The Post-Impressionists* exhibition 1910. Fry Bequest 1934.

EXHIBITED *Manet and the Post-Impressionists,* Grafton Galleries, London, 8 November 1910, 15 January 1911 (118); *André Derain,* Edinburgh and London, 1967 (37); *André Derain,* Grand Palais, Paris, 15 February-11 April 1977 (13); *Kubismus: Künstler, Themen, Werke, 1907–20,* Josef-Haubrich-Kunsthalle, Cologne, 26 May-25 July 1982 (30).

LITERATURE *General Catalogue of the Courtauld Institute Galleries* (revised ed. 1979), no.13; Frances Spalding, *Roger Fry. Art and Life* (1980), p.140.

This subject was also painted by Georges Braque, with whom Derain visited Carrières-Saint-Denis (? near La Roche-Guyon) in the summer of 1909. Derain had first painted in the area as early as 1899 (e.g. *The Road to Carrières,* repr. in D. Sutton, *André Derain* (1959) pl.2). Daniel-Henry Kahnweiler was Braque's dealer, and Derain's from 1907–14 and from 1920–22, and thought highly of Derain's early work. He lent three Derain landscapes to Fry's *Manet and the Post-Impressionists* exhibition, two of 1908, and this of 1909. The artist became a favourite with the Fry/Bloomsbury Group of artists, writers, collectors and critics.

Frances Spalding (*op.cit.*) records that although Fry purchased this small painting because its price was within his moderate means, it "had a profound effect on his own style, for the rhythmic reductionism of form found in the treatment of the foliage proved the starting point for his own form of Post-Impressionism".

Writing to Maurice Vlaminck, in a letter of 1909, Derain speaks of the difficulty of properly "capturing" a landscape, but remarks how much easier it is to create plastic harmony by plucking it from its context, and by bringing to it the feelings one has from the physical world. He quotes, with approval, Delacroix's dictum that "nature is a dictionary from which one takes words" (A. Derain, *Lettres à Vlaminck* (Paris, 1955), p.176).

FORAIN, Jean-Louis 1852–1931

28 **At the Assizes** *c.*1908–10

Extensive preliminary drawing in black chalk, with rubbing; restricted watercolour washes, with drawing with the point of the brush (particularly in the figure of the foreground barrister); white bodycolour (mixing in parts with the chalk and watercolour washes); on cream (now unevenly discoloured and stained) laid paper, watermarked: "CHAPRON — COQUELIN — PARIS". 37.9 x 51.5 cm

Signed in soft pencil, lower right: "forain".

Inscribed and numbered in different hands in pencil, *verso:* 'Scène de cour d'assises", and: "3095/T" and: "N^{o}—76" (encircled), and priced (?): "5500" (altered from "5000").

PROVENANCE With Arthur Tooth and Son, London (purchased from the artist, no record of date); Samuel Courtauld 1925. Courtauld Gift 1932.

EXHIBITED *Drawings by Forain,* Arthur Tooth and Son, London, February 1925 (18); British Institute of Adult Education, Silver End, Essex, April 1935; *Fighting French Exhibition,* London, May 1943; on loan to City Art Gallery, Wakefield, 1946–47; Tate Gallery, London, 1948 (95); Orangerie, Paris, 1955 (77); *Forain,* Roland, Browse and Delbanco, London, 1964 (29).

LITERATURE *Home House Catalogue,* no.71; Cooper, 1954, no.120.

This drawing was dated by Cooper (*ibid.*) to *c.*1908–09, although scenes of the lawcourts were the subject of the bulk of Forain's paintings and drawings from *c.*1900–10, and appear in lithographs as late as 1915 (cf. *Legal Advice, J-L. Forain Peintre, Dessinateur et Graveur,* Bibliothèque Nationale, Paris, 1952). The restricted colour of the Courtauld drawing reflects the sombre palette which Forain employed in the oil paintings during the period *c.*1895–1920.

Yves Brayer has noted (*J-L. Forain, Artist, Realist, Humanist* (International Exhibition Foundation, Washington, 1982–83) p.9) Forain's procedure of executing many drawings of the same motif — some of which were traced — to be reworked or recombined with other images: such working methods preclude a precise dating of the artist's drawings and watercolours.

Variations of both barristers in the Courtauld drawing appear in the lithograph *Legal Advice* (cited above), while the defendant in this work leans forward in an attentive manner similar to that of the young client in the print. The foreground barrister of the present sheet also appears in the painting *The Unmarried Mother,* signed and dated to 1909 (City of Bristol Museum and Art Gallery), a variant of which is in the National Gallery of Art, Washington. A related oil composition, although one in which the barristers address each other, was in the Polès sale, Galerie Petit, Paris, 22-24 June 1927, Lot no.12.

The motif of the bored lawyer, slumped at his desk with head in hand, indifferent to the dramatic events occurring behind him, is derived from similar figures in compositions by Edgar Degas, for example Edmond Duranty, in the portraits of 1879 (Glasgow Art Gallery and Museum; National Gallery of Art, Washington: Lemoisne, *Degas, op.cit.,* 517, 518, respectively). The subject matter of the lawcourts ultimately derives from the work of Honoré Daumier (see, for example, no.20).

FORAIN, Jean-Louis 1852–1931

29 **In the Wings** *c.*1920–23

Preliminary drawing with the point of the brush and brown ink wash of varying strengths; black (Indian?) and brown ink wash and restricted watercolour washes (all of varying strengths and combinations) with extensive drawing with the brush; white and dark green bodycolour; on cream (now unevenly discoloured) laid paper watermarked: "VAN GELDER ZONEN". The sheet unevenly torn, right.

45.2 x 29 cm

Signed in pencil, lower right: "forain". Numbered and priced in different hands in pencil, *verso:* "T8000" and: "3079/T", and: "N^O.64" (encircled), and: "7500" (altered from "6000").

PROVENANCE With Arthur Tooth and Son, London (purchased from the artist, no record of date); Samuel Courtauld 1925. Courtauld Gift 1935.

EXHIBITED *Drawings by Forain,* Arthur Tooth and Son, London, February 1925 (2); Tate Gallery, 1948; Orangerie, Paris, 1955 (76); Arts Council (11).

LITERATURE Cooper, 1954, no.119.

The subject of the ballet dancer with her protector or admirer is one treated by Forain from his debut as an artist until the mid-to-late 1890s, and to which he returned after *c.*1920. During the intervening period, he directed his attention, in both oils and watercolours, towards political subject matter, scenes of domestic life or of the lawcourts, and religious themes (Alicia Faxon, *The Work of Jean-Louis Forain in New England Collections* (Danforth Museum, Franningham, USA 1979), p.11), adopting a sombre palette in which browns, blacks and white predominate.

The date 1906–07 assigned by Cooper (*ibid.*) to the Courtauld drawing is therefore unconvincing. The drawing's subject matter reworks that of the watercolour, *The Dancer and the Subscriber to the Ballet* of 1890 (private coll., France: exhibited *J-L. Forain,* Musée Marmottan, Paris, 1978, no. 96, and illustrated), although this work is executed in subdued tones, with extensive pen drawing of precise and continuous contours which tend to detach the figures from their background.

Although the Courtauld sheet is now discoloured and brown (the degree of discoloration may be observed at the edges of the sheet), it was originally executed in heightened colour, with a fluidity and freedom of drawing and an apparent unconcern for the degree of finish. The figures, no longer defined by incisive contours, appear to merge at intervals with their surroundings. Similar characteristics of manner and handling may be observed in the highly-coloured and well-preserved sheet, *Dancer in a Tutu,* dated to 1920 (coll., Chagnaud-Forain, Paris: exhibited *J-L. Forain,* Musée Marmottan, Paris, 1978, no.112, and illustrated) and in the gouache, also entitled *In the Wings,* dated by Faxon (*op.cit.*) to 1923 (Wiggins coll., Boston Public Library: exhibited Danforth Museum (see above), no.25, and illustrated).

On the basis of analogous style, the Courtauld sheet may also be assigned to the period of these works, that is, *c.*1920–23.

GAUGUIN, Paul 1848–1903

30 **Haymaking** 1889

Oil on canvas, 92 x 73.3 cm

Signed, bottom right: 'P. Gauguin '89'

PROVENANCE Ambroise Vollard; Dr. Frizeau, Bordeaux; through?; Samuel Courtauld by 1923. Courtauld Gift 1932.

EXHIBITED *Gauguin Exhibition,* Leicester Galleries, London, July 1924 (61, repr.); Tate Gallery, 1948 (27); Orangerie, Paris, 1955 (29); *Gauguin,* Edinburgh, 1955 (28); *Gauguin and the Pont-Aven Group,* Arts Council at Tate Gallery, 7 January-13 February 1966 (20).

LITERATURE Jamot-Turner, no.36 (repr.); Home House Catalogue, no.10; Cooper, 1954, no.29 (repr.) as *Les-Meules;* J. Rewald, *Post-Impressionism: From Van Gogh to Gauguin* (New York, 1956), repr. p.248 (as *Harvesting*); Georges Wildenstein, *Gauguin,* I (Paris, 1964), p.135, no.352 (repr.).

One of two haymaking scenes painted at Pont-Aven, Brittany, in July 1889, the other being *Le Moisson Blond* (Musée du Louvre, Wildenstein 351). Gauguin had first visited Pont-Aven in 1886, partly to escape from Paris, and partly to find a cheaper place to live (he stayed at the Pension Gloanec, where he could obtain almost unlimited credit), and to enjoy a more primitive atmosphere. Although it must be said that Brittany was by now becoming prosperous economically and an attractive tourist centre, Gauguin avoided most other painters, but a group of younger artists began to form around him consisting of Charles Laval, Émile Bernard, the Symbolist writer G.-Albert Aurier, Meyer de Haan, Paul Sérusier, and Émile Schuffenecker — who helped support Gauguin financially at this time.

Gauguin's style had developed quite radically from the type of Impressionist paintings he had produced in the mid-1870s while still influenced by Camille Pissarro. He had already paid his first visit to Martinique (1887), and dreamt of returning to the tropics. He begins to simplify his forms, to "synthesize" them, and to subordinate naturalistic representation to purely aesthetic considerations.

Writing to Émile Bernard from Arles in November 1888, Gauguin explains his attitude to the role of shadows in a painting: 'You want to know whether I disdain shadows . . . In so far as they are an explanation of light, I do. Look at the Japanese who draw so admirably, and you will see there life in the open air and in the sun, without shadows. They use colour only as a combination of tones, various harmonies, giving the impression of heat, etc . . . Thus I shall get away as much as possible from anything that gives the illusion of an object, and shadows being the *trompe l'oeil* of the sun, I am inclined to eliminate them." (quoted by Rewald, *op.cit.,* p.198). Gauguin qualifies these remarks only to the extent that he will use shadows if they serve a purely pictorial (as distinct from representational) purpose.

In *Haymaking,* shadows have been eliminated, the perspective flattened, and the shapes of individual elements, such as the harvesters, oxen, trees, and farm buildings, are all more rigorously simplified than the haymaking scene of 1888 (Musée du Louvre; Wildenstein 269).

A sheet of studies for *Haymaking* was sold at Galerie Charpentier, Paris, 21 June 1960 (lot 19), and a related watercolour is in the Albertina, Vienna.

GAUGUIN, Paul 1848–1903

31 **Nevermore** 1897

Oil on canvas, 60.5 x 116 cm

Signed, top left: "NEVERMORE/P. Gauguin 97/O. TAÏTI".

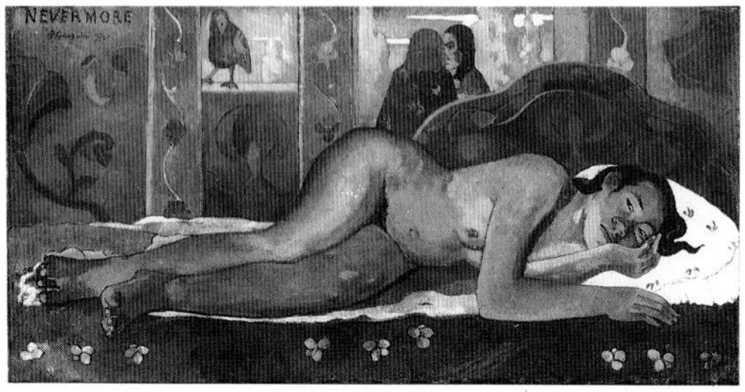

colour plate, page 48

PROVENANCE Bought from Daniel de Montfried by Frederick Delius 1898 (500 Frs.); Alfred Wolff, Munich; with Alex. Reid, Glasgow; with Agnew, London and Manchester; Herbert Coleman, Manchester; Samuel Courtauld by 1926. Courtauld Gift 1932.

EXHIBITED Salon d'Automne, Paris, 1906 (216); Sonderbund Ausstellung, Cologne, 1912 (168); *Masterpieces of French Art of the 19th Century,* Agnew, Manchester, September 1923 (17); *Gauguin Exhibition,* Leicester Galleries, London, July, 1924 (52); Tate Gallery, 1948 (28); *Gauguin, Exposition du Centenaire,* Orangerie, Paris, July 1949 (48); Orangerie, Paris, 1955 (25); *Gauguin,* Edinburgh, 1955 (55); Courtauld Centenary, 1976 (21); National Gallery, London, February-March 1983 (no catalogue).

LITERATURE Jamot-Turner, no.37 (repr.); Home House Catalogue, no.4; Cooper, 1954, no.30 (repr.); G. Wildenstein, *Gauguin,* I (Paris 1964), pp.230-31, no.558 (repr.).

Painted in February 1897, during Gauguin's second visit to Tahiti, whence he had returned from Paris in search of a simpler, more primitive, life in 1895. In a letter to the artist, Daniel de Montfried, who also acted as Gauguin's agent, he wrote of this painting (14 February 1897): "I wished to suggest, by means of a simple nude, a certain long-lost barbarian luxury. The whole is drowned in colours which are deliberately sombre and sad; it is neither silk, nor velvet, nor *batiste,* nor gold that creates luxury here but simply matter which has been enriched by the hand of the artist. No nonsense . . . Man's imagination alone has enriched the dwelling with his fantasy. As a title: Nevermore, not the raven of Edgar Allan Poe, but the bird of the devil that is keeping watch. It is badly painted (I'm so nervy and can only work in bouts) but no matter, I think it is a good canvas." (*Lettres de Paul Gauguin à Daniel de Montfried,* new ed. by Mme Joly-Sègalen, Paris, 1950, pp.101, 135, 190, 210-11).

The painting has affinities with *Manao Tupapau: L'Esprit Veille* (coll. Conger Goodyear, New York; Wildenstein no.457) painted in 1893. Both were inspired by Manet's *Olympia* (1863), which Gauguin greatly admired and of which he made a copy; he also had a photograph of *Olympia* in his hut in Tahiti. He attached great importance to *Nevermore* and insisted to de Montfried (*op.cit.*) that it should be included in any retrospective exhibition of his work.

The English composer, Frederick Delius (1862–1934), the first owner of the painting, was introduced to the work of Gauguin by the composer William Molard, who had known the artist well in 1893–94 when they were both living at 4 Rue Vercingétorix in Paris. Gauguin wrote to de Montfried (12 January 1899) to express his pleasure that Delius had become the owner of the picture "given that it is not a speculative purchase for re-sale, but for enjoyment."

There is evidence that *Nevermore* was painted over another painting, but the white ground obscures most of the previous composition, although what appear to be trees can be discerned on radiographs. Where old paint losses from the present composition occur, the colour of the underlying pigment thus revealed bears no relation to the final work. A detailed technical examination and analysis appears in an unpublished M.A. Report for the Courtauld Institute prepared by Charlotte Hale in 1983.

GAUGUIN, Paul 1848-1903
32 **Te Rerioa** 1897
Oil on canvas, 95.1 x 130.2 cm
Signed, bottom left centre: "TE RERIOA/P. Gauguin 97/TAITI"

colour plate, page 49

PROVENANCE Bought from Daniel de Montfried by Gustave Fayet, Igny (1,100 Frs.); with Paul Rosenberg, Paris (November 1928); with Wildenstein, New York; Samuel Courtauld, July 1929. Courtauld Gift 1932.
EXHIBITED Musée de Bezier, 1901; Salon d'Automne, Paris, October 1906 (4) as "Intérieur de case à Tahiti" and lent by Fayet; *French Art,* Royal Academy, London, 1932 (520); Tate Gallery, 1948 (29); *Gauguin, Exposition du Centenaire,* Orangerie, Paris, July 1949 (49); *Gauguin,* Edinburgh, 1955 (56); Orangerie, Paris, 1955 (26); Courtauld Centenary, 1976 (22).
LITERATURE Jamot-Turner, no.35 (repr.); Home House Catalogue, no.5 (repr.); Cooper, 1954, no.31 (repr.); G. Wildenstein, *Gauguin,* I (Paris, 1964), pp.229-30, no.557 (repr.).

Painted in Tahiti in March 1897, about three weeks after *Nevermore,* it has been said that this painting shows the last house Gauguin occupied at Atuana, a remote village on Hiva-Oa, the largest of the Marquesas islands. This is clearly wrong, since Gauguin did not move to Atuana until 1901, but Christopher Gray (*The Sculptures and Ceramics of Paul Gauguin,* The Johns Hopkins Press, Baltimore, 1963, pp.75, 266-67, 276) accepts that it may show Gauguin's house at Tahiti. Gray also prefers the spelling *Te Reri Oa.*
Gauguin refers to this picture in a letter of 12 March 1897 to de Montfried, and says that he has hastened to complete another canvas to send with *Nevermore* and three other pictures on a French warship bound for France, the departure of which had been delayed by ten days or so. He continued, in the same letter: "Te Rerioa (Day-dreaming), that's the title. Everything about this picture is dreamlike: is it the child, the mother, the horseman on the bridlepath, or better still is it the painter's dream? All that has nothing to do with painting, they'll say. May be, but also perhaps not." (*Lettres de Paul Gauguin à Daniel de Montfried,* new ed. by Mme Joly-Ségalen, Paris, 1950, pp.102, 237, 239-40.)
Gray (*op.cit.,* pp.266-67) notes some resemblance between the right-hand figures in the wood carving, *Panel with Two Figures,* and the right-hand figure in the baseboard decoration, which appears diagonally to the left of *Te Rerioa.* He also sees a similarity between the mermaid in the right hand panel on the wall in *Te Rerioa* and a print, probably taken from a redwood board carving made by Gauguin to decorate his house, *Siren and marine God.* The grimacing figure in the bottom foreground is a variant on the devil-creature in *Manao Tupapau;* Richard S. Field has noted that the two embracing figures on the diagonal wall are a free variation on the group of lovers in the centre of Delacroix's *Massacre of Scio* 1824 (Field, *op.cit.,* 1977).
There are traces of *pentimenti* in the vertical bands on either side of the doorway, through which can be seen a landscape. Traces of the mountain ridge and palm tree boughs are visible through the overpaint on the left and, especially, on the right side of the door opening.

GAUGUIN, Paul 1848-1903
Album of Ten Woodcuts 33-42

Numbers 33-40 of the present woodcuts were executed by Gauguin in the winter of 1893–94, as part of a suite of ten probable illustrations for his book entitled *Noa Noa* (Field, 1968, *op.cit.,* pp.500-03), The project for the book, which would both recount the events of Gauguin's visit to Tahiti from April 1891-August 1893 and elucidate the paintings which had resulted from this trip, was initiated by the artist to counter the incomprehension and adverse criticism which had greeted those paintings of Tahitian subjects he had exhibited at Durand-Ruel's, in November 1893 (Bengt Danielsson, *Gauguin in the South Seas,* 1965, p.143).
The text of *Noa Noa* was to be the result of collaboration between Gauguin and the symbolist writer and critic, Charles Morice (1861–1919). In the winter of 1893, Gauguin supplied an initial rough draft for Morice to work from (now in the hands of the heirs of the print-seller, Sagot (Loize, *op.cit.,* p.58)). The following spring, Gauguin copied, and attempted to put into order, a first version sketched by Morice from the material already supplied: gaps were left in the text in which to incorporate the poet's supplementary verses. In 1895, when Gauguin returned to Tahiti for good, he took this copy of *Noa Noa* with him. He had already begun to illustrate it with watercolours and woodcuts, and continued adding to it until 1899: this version of *Noa Noa* entered the Louvre in 1925.
The blocks upon which the woodcuts were executed were made up from small sections of hard, smooth boxwood (*Buxus sempervirens*) cut across the end-grain – the traditional material of the European wood-engraver (Walter Chamberlain, *The Thames and Hudson Manual of Wood Engraving,* 1978, pp.75-80). As cutting tools Gauguin employed the carpenter's chisel (with which he had fashioned the sculpture and reliefs of the previous years), and also the knife or razor, needle and sandpaper, implements normally found in the lithographic studio (Field, 1968, *op.cit.,* p.504). Indeed, Field (*ibid.*) has observed that the lithographs of Gauguin's friend, Eugène Carrière (1849–1906), must have provided direct inspiration for the woodcuts. The subtle tones achieved by Degas in the monotypes must have also influenced him.
Field (1968, *op.cit.,* pp.505-07) suggests that Gauguin worked simultaneously on all the blocks of the *Noa Noa* suite, each block passing through four comparable stages which may be determined from the artist's surviving impressions. The printing of the blocks, either with a press or by rubbing was carried out as informally and as experimentally as the cutting. No complete edition of the *Noa Noa* suite was published by Gauguin, although one was printed under the artist's direction by Louis Roy in late spring of 1894. Gauguin's disapproval of this edition is attested to by his use of the *versos* of many of the prints to carry out further experiments of his own.
When Gauguin departed for Tahiti the second time, eight of the *Noa Noa* blocks were deposited with the musician, William Molard. These were passed on to Gauguin's son, Pola, who added a further block (see cat. nos.41 and 42) to print the present edition of 100 in 1921, of which the Courtauld album is no.28.

The present album, purchased from Pola Gauguin by the Leicester Galleries by 1924, was acquired by Samuel Courtauld in July of that year. He bequeathed it to the Courtauld Institute in 1948 (H.H. 214-23).
Each woodcut is printed in black ink on thin, white laid paper, impressed with a multi-directional grain. Each print is inscribed in Pola Gauguin's hand in pencil below the blockmarks, left: "Paul Gauguin fait", and right: "Pola Gauguin imp", and numbered above the blockmarks, left: "No. 28".

Sketchbooks and writings by Paul Gauguin referred to in the catalogue entries:

Le Carnet de Gauguin (c.1888: facsimile), introduction by R. Huyghe (Paris, 1952).
Carnet de Tahiti (1891–93: facsimile), introduction by B. Dorival (Paris, 1954).
Presentation de l'Ancien culte mahorie (1892: facsimile), introduction by R. Huyghe (Paris 1951).
Cahier pour Aline (1893: facsimile) (Paris 1963).
Noa Noa (1894–99: facsimile) (Berlin 1926).
Noa Noa introduction by Jean Loize, translated Jonathan Griffin, Oxford, no date.
Avant et Après (1903: facsimile) (Leipzig 1919).

Exhibitions referred to in the catalogue entries:
Leicester Galleries: *Gauguin,* Leicester Galleries London, July 1924.

Tate Gallery: *Paul Gauguin paintings sculpture and engravings,* Arts Council of Great Britain, Tate Gallery, 30 September-26 October 1955.

Europe: *Paul Gauguin,* Galerie Charpentier, Paris, January-February, Haus der Kunst, Munich, March-April, Oesterreichische Galerie, Vienna, June-July 1960.

Japan: *Paul Gauguin,* Seibu Gallery, Tokyo, September-October, National Museum of Modern Art, Kyoto, October-November, Museum of Fukuoka, November-December 1969.

Newcastle: *Prints by Paul Gauguin and Contemporary Artists,* Hatton Gallery, Newcastle University, Newcastle-on-Tyne.

Catalogues and other works referred to in the entries:

(F number): refers to the catalogue nos. of paintings in Richard S. Field, *Paul Gauguin The Paintings of the First Voyage to Tahiti* (originally presented as the author's Ph.D. thesis, Harvard University 1963, New York, 1977).

(Gray number): Christopher Gray, *Sculpture and Ceramics of Paul Gauguin* (Baltimore, 1963).

Guérin [number]: Marcel Guérin, *L'oeuvre gravé de Gauguin* (Paris 1927, 2 vols.). Where Guérin allots a number to an individual early state of the woodcut, it is here signified thus [15].
Where Guérin groups several early states under one number, the states are distinguished thus: i,ii,iii, e.g. [15 i,ii].
Where Guérin records a final state identical with that of a woodcut from Pola Gauguin's edition, it is signified by*, thus: [15 i,ii,16*].
Guérin allots a new number for each print from the Pola Gauguin album: this number appears after the brackets, thus [15,i,ii,16*] 97.

(Rewald number): John Rewald, *Gauguin Drawings* (New York, 1958).

(W number): Georges Wildenstein, *Gauguin* (vol.1, Paris, 1964).

[number]: refers to earlier states of the present woodcut mentioned in any other catalogue recorded in the text.

GAUGUIN, Paul 1848–1903
33 **Te Po**
Woodcut, with extensive wood engraving.
Blockmarks: 20.4 x 35.9 cm.
Signed on the block, upper left: "PGo", and inscribed on the block, lower left: "TE PO".

EXHIBITED Leicester Galleries (19 or 28 (?)); Tate Gallery (71 (1)); Newcastle (1); Arts Council (15).
LITERATURE Guérin [15 i,ii*] 89, under 56; G. L. McCann Morley, *P. Gauguin* (San Francisco Museum of Art, 1936) [66-69] 70; Cooper, 1954, no.182/1; Hugh Edwards, *Gauguin* (Art Institute of Chicago and Metropolitan Museum, 1959), pp.76-78 [141, 142, 143]; Ronald Alley, *Gauguin* 1961), p.18; W 458, 459, 460, 477, under 457; Bengt Danielsson, "Gauguin's Tahitian Titles", *Burlington Magazine,* CIX (April 1967), no.72; Richard S. Field, "Gauguin's Noa Noa Suite", *Burlington Magazine,* CX (September 1968), p.509; Ronald Pickvance, *The Drawings of Gauguin* (New York, Sydney, Toronto, 1970), p.13; Field (1977) *op.cit.,* p.125, footnote 36.

The composition of the woodcut is a reworking in reverse, and with important alterations, of that of the painting *Manao tupapau* of March-April 1892 (coll. Gen. A. Conger Goodyear, New York: F 28; W 457). The meaning of the painting, explained by Gauguin at length on several occasions (in a letter to his wife of 8 December 1892, cf. M. Malingue, *Lettres de Gauguin à sa femme et à ses amis* (Paris, 1942), no. CXXXIV; in *Cahier pour Aline,* p.9; in *Notes Eparses* [cited by Robert Ray, *Gauguin* (Paris, 1928), p.37]) encompasses two themes: the Tahitians' constant terror of the night and fear of the *tupapau* or spirit, and the communication between sleeper and *tupapau.* It is the former theme which Gauguin elaborates in this woodcut. The sleeping nude of *Manao tupapau* is replaced in the present composition by a clothed figure, taken from the foreground of the oil *TE FARE HYMENEE* of February 1892 (coll. Mr. and Mrs. Carleton Mitchell, Annapolis, USA: F 22; W 477), a study for which is on p.68 *recto* of the *Carnet de Tahiti.* Gauguin's decision to use this figure arose from his recognition of the erotic nature of the pose of the nude in *Manao tupapau,* and his wish, expressed on p.9 of *Cahier pour Aline* and elsewhere (see above) to make of the subject 'a chaste picture'.
The figure of the spirit at the right of the print may be identified with the profile figure who occupies a similar position in the composition of both painted and printed versions of *Manao tupapau* (see cat. no.35), and is probably derived, as Field (1977, *ibid.*) observed, from Papuan or New Caledonian prototypes. The figure first appears, holding a mask, in the preparatory study for the painting *Parau na te varau ino* (Cabinet des

Dessins, Musée du Louvre: Rewald 40) and is also incorporated into that composition (coll. Governor and Mrs. W. Averell Harrimann, New York: F29; W458), as well as in the paintings *Barbaric Tales* (private coll., Paris: F31; W459) and *Parau hanohano* (private coll., no location: F30; W460), all executed in April-May 1892. The figure at the left of the background group may be identified as Gauguin himself: the slanted eyes, hooked nose and set of the head are reminiscent of those in paintings such as the *Self-portrait with Idol* of *c.*1893 (Marion Koogler McNey Art Institure, San Antonio, USA: W415).
The motif of the sleeping figure was taken up, after completion of this print, in the woodcut *Interior of a hut* of *c.*1896-97 (Guérin 56), while a watercolour variant of it appears on p.63 of *Noa Noa.*

GAUGUIN, Paul 1848–1903
34 **Noa Noa**
Woodcut, with extensive wood engraving.
Blockmarks (slightly irregular): 35.6 x 20.6 cm.
Signed on the block, upper centre: "P G o", and inscribed above: "NoANoA".

EXHIBITED Leicester Galleries (32 (?)); Tate Gallery (71 (2)); *Prints,* City Art Gallery, Leeds 1961 (18); Newcastle (2); Arts Council (16).
LITERATURE Guérin [16, 17*] 90; McCann Morley, *op.cit.,* [71-73] 74; Cooper, 1954, no.182/2; Edwards, *op.cit.,* pp.76-78 [76-78, 144]; W431, 432, 468; Danielsson, *op.cit.,* 39; Field (1968), *op.cit.,* p.509, no.13; Pickvance, *ibid.;* Richard S. Field, *Gauguin Monotypes* (Philadelphia Museum of Art, 1973), under no.124.

The composition refers to the two versions of the oil painting *I RARO TE OVIRI,* the first of which (Dallas Museum for Contemporary Arts: F10; W431) dates from November 1891, while the second (Minneapolis Institute of Art: F11; W432) may have been executed in early 1892. The motif of the carrier of *fei* (wild banana) in both paintings and woodcut may be traced to rapid sketches on pp.27 *recto,* and 89 and 91 *verso* of the *Carnet de Tahiti,* although Field (1977, *op.cit.,* p.47) suggests that it may ultimately derive from a Trajan relief, a photograph of which Gauguin possessed. The dual source for many of the motifs, in both the paintings and woodcuts, which results from a fusion of analytical observation with synthetic recreation, is, as Field (1977, *ibid.*) observes, a recurring feature in much of Gauguin's work of the period 1891–95.
The differences between the present woodcut composition and that of the paintings to which it refers are crucial: in the print, Gauguin has employed a vertical format, rather than the horizontal format of the oils, has altered the seashore setting of the paintings to one inland (reminiscent of that used in *MARURU:* see cat. no.36), and has radically reduced the size of one of the figures. The fallen pandanus branches now form an enclosing oval pattern, which stresses the interaction of the two figures, and prevents the eye from wandering, as it does particularly in the Minneapolis picture, into areas of deep space at either side of the composition. The trunk of the pandanus tree behind the fruit carrier in the oils is transposed without reversal to the left edge of the woodcut, where it is cropped, assuming the form of a mysterious shaft of directional light (Field, 1968, *ibid.*) which again forces the eye to the centre of the composition. The *fei* are aligned with the trunk of the tree at the centre of the woodcut composition, their rounded forms anticipating those of the foliage, in which small figures are seated. A meaning which the painting did not convey is now evident in *NoANoA,* for the emblematic tree (studies for which are on pp.26 *recto,* 48 *verso,* 49 *recto* and 71 *verso* of the *Carnet de Tahiti*) and fruit (with its associations of the Fall of Eve and the loss of innocence) are literally the support of human life.
The dog, which appears in both versions of *I RARO TE OVIRI,* can be traced back to a small watercolour study of 1891 (coll. Mr. and Mrs. Ward Chesney, New York: Rewald 71), and is repeated with variations in the painting *AREAREA* of November-December 1892 (Musée du Louvre: F50; W468). The same dog appears, without a head, on p.80 *recto* of the *Carnet de Tahiti.* The similar cropping of the dog's head in the woodcut – in the paintings (cited above) the animal appears in its entirety – may be the result of working directly from the *Carnet* sketch, although it can be argued that it alludes specifically to the appearance of the dog in a third painting of 1891, *Tahitians on the Beach* (Academy of Arts, Honolulu: F83; W456). In this work, the animal's head is masked by its mistress's legs. Once this clue is taken up, it can be seen that *NoANoA* makes other references to this third painting: the pose of the nude woman on the right of this canvas is identical to that of the figure on the right of *I RARO TE OVIRI* (translated in reverse on the left of the woodcut), while the vertical format of *Tahitians on the Beach* is that adopted for *NoANoA.*
The mysterious kangaroo-like creature, at the upper right of the woodcut, is a variation of that which appears first in 1880 as a design on the side of a pot in the shape of a gourd (coll. Mme Juliette Cramer, Paris: Gray 55); in the following year a similar motif was part of the burned decoration on the side of a brush-holder Gauguin dedicated to his friend Schuffenecker (coll. Galerie Saint Etienne, New York: Gray 48).
The year after the present woodcut was completed, Gauguin executed a variant of the composition, also in the medium of woodcut (Guérin 47), while a colour monotype of 1896–99 records the fruit carrier only (Field, 1973, *op.cit.,* no.124). With the pasted additions of the figure seated in the tree (left) and the 'kangaroo' (right) from the present woodcut, the monotype was used as the frontispiece to *NOA NOA.* A watercolour in the Museum of Belgrade, mentioned under W431, may be a variant of this.
The motif of the dog was used again in the monotype *Tahitian Scene* of 1894 (coll. Cabinet des Dessins, Musée du Louvre: Field, 1973, *op.cit.,* no.4), and finally in the two versions of *ARII Vahine* of 1896 (Pushkin Museum, Moscow: W542; and private coll., no location: W543).

GAUGUIN, Paul 1848–1903

35 **Manao Tupapau**

Woodcut, with extensive white-line engraving.

Blockmarks: 20.4 x 35.6 cm

Signed on the block, lower left: "PGo", and inscribed on the block, upper left: "Manao/tupapau".

EXHIBITED Leicester Galleries (29 (?)); Tate Gallery (71 (3)); London (34); Newcastle (3); *The Mechanised Image,* Arts Council travelling exhibition, 1978 (51).

LITERATURE Guérin [18, 19, 20*] 91, and under no. 57; McCann Morley, *op.cit.,* [75-83] 84; Cooper, 1954, no.182/3; Edwards, *op.cit.,* pp.76-78 [145, 146]; W457, 502, 506, 597, Danielsson, *op.cit.,* no.27; Pickvance, *ibid.*; Field, 1977, *op.cit.,* pp.111-18, and no.28.

The composition is based on the oil painting *Manao tupapau* (see cat. no.33), which Gauguin recorded in a summary drawing at the heading of a note rationalizing the painting's genesis on p.9 of *Cahier pour Aline* (Rewald 67). One of the reasons for substituting for the nude who lies face-down, diagonally across the bed a figure in a different pose, is discussed under cat.no.33. The foetal pose of the present nude is related to that of the Breton Eve series of nudes (W320, 333, 334, 335), also to that of the female figure incised on the side of a stoneware pot in the form of a treestump (Musée des Arts Africains et Océaniens, Paris: Gray 54) — all works of 1889 — which was influenced by the form of a Peruvian mummy exhibited at the Musée d'Ethnologie du Trocadéro in the 1880s (Wayne Andersen, "Gauguin and a Peruvian Mummy", *Burlington Magazine,* CX, April 1967. The figure in this group of works, however, is seen vertically and generally frontally.

Similarly posed figures, either in profile or rear-view, were sketched from life on pp.32 and 33 *recto,* 44 *verso,* 46 *recto,* 58 *recto* and *verso,* and 59 *recto* of the *Cahier de Tahiti.* Most important for the present figure are the drawings on p.46 *recto* (of a nude posed so that the knees touch the chest), and on pp.32 and 33 *recto,* for which the sketchbook has been turned from the normal vertical format to the horizontal. When the sketchbook is turned again to its usual format, these figures appear to lie on their side. The pose of the nude in the present print may have been partly determined by these observations.

The treatment of the figure, however — the bold hatching at right angles to the spine, and the high viewpoint from which it is observed upon the oval form of the blanket — indicate a renewed interest in the bather subjects of Edgar Degas (for example, pastels such as *The Tub* of 1886 (Lemoisne, *Degas,* 872) or the sculpture *The Tub* completed in June 1889 (Charles W. Millard, *The Sculpture of Edgar Degas,* (Princeton, 1976), p.10 and fig.92)). The conflation of Degas's influence with that of the Peruvian mummy has been noted by Andersen (*op.cit.,* p.241) in the earlier context of the Breton Eves. By linking the pose of the Tahitian nude with that of the foetal Peruvian mummy, in whose posture life and death are fused (Andersen, *op.cit.,* p.238), Gauguin makes explicit in the woodcut the theme, hidden in the painting (Field, 1977, *op.cit.,* p.118), of the Tahitian, who, through the medium of death and night, establishes contact with her ancestors, to be reborn at daybreak. The oval form of the blanket may thus be interpreted as a womb image.

The differentiation observed by Field (1977, *op.cit.,* p.117), between the flat, painterly background, and the robust plasticity of the foreground figure in the painting — the contrast between night and day or death and life — has its equivalent in the woodcut, now exaggerated by the conflicting perspective systems employed: the figure is observed from above, the background from a lower viewpoint. Other changes away from the painting reinforce the dramatic nature of the print's content. The edge of the bed and floor, visible in the oil, are eliminated in the woodcut, and the nude is enlarged and brought closer to the picture surface, inducing in the viewer a feeling of discomfort. The headboard of the bed is reworked as an undulating band incorporating heads (variants of the Marquesan Atua figure, which appear in a similar band separating the figures on a carved cylinder of 1892-93 (private coll., Paris: Gray 102)) which stand as both the decorative carving of the furniture and as a secondary reference to the nude's ancestors.

The *tupapau,* or spirit of the dead, at the upper right of the print, may be derived from rapid sketches of profiles on pp.8 *recto* and 56 *recto* of the *Carnet de Tahiti:* it reappears in the pastel *Eve* of 1892 (a photograph of which was later pasted onto p.51 of *Noa Noa*), and in a watercolour on silk, *Barbarous Music* of the same date (both Kupferstichkabinett, Basle: Rewald 55 and 83, respectively). Rewald (under 55) also records a pen and ink sketch in the Art Institute of Chicago.

During 1894, the nude was incorporated on the right of the woodcut *Mahana Atua* (see cat.no.41), and in the large *Manao tupapau* woodcut (Guérin 36), the block of which Gauguin reworked as a relief (Guérin 39). The entire oil composition of *Manao tupapau,* incorporating the goddess Hina, was translated into a lithograph, also of 1894, while at about the same time the motif of the spirit and the head of the girl from the painting of *Manao tupapau* were juxtaposed in the woodcut executed on the back of the block of the large version of *Manao tupapau* (Guérin 40). The *tupapau's* profile was incorporated into one of the *Pape Moe* panels of 1895 (coll. Mme P. Bacou, Puissalicon: Gray 107), and reappears in the woodcut *Exotic Eve* of c.1896–98 (Guérin 57). A reworking of the theme of sleeper and spirit appears in the lower left corner of *TE RERIOA* of 1897 (see cat.no.32).

Gauguin returned to the motif of the spirit frequently during the period 1900-02. It reappears, now on horseback, first in the monotype *The Nightmare* of 1900 (private collection, France: Field, 1973, *op.cit.,* 70), in the oil *The Flight* of the following year (Hermitage, Leningrad: W597), and in the related monotype of c.1902, *The Flight* (coll. Musée des Arts Africains et Océaniens, Paris: Field, 1973, *op.cit.,* 104), of which there are two variants — the watercolour *The Escape* (location unknown: Rewald 108) and a watercolour in the Lithanet collection. The *tupapau* makes its final appearance in the gouache monotype *The Flight* c.1902 in the collection of the National Gallery of Art, Washington (Field, 1973, *op.cit.,* 134).

GAUGUIN, Paul 1848–1903

36 **Maruru**

Woodcut, with extensive white-line engraving.

Blockmarks: 20.5 x 35.6 cm

Signed on the block, bottom right: "P G O", and inscribed on the block, bottom right of centre: "MARURU".

EXHIBITED Leicester Galleries (37 (?)); Tate Gallery (71 (4)); Europe (185); *Prints,* City Art Gallery, Leeds 1961 (19); Japan (78); Newcastle (4).

LITERATURE Guérin [23, 24*] 92; McCann Morley, *op.cit.,* [88-90] 91; Cooper, 1954, no.182/3; Edwards *op.cit.,* pp.76-78, [149-51]; W467, 468, 482, under 500; Danielsson, *op.cit.,* no.28; Field (1968), *op.cit.,* p.509, no.12; Pickvance, *ibid.*

The print reverses all the motifs, with the exception of the range of background mountains and pandanus leaves in *HINA MARURU* of January 1893 (private coll., USA: F53; W500), the culminating painting of a series in which the profile of the moon goddess, Hina, gains in size and importance (Field (1977), *op.cit.,* p.174). The first of the series, *PARAHI TE MARAS* (coll. Mr. and Mrs. R. Meyer de Schauensee, Devon, USA: F34; W483), was completed in April-May 1892, soon after Gauguin had read J-L. Moerenhout's *Voyage aux Iles du Grand Océan* (Paris, 1837, republished 1877), from which he copied the material for his own *Ancien culte mahorie* (see cat.no.37). The other paintings of this period in which Hina's profile occurs are *MATAMUA* (private coll., New York: F51; W467), *AREAREA* (Jeu de Paume: F50; W468), both of December 1892, and a watercolour fan of comparable date reproducing the latter work (coll. Mr. and Mrs. Sydney F. Brody, Los Angeles: W469). Hina's profile is also incorporated into the carving on the back of *Idol with Pearl,* datable to 1892–93 (coll. Mme Huc de Montfried, Paris: Gray 94).

The *vivo* player (flautist) appears first (in the same sense as the woodcut) in the oil *Tahitian Pastoral* of December 1892 (Hermitage, Leningrad: F52; W470), and is reversed and combined with a variant of the woman, viewed from the rear, to her left, in the painting *RUPE TAHITI* of 1893 (New York art market: W509), executed on the glass panels of the door of Gauguin's hut in Tahiti.

Whereas the painting of *HINA MARURU* employs a vertical format, the woodcut adopts the horizontal format, banded composition and landscape details of Gauguin's oddly Impressionist painting, *Fatata te Mouà* of November 1892 (Pushkin Museum, Moscow: F49; W481). In reverting to this landscape, which itself owes much to the background of *Women by the River* of the previous year (coll. V. W. van Gogh, Laren: F72; W482), Gauguin made explicit the source of the landscape motifs which are found in *MATAMUA* and *HINA MARURU.* All details of *Fatata te Mouà,* with the exception of the horse and rider, are translated into the present woodcut in the same sense as they appear in that oil.

During 1894, Hina's profile appeared, again in the context of a landscape derived from *Fatata te Mouà,* in the background of the large woodcut *Manao tupapau* (Guérin 36: the upper section of which was pasted on to p.61 of *Noa Noa* (Guérin 37)), and in the block which was later reworked as a relief (Guérin 39: see cat.no.35). The landscape, combined with the image of the dog derived from *I PARO TE OVIRI* (see cat.no.34), was the subject of two watercolour monotypes also of 1894 (Cabinet des Dessins, Musée du Louvre; and location unknown: Field, *op.cit.,* 1973, nos.4 and 34 respectively).

The motif of the *vivo* player was taken up again in the oil *MAHANA no Atua* of the summer of 1894 (Art Institute of Chicago: W513) and was repeated in the woodcut interpretation of this picture (see cat.no.41). Its final appearance is in one of the three panels from the carving *Pape Moe* of 1895 (coll. Mme d'Andoque, Béziers: Gray 107 and p.63).

GAUGUIN, Paul 1848–1903

37 **L'Univers est crée**

Some woodcut, with extensive white-line engraving.

Blockmarks: 20.4 x 35.4 cm

Signed on the block, lower right: "PGO", and inscribed on the block, lower left: "l'Univers est crée" (*sic*).

EXHIBITED Leicester Galleries (15 or 33 (?)); Tate Gallery (71 (5)); Europe (186); Japan (79); Newcastle (5).

LITERATURE Guérin [25, 26*] 91, under 48, under pp.1, XXVII; McCann Morley, *op.cit.,* [92-94] 95; Cooper, 1954, no.182/4; Edwards, *op.cit.,* pp.76-78 [152-53]; Jean Leymarie, *Paul Gauguin, Aquarelles, pastels et dessins en couleur* (Basle, 1960), no.19; Gray, under no.103; Field, 1968, *op.cit.,* p.509; Pickvance, *ibid.*

The title of this woodcut is taken from p.10 of Gauguin's book *L'Ancien culte mahorie* (Louvre) in which the artist copied and illustrated passages from J-L. Moerenhout's *Voyage aux Iles du Grand Océan* (Paris, 1837 and 1877), probably during March 1892. Moerenhout's book recounts the old Tahitian legend of the Creation and subsequent events, and describes in detail the pantheon of Tahitian gods.

The sentence 'l'Univers est crée' concludes Gauguin's narrative of the creation of the world by Taaora, who is both the god of creation and the matter from which the universe is composed: the legend was not illustrated by Gauguin in *L'Ancien culte mahorie.* The title which the artist has gone to great pains to inscribe in reverse on the block, in the same cursive script in which *L'Ancien culte mahorie* was written, may therefore be interpreted as both the summary of the Creation myth, and as the graphic substitute for an illustration of Taaora's abstract nature and deed.

All the motifs used in this print, except for those in the upper left corner,

are reversals of illustrations to *L'Ancien culte mahorie*.
The motif of the fish is taken from p.18, illustrating the lesser god and patron of sailors, Atoua maho. The profile figure behind the fish, and the fan on the stem issuing from the fish's mouth (also in the illustration to *L'Ancien culte mahorie*) were inspired by, respectively, a Theban tomb fresco, and decorative carvings on the temple of Borobudur, Java, photographs of which were in Gauguin's possession from *c*.1887 (cf. Bernard Dorival, "Sources of the Art of Gauguin from Java, Egypt and Ancient Greece", *Burlington Magazine,* XCIII (April 1951), pp.118-22). A related motif of two fish linked to each other by a stem from the mouth, was carved on the botton of a bowl for *poi* (1892-93; coll. Mme Huc de Montfried, Paris: Gray 103), and was repeated on the inside cover of the *Cahier pour Aline,* 1893.
The creatures on the right of the woodcut can be identified as the Tiis, children of Taaora and the moon goddess, Hina, who were inferior gods acting as both the demarcation and intermediaries between the organic and inorganic, and who, although not of the sea, were guardians of all within it (*L'Ancien culte mahorie,* p.20). These figures are illustrated on p.21 of *L'Ancien culte mahorie,* and are repeated, with Hina, in a watercolour on silk, *Barbarous Music,* also of 1892 (Kupferstichkabinett, Basle: Rewald 83).
The male and female figures and the motif of the waves, taken from p.37, illustrate the 'Legend of Roua hatou', a Tahitian god of the sea who was awoken from sleep by the nets of a fisherman caught in his hair. As punishment, Roua hatou initiated a deluge, from which, paradoxically, the fisherman and his wife only were spared, after having sought refuge on the island Toa marama. The woodcut composition can now be seen as a condensed synthesis of characters and events described in *L'Ancien culte mahorie,* linked by recurring marine imagery.
The convention for the waves was inspired by Japanese woodcuts; it first appears in Gauguin's oil *The Wave* of 1888 (location unknown: W268), was repeated in the *Ondine* canvases (W336, 337, 338, 360, 362) and was used in such Tahitian paintings as *Vahine no te Miti* of February 1892 (Museo Nacional de Bellas Artes, Buenos Aires: F21; W465), and *Fatata te miti* of the summer of that year (National Gallery of Art, Washington: F38; W463).
The motif of the female nude, a reworking of the figure which first appears in Gaugin's zincograph *At the Black Rocks* and in its cognate drawings of 1889 (reproduced, Guérin, pp.1, XXIV), is combined with the wave convention in the *Ondine* paintings (see above), in the gouache *Nirvana* (Wadsworth Atheneum, Hartford, USA), and in the carving *Les Ondines* (coll. Mme P. Bacou, Puissalicon: Gray 75). It is related for the first time, as in the present woodcut, with both the wave convention and with a figure whose pose of arm and hand is inspired by Egyptian art, in the relief *SOYEZ MYSTERIEUSE* of late 1890 (coll. Mme d'Andoque, Béziers: Gray 87).
The three slight figures at the upper left of the composition are also identifiable as gods. The head on the right of the group is a variant of that of the Tiis mentioned above, while the head in the centre may be identified as that of the goddess Hina, particularly as she appears on the back of the sculpture *Idol with Pearl* of 1892-93 (coll. Agnès Huc de Montfried: Gray 94; see also cat. no.36).
The mysterious figure at the left is a variant of the female at the right of the versions of the painting *E Haere oe i hia* of 1892 (coll. Bernhard Koehler, Berlin: F87; W478) and February-March 1893 (Hermitage, Leningrad: F57; W501).
In 1894, Gauguin was to metamorphose this figure into *Oviri* in two watercolour monotypes (private coll., USA: Field, 1973, *op.cit.,* 30; and location unknown: Field, 1973, *op.cit.,* 31). The following year, Gauguin executed a stoneware sculpture of *Oviri* (private coll., Paris: Gray 113) and two woodcuts, *Oviri* (Guérin 48), and *Woman picking fruit and Oviri* (Guérin 49). In 1898, the figure of Oviri was incorporated into the painting *Rave te hiti aamu* (Hermitage, Leningrad: W570), while in the August of the following year it was drawn on the *verso* of a copy of *Le Sourire* (formerly coll. Schuffenecker, reproduced Guérin, p.XXVII and under 48; see cat. no.42).
Variants of the three gods at the upper left of the woodcut were the subject of the print *TE ATUA* of 1896-99 (Guérin 60, 61), and of the pen and ink drawing *Holy Images* of 1903 (*Avant et Après,* p.105: Rewald 122).
Gauguin's subsequent use of the motifs in *L'Univers est crée* (with the exception of the gods mentioned above) was limited. Invented to illustrate events described in *L'Ancien culte mahorie,* their meaning was perhaps too specific to allow them to be successfully combined with other images. The watercolour of the fisherman and his wife which appears on p.56 of *Noa Noa* (1894–99) is therefore a reversion to the image illustrating p.37 of *L'Ancien culte mahorie*. The Tiis, who appear on p.79 of *Noa Noa,* are likewise taken directly from Gauguin's earlier work.

GAUGUIN, Paul 1848–1903
38 **Navenave Fenua**
Woodcut, with extensive white-line engraving.

Blockmarks: 33.4 x 20.4 cm
Signed on the block, lower left: "P/G/o", and inscribed on the block top: "NAVENAVE FENUA".

EXHIBITED Leicester Galleries (31(?)); Tate Gallery (71(6)); London (35); Newcastle (6); *Dada and Surrealism Reviewed,* Hayward Gallery, 11 January-27 March 1978 (8.74).
LITERATURE Guérin [27, 28, 29*] 94; McCann Morley, *op.cit.,* [96-100] 101; Cooper, 1954, no.182/5; Edwards, *op.cit.,* pp.76-78, [154]; Gray, p.80, note 2; W 455; Danielsson, *op.cit.,* 36; Field, 1968, *op.cit.,* p.509 [10, 11, 20, 21, 28, 30, 31]; Pickvance, *ibid.*

The title of the woodcut, whose subject is the Tahitian Eve before the Fall, refers to the painting *Te NAVE NAVE FENUA* of April-May 1892 (Ohara Museum, Kurashiki, Japan: F 33; W 455), although compositionally the print owes more to the preparatory drawings for that work (two charcoal studies of a *Standing Tahitian Nude* (private coll., Paris; and location unknown: Rewald 56 and Rewald 60, respectively), and to a watercolour in the pointillist manner (Musée de Grenoble, France: Rewald 58)).
The true prototype for the composition of this woodcut, however, is to be

found, in reverse, in a painting which pre-dates Gauguin's first stay in Tahiti, the *Exotic Eve* of 1890 (private Coll., Paris: W 389). In this work, as is in the woodcut, the height of the figure is approximately half that of the picture format: the horizon line is situated above the figure's head, while the open sky is punctuated by undulating palms (which, as Henri Dorra points out ("The First Eves in Gauguin's Eden", *Gazette des Beaux-Arts,* XLI (January-June 1953, p.194), may be traced back to the Martinique landscapes of 1887)). The painted composition incorporates a blank strip at the right side: in the woodcut, a similar margin on the left is decorated, appropriately, with patterns approximating to the Marquesan *matahoata,* motifs common to tattooing. Gauguin had previously employed similar patterns in the decoration of a margin of *c.*1892–93, which separated two figures on a carved, wooden cylinder (private coll., Paris: Gray 102).

In turning to the *Exotic Eve* as a model for the present woodcut, Gauguin can be seen to both reassess and affirm the validity of a painting which although executed in France, was of a genuine exotic nature, whose style influenced many of the early Tahitian works.

The new, specifically Tahitian elements incorporated into the woodcut composition are the banded form of the landscape (see cat.no.4), and the lizard, a substitute for the snake as a symbol of temptation. Gray (*op.cit.,* p.80, note 2) has observed that snakes are not indigenous to Polynesia, and that early missionaries to that country translated the Biblical symbol as 'lizard without legs'. The lizard, reduced in size, appears in the oil *Te NAVE NAVE FENUA.*

The pose of the nude, influenced by the figure of Buddha from a frieze in the Javanese temple of Borobudur (Dorra, *op.cit.,* p.196), first appears in Gauguin's oeuvre in 1886–87, as a decoration for a pot (Musée des Arts Africains et Océaniens, Paris: Grey 15). A variant of the pose may be found in the fresco *Jeanne d'Arc* of 1889 (coll. Abraham Rattner and Isadore Levy, New York: W 329), although the girl is here dressed in Breton peasant costume. A variant of the Eve, clad in a skirt, is included in *HAERE PAPE* of the summer-autumn 1892 (Barnes Foundation, Merion, USA: F 41; W 464), while the subject of the *Exotic Eve* was carved onto the back of a mask of a Tahitian woman, *c.*1892–93 (coll. Mme Huc de Montfried, Paris: Gray 98).

The flowers and stems the Tahitian Eve is about to pluck, which, as Field has observed (1977, *op.cit.,* p.63) are strongly suggestive of sperm cells, have their prototype in the painting *Self-portrait with Halo* of 1889 (National Gallery of Art, Washington: W 323), and are first juxtaposed with a female figure in *Jeanne d'Arc* (see above). The plant appears again on p.13 of *L'Ancien culte mahorie,* and is part of the painting *Te NAVE NAVE FENUA* (see above).

The subject of *NAVE NAVE FENUA* was taken up again in 1894 in a watercolour (National Gallery of Art, Washington: Rewald 59), and in two watercolour monotypes, a *Standing Tahitian Nude* (Museum of Fine Arts, Boston: Field, 1973, *op.cit.,* 6) and a related though independent work in the collection of Mr. and Mrs. John Hunt, Ireland (Field, 1973, *op.cit.,* 7).

A variant of the figure of Eve appears in the painting on glass, *Woman with Fruit* of 1896 (coll. P.E. Berman, USA: W 552), and, greatly modified, in the woodcut, *Woman, animal and foliage* of *c.*1898–1900 (Guérin 59). The motif of the plant appears again in the woodcut *Mahana Atua* (see cat.no.9).

GAUGUIN, Paul 1848–1903

39 **Mahna no Varua ino**

Some woodcut with extensive white-line engraving.

Blockmarks: 20.2 x 35.4 cm

Signed on the block, lower left: "P G o", and inscribed on the block, bottom left of centre: "MAHNA NO VARUA INO".

EXHIBITED Leicester Galleries (35 or 39(?)); Tate Gallery (71(7)); Europe (187); Japan (80); Newcastle (7).

LITERATURE Guérin [32, 33,34*] 95; McCann Morley, *op.cit.,* [104, 105a] 106; Cooper, 1954, no.182/7; Edwards, *op.cit.,* 433; Danielsson, *op.cit.,* no.26; Field, 1968, *op.cit.,* p.509; Pickvance, *ibid.;* Field, 1977, *op.cit.,* no.9, p.38.

The woodcut reworks, in reverse, motifs taken from the painting *The Fire Dance* of October-November 1891 (formerly coll. Hugo Perls, USA: F 9; W 433) which Field (*ibid.*) suggests may have been inspired by engravings of the South Seas, or possibly by a postcard. There are a number of preliminary studies for the painting, the most substantial of which is *Tahitians watching a Group of Dancers* (location unknown: Rewald 41). Other studies for the seated figures are found on pp.15 *verso,* 16 *recto* and 22 *verso* of the *Cahier de Tahiti,* while Field (1977, *op.cit.,* p.39) notes that two unpublished drawings for the dancers are in the Musée des Arts Africains et Océaniens.

The lovers (far left), inspired by the figures at the left of Delacroix's *Massacre at Scio* (1824: Musée du Louvre) are repeated in a charcoal drawing, *Te Faruru* of 1891–93 (location unknown: Rewald 78) and in the woodcut of the same title, also of 1893 (Guérin 22). In 1894, they were the subject of a watercolour monotype (with Wildenstein & Co., New York: Field, 1973, *op.cit.,* 5), while a variant of the motif appears as a carving on the left of *Te RERIOA* of 1897 (see cat.no.32).

The elements which give to the painting a theatrical appearance are, in the woodcut, suppressed: the stage-like foreground running diagonally into the distance in the oil is merely implicit in the woodcut, and the seated figures, viewed from the rear, are recomposed in a line almost parallel to the picture surface, which curves inwards at the right. The extensive background and staffage are eliminated, as is the lower part of the foreground: the woodcut achieves a new intimacy, and the drama of the scene is enhanced by being brought closer to the spectator.

A new dramatic content is introduced into the woodcut by the massing of the flames to suggest the profile of a demonic head, the mouth of which, lower right, is clearly indicated at an early stage in the cutting of the block (see Guérin 32), while the recomposed bole and tree-trunk are aligned with the flames in such a manner as to suggest a shoulder and outward-flung arm. The two dancers in the woodcut composition now confront a menacing demon, observed by the seated spectators in the foreground.

The new composition of the woodcut — the tree-trunk springing from the centre of the print to cut diagonally across the pictorial area, almost to its upper corner (rather than about a quarter of the way into the composition, as in the painting), the line of the foreground spectators curving inwards around the tree-trunk, and the small figures confronting the spirit world, upper right — recalls that of the painting *The Vision after the Sermon* of 1888 (National Gallery of Scotland, Edinburgh: W 245). The compositional similarities with this painting are, we suggest, deliberate: it would appear that, in making the woodcut a formal counterpart to the Edinburgh composition, the artist was also indicating the similarity of subject matter, whose meaning is clarified by reference and contrast to it. In the Edinburgh work, the Breton peasants witness in daylight the good angel — an invention of civilized man — wrestling with the mortal Jacob; in the print, the Tahitian peasant witnesses at night the dancers' confrontation with the demonic spirit, cast in the form of the elemental fire of primitive man.

GAUGUIN, Paul 1848–1903
40 **Auti te Pape**
Woodcut, with extensive white-line engraving.
Blockmarks: 20.5 x 35.5 cm
Signed on the block, bottom left of centre: "PGO", and inscribed on the block, bottom right: "AUTI TE PAPE".

EXHIBITED Leicester Galleries (34 or 41(?)); Tate Gallery (71(8)); Europe (188); Japan (81); Newcastle (8); *The Mechanised Image,* Arts Council travelling exhibition, 1978 (51).
LITERATURE Guérin [35 i, ii,*] 96; McCann Morley, *op.cit.,* [107, 108] 109; Cooper, 1954, no.182/8; Rewald, p.18, pl. C and under no.39; Edwards, *op.cit.,* pp.76-78 [161-63]; W 458, 461, 463, 512, 574, 579, 596; Danielsson, *op.cit.,* no.7; Field, 1968, *op.cit.,* p.509.

The woodcut reproduces, in reverse, the seated figure in the painting *Aha oe feii?* of August 1892 (Pushkin Museum, Moscow: F 40; W 461). A preparatory drawing for the figure, whose pose was inspired by that of Dionysius on a Hellenistic frieze (Field, 1977, *op.cit.,* p.161), is in the coll. Français, Paris (Rewald 39).
The strange form to the left of the seated girl in the woodcut is residual head and hair imagery from the reclining woman also in *Aha oe feii?*.
The general beach setting of the painting is taken over in the print, although the undulations of the shoreline at the left are larger and more generalized, while those at the right deviate considerably from their painted model. The reflections in the water are magnified in the woodcut, and are recast as slightly disturbing head forms.
The figure of the girl plunging into the waves, right, is a free variant of the Ondine figures (see cat.no.36), and is taken from the painting *Fatata te miti* of summer 1892 (National Gallery of Art, Washington: F 38; W 463). In that canvas, the girl's left hand is masked by a tree. By cropping the corresponding hand of the bather in the present woodcut, Gauguin specifies not only the painted source of the figure, but also the landscape context — and by implication, the entire composition of the painting — from which she derives. Subtler references to *Fatata te miti* may be observed in the masking of the bather's legs by the sea-shore (as they are masked by the tree-trunk in that painting) and by the line of the sea-shore itself (right), which is taken, without reversal, from the contour of the tree-trunk. The tree-trunk itself is derived from the painting of April-May 1892, *Parau na te varua ino* (coll. Governor and Mrs. W. Averell Harriman, New York: F 29; W 458).
In 1894, after completion of the woodcut, Gauguin recorded the painting *Aha oe feii?* in a watercolour monotype of the same title (coll. Mr. and Mrs. O. Roy Chalk, New York: Field, 1973, *op.cit.,* 10), and included the seated figure in *NAVE NAVE MOE* (Hermitage, Leningrad: W 512). A variant of the figure was incorporated in *Women by the River* (private coll. Paris: W 475) in 1898, while in the following year it appears in the painting *The large Buddha* (Pushkin Museum, Moscow: W 579).
The seated figure is the subject of a traced monotype of 1899–1902 (location unknown: Field, 1973, *op.cit.,* 42), and of 1901 (coll. Galerie de l'Ile de France, Paris: Field, 1973, *op.cit.,* 94), the latter a preparatory work for the oil *And the Gold of their Bodies* (Musée du Louvre, Jeu de Paume: W 596) in which the girl makes her last appearance.

GAUGUIN, Paul 1848–1903
41 **Mahana Atua**
Woodcut, with some white-line wood engraving.
Blockmarks: 18.2 x 20.3 cm

Signed on the block, lower left: "PGo", and inscribed on the block, bottom right: "Mahana Atua".

EXHIBITED Leicester Galleries (20 or 27(?)); Tate Gallery (71(9)); Europe (189); Japan (82); Newcastle (9).
LITERATURE Guérin, 42 and under 43; McCann Morley, *op.cit.,* 111; Cooper, 1954, no.182/9; Edwards, *op.cit.,* pp.76-78 [167]; W 460, 497, 513, 514, 561; Danielsson, *op.cit.,* no.24; Field, 1968, *op.cit.,* p.510; Field, 1973, *op.cit.,* under 14.

The block for this print was cut after the completion of the *Noa Noa* suite (see above), and dates from the summer of 1894 (Field, *ibid.*). The painting *Mahana no Atua* (Art Institute of Chicago: W 513) whose composition the woodcut translates, can also be dated to the same period. Both painting and woodcut embody Gauguin's idealized conception of life in the golden age of Tahiti, before the arrival of the Europeans. The cutting of the block, in comparison with those of the *Noa Noa* suite, is more obviously stated: Gauguin has abandoned the tools to make line and tone (razor, needle and

sandpaper) in order to produce an intentionally more "barbaric" work in which forms are summarily rendered, and bold areas of black and white are contrasted. The artist introduces into the woodcut the opposition between fluid landscape forms and the enclosed shapes of figures as a graphic equivalent for the contrasts of colour in the painting.
The moon goddess Hina (centre), the protectress of all that flourishes and lives (*L'Ancien culte mahorie, op.cit.,* p.13), appears in a number of Tahitian works after March 1892, the date of Gauguin's reading of Moerenhout (see cat.no.37). The prototype for her form may be traced back to the caricature of a female figure on p.32 of the sketchbook which Gauguin used in Arles in the winter of 1888 (*Carnet de Paul Gauguin*).
In the Tahitian works, she appears in a drawing (formerly coll. P. Durrio, reproduced Guérin, p.XV) which may be a preparatory sketch for the painting *Parau hanohano* of April-May 1892 (location unknown: F 30; W 460), in the frieze incorporated behind Gauguin's mistress in the painting *MERAHI METUA NO TEHAMANA* of February-March 1893 (coll. Mr. and Mrs. Chancey McCormick, Chicago: F 56; W 497), and in the *Self-portrait with Idol* (Marion Koogler McNey Art Institute, San Antonio, USA: listed under W 415 as a work of 1891, but probably from 1893). Hina was the subject of a woodcarving of 1892–93 (coll. Alden Brooks, USA: Grey 97), represented on a carved cylinder of the same period (Hirshhorn Museum, Washington: Gray 95), and was included in the woodcut *TE ATUA* of 1893 (Guérin 30, 31), and in the lithograph *Manao tupapau* published in April-June 1894. A pen and violet ink drawing of the goddess, probably destined for *Noa Noa,* may have been executed contemporaneously with the present woodcut (reproduced Malingue, no. 22), as may the watercolour and ink drawing *Tahitian Woman and Idol* (location unknown: Rewald 87). During the period 1893–95, the head of Hina was carved on the pommel of two canes (coll. Musée des Arts Africains et Océaniens, Paris: and coll. Raymond Duport, Paris: Gray 105 and 117, respectively).
To the left of the goddess are seated the lovers from the painting *The Fire Dance* (see cat.no.39), while the dancers are also variants of those in that work.
The sleeper in the left foreground is a paraphrase of the figure in the woodcut *Manao tupapau* (see cat.no.35), while that on the right is preceded by two watercolour monotypes (coll. W.A. Bechtler, Zollikon, Switzerland; and private coll., New York: Field, 1973, *op.cit.,* 14 and 15, respectively). Wildenstein (under 513) also cites a preliminary drawing for the figure, known only from a photograph (Vizza-vona 4396). The seated woman at the centre of the composition may be traced to a rapid sketch, upside-down on p.23 of the *Carnet de Tahiti,* while the *vivo* player is a variant of the figure who appears in *MARURU* (see cat.no.36).

GAUGUIN, Paul 1848–1903

42 **Three Women, a Mask, a Dog(?) and Bird – a Title for *Le Sourire* of November** 1899

Woodcut, with some white-line engraving.
Blockmarks: 10.1 x 18.3 cm
Signed on the block, lower left: "P. Gauguin", and inscribed on the block, upper left: "le Sourire".

EXHIBITED Leicester Galleries (16(?)); Tate Gallery (71(10)); Europe (190); Japan (83); Newcastle (10).
LITERATURE Guérin, no.75 and under no.76; McCann Morley, *op.cit.,* [133] 134; L-J. Bouge, *Le Sourire de Paul Gauguin* (Paris, 1952), no.1; Gray, under no.132; W 537, 559, 581, 616, 628.

Le Sourire ('the smile') was the facetious title of a satirical monthly broadsheet written, illustrated and published by Gauguin in Tahiti from August 1899 to April 1900. The fourth (November 1899) edition was the first to carry a woodcut title incorporating motifs drawn from a wide range of Gauguin's work. The motifs in the titles largely replaced the drawn illustrations in the text of the newspaper. In all, fifteen blocks of varying format were cut as titles for the paper although only nine of these were published: three different titles were used for the November 1899 issue, two for the February 1900 issue (Bouge, *op.cit.,* p.15). A numbered and initialled edition of thirty of the present title was published separately by Gauguin.

The present title was cut from the back of the block of *Mahana Atua* (Guérin 43; cat.no.41): upside-down, below the print, is a blind-print, also of a title for *Le Sourire* of November 1899 (*Tahitian women, hare and dog (?); Guérin 76; Bouge, op.cit.,* 14, pl. E. VII) which was cut from the same block. This title was published in a separate edition of 25 by Pola Gauguin (Guérin, *ibid.*).
The animal at the left of the print, which sometimes has the attributes of a dog, sometimes of a fox, first appears carved in low-relief on the side of a barrel dating from early 1888 (Marlborough Galleries, London: Gray 84). It appears in the paintings, first as a domestic animal, in *HAERE PAPE* of the summer-autumn 1892 (Barnes Foundation, Merion, USA: F 41; W 461), and in modified form in *Scene of Tahitian Life* of 1896 (Hermitage, Leningrad: W 537). During 1899, the motif becomes more frequent, and is used as a symbol of perversity (Gray, p.74); it appears in the woodcut *Change of Residence* and in the *Print with horned Devil* (Guérin 66 and 67, respectively), and in the oil *Maternity* (Hermitage, Leningrad: W 581). In *Le Sourire* it appears first as a drawing in the edition of 13 October 1899 (Bouge, *op.cit.,* 3) and on the alternative titles for the November issues (Bouge, *op.cit.,* 2, pl. A, I, and mentioned above). It also appears in the unused title, *The Mango Seller* (Guérin 78; Bouge, *op.cit.,* 11, pl. B. IV).
The bird, a symbol of concupiscence (Gray, *ibid.*), appears first in the paintings *VAIRUMATI* (Musée du Louvre, Jeu de Paume: W 559) and *D'où venons nous ? Que sommes nous ? Où allons nous ?* (Museum of Fine Arts, Boston: W 561), both of 1897: it is also carved in reverse on the relief *QUE SOMMES NOUS* of the same year (coll. Henry Dauberville, Paris: Gray 126). In 1899, it appears in the painting *The square Basket* (National Gallery, Oslo: F AI; W 593).
A variant of the compactly-posed kneeling woman at the centre of the composition is observed from life in two sketches in the *Carnet de Tahiti* (pp.71 and 72 *recto*). She appears in the painting of 1891, *Landscape with Black Pigs and Kneeling Tahitian* (coll. William Cargill, Scotland: F 1, W 445), and in three paintings of 1892: *NAFEA faa ipoipo* (Kunstmuseum, Basle: F 35; W 454), *TE FARE HYMENEE* (coll. Mr. and Mrs. Carleton Mitchell, Annapolis, USA: F22; W 477), and in the two versions of *E Haere oe i hia* (coll. Bernhard Koehler, Berlin: F 87; W 478, and Hermitage, Leningrad: F 57; W 501 (datable to February-March 1893)). She also

appears in two studies related to *E Haere oe i hia,* the *Crouching Tahitian Girl* (Art Institute of Chicago: Rewald 47) and a study sheet with a crouching Tahitian girl (location unknown: Rewald 46).

The prototype of the woman looking upwards can be found on p.91 of the *Carnet de Paul Gauguin* of *c.*1888, while her companion with headscarf, whose prototype goes back to the oil *In the Garden of Arles Hospital* of 1888 (Art Institute of Chicago: W 300), was studied from life on pp.11 and 17 *recto* in the *Carnet de Tahiti.* They appear together on p.47 *verso* of the sketchbook in the Cabinet des Dessins, Louvre (reproduced Gray, pl. 121b), and in the woodcut of *c.*1896–97, *soyez amoureuses vous serez heureuses* (Guérin 58) and in two wood reliefs of the same period – the baseboard of the dining-room of Gauguin's hut in Punaauia (National Museum, Stockholm: Gray 121) and *Te Fare Amu* (coll. Henry Pearlman, New York: Gray 122).

The motif at the far right of the composition is a reworking of the head of the idol in the painting *Barbaric poems* of 1896 (Fogg Art Museum, Cambridge, USA: W 547): the form of the idol is reminiscent of Gauguin's own ceramics, and appears on at least two pages of a sketchbook in the collection of Mme Joly-Ségalen, Paris (reproduced Rewald, 43, and Gray, fig. 18, p.27). Gray *(ibid.)* discovered that Gauguin copied the design from illustrations F.2 of Pl. XXVIII of the Atlas accompanying Alexandre Brongniart's *Traité des Arts Céramiques* ... (3rd edition, Paris, 1877): significantly, the ceramics illustrated on this page of Brongniart are of Mexican, Brazilian and Peruvian origin, and would have therefore been of great interest to Gauguin, whose mother was part Peruvian, and who had spent his early childhood in that country.

The motifs in *Le Sourire* were consistently re-used by Gauguin until his death in 1903. The dog appears in distorted form in the traced monotype study for *D'où venons nous ?* of 1899–1902 (Field, 1973, *op.cit.,* 38) and is carved on the right corner of the left basepanel *(SOYEZ MYSTERIEUSES)* of the door-frame to Gaugin's house in the Marquesas, while on the right basepanel *(SOYEZ AMOUREUSES VOUS SEREZ HEUREUSES),* are carved the two women at the right of the present woodcut (Louvre: Gray 132). The dog alone appears in an undated traced monotype, *Bonjour Monsieur Gauguin,* pasted on to p.167 of *Avant et Après* (Field, 1973, *op.cit.,* 113), and it appears, with the woman in the headscarf, in the oil *The Enchanter* of 1902 (Musée des Beaux-Arts, Liège: W 616). With the bird, it appears in the painting *Adam and Eve,* also of 1902 (Museum of Ordrupgaard: W 628) and finally it is incorporated into *Landscape with Dog* of 1903 (private collection, no location: W 638).

The figure with the headscarf appears in *The Call* of 1902 (Museum of Art, Cleveland, Ohio: W 612) and in its cognate drawing (location unknown: Rewald 113), and monotypes (location unknown; and Musée Léon-Dierx, St.-Denis, Réunion: Field, 1973, *op.cit.,* 101 and 102, respectively). She also appears with the upward-looking woman in a traced monotype of 1902 (location unknown: Field, 1973; *op.cit.* 46).

GUYS, Constantin 1802–1892

43 **Two Women with Muffs** *c.*1863

Slight preliminary drawing in pencil; contour drawing with pen and brown ink; black (Indian?) and brown ink washes, and touches of blue, pink and yellow watercolour washes (of varying strengths and combinations), with extensive drawing with the point and flat of the brush; on off-white (now stained) wove paper, given a pale grey (Indian?) ink wash ground. The sheet apparently trimmed on all sides. The drawing disturbed by abrasions and rubbing, and tears repaired, right and top right.

34.6 x 23.6 cm

Unsigned.

colour plate, page 23

Numbered in different hands in pencil, *verso:* "2" and: "4 *fr*" and "4".

PROVENANCE ?; with Paul Rosenberg, Paris, from whom purchased by Samuel Courtauld 1928. Courtauld Gift 1938.

EXHIBITED Orangerie, Paris, 1955 (80); Arts Council (22).

LITERATURE Gustave Geffroy, *Constantin Guys* (Paris, 1926) opposite p.38; Cooper, 1954, no.126; Luce Jamar-Rolin, "La Vie de Guys et la Chronologie de son Oeuvre", *Gazette des Beaux-Arts,* XLVIII (July-August 1956), pp.69-112, and fig.23, p.97.

The drawing, dated by Jamar-Rolin *(ibid.)* to *c.* 1863 on the basis of the "High Life" subject matter and the style of the women's costumes, depicts two fashionable ladies from the upper strata of Parisian society.

Two similar women appear in the drawings *The Conversation* (Geffroy, *op.cit.,* opposite p.108) and *In the Street* (Musée du Louvre, Cabinet des Dessins: illustrated P.G. Konody, *The Painter of Victorian Life* (1930), no.66); this repetition of motifs in Guys's oeuvre is the result of his working on many drawings simultaneously, a practice first recorded by Baudelaire in *The Painter of Modern Life (cf. 'The Painter of Modern Life' and other essays,* translated by Jonathan Mayne (1964), p.18).

KOKOSCHKA, Oskar 1886–1980
44 **Market in Tunis** 1928–29
Oil on canvas, 86.5 x 129 cm
Unsigned.

PROVENANCE Marcell von Nemeš, Munich; with Cassirer, Berlin; acquired by Count Seilern 1939/45. Seilern Bequest (Princes Gate Collection, no.257), 1978.
EXHIBITED Kunsthalle, Mannheim, January-March 1931 (78); *Oskar Kokoschka,* Galerie Georges Petit, Paris, March-April 1931 (35); Kunstnernes Hus, Oslo, January 1932 (95) (according to stamp on back of former stretcher); *Exhibition of Modern German Art,* Museum of Fine Arts, Springfield, Mass., January 1939; Kunsthalle, Basle, March-April 1947 (134); Kunsthaus, Zurich, July-August 1947 (37); *Austrian Painting and Sculpture, 1900–1960,* Arts Council Gallery, London, May-June 1960 (75); *Oskar Kokoschka, Österreichische Galerie, Vienna, 1971 (51); The Princes Gate Collection,* Courtauld Institute Galleries, London, from 17 July 1981 (34).
LITERATURE Edith Hoffmann, *Kokoschka: Life and Work* (London, 1947), p.327, no.227; Hans Maria Wingler, *Oskar Kokoschka; das Werk des Malers* (Salzburg, 1956), pp.56, 318, no.233 (repr.), English edition (Salzburg, 1958), pp.58, 318, no.233 (repr.); A.S. [Antoine Seilern], *Paintings and Drawings of Continental Schools other than Flemish and Italian at 56 Princes Gate London SW7,* III (1961), p.141, no.257 (repr.); L. Goldscheider in collaboration with the artist, *Kokoschka* (1963), p.77, no.34 (repr.); F. Novotny in *Bustan,* IX, 3-4, 1968, pp.84f. (repr.); Oskar Kokoschka, *Mein Leben* (Munich, 1971), p.216, English edition (1974), pp.134-5.

This view was painted in the first half of January 1928 from the roof of a house on Place Bab Souika, Tunis (information kindly given by Mrs. Olda Kokoschka). The artist wrote *(loc.cit.,* 1974): "In the old city of Tunis, I discovered the roof of a greengrocer's shop, which had a magnificent view of the great mosque and the adjoining square, with its processions of weddings, funerals and circumcisions. Swaying camels and heavy-laden donkeys swung through the dark alleys of the souk beneath me; clouds of flies swarmed around the butchers' shops and sweetmeat stalls. A week later, with the painting almost completed, I fell through the roof of the shop, easel and all; even after lengthy bargaining, I had to pay the proprietor a considerable sum of money for a new roof." Prevented by this accident from completing the work then, Kokoschka finished it in Asia Minor the following year, after intervening travels in Europe.
The present condition of the work (restored 1983) confirms that the canvas was rolled up and carried, then stretched repeatedly by the artist during his travels. There are three sets of nail holes, damage and paint losses as well as "foreign" paint stuck to it. The painting, which, like nos.45 and 46 in this exhibition, is not varnished, was executed in several layers, built up wet-on-wet in the Expressionist manner. Parts remain thinly painted, and the ground left exposed in places, elsewhere there is thick impasto; thin washes have been drawn across the finished image.
During the period 1924–31 Kokoschka travelled widely through most European countries (see also no.45 in this exhibition) as well as in North Africa and Asia Minor. They were years productive of many landscapes and city views but two of the finest paintings of the same date (and size) as the present one are Berber portraits: *Arab Women* and *The Marabout of Temacine* (February and March 1928; both in private collections; Wingler, nos.234, 237), and on his return from Asia Minor in 1929 Kokoschka painted his portrait of the collector Marcell von Nemeš (Neue Galerie, Linz; Wingler, no.245), who presumably acquired the present canvas at that date.

KOKOSCHKA, Oskar 1886–1980
45 **Landscape in Scotland (Findhorn River)** 1929
Oil on canvas, 71 x 91 cm
Unsigned.

PROVENANCE With Cassirer, Berlin; acquired by Count Seilern, London, 1941. Seilern Bequest (Princes Gate Collection, no.258), 1978.
EXHIBITED Kunsthalle, Mannheim, January-March 1931 (80); *Oskar Kokoschka,* Galerie Georges Petit, Paris, March-April 1931 (39); *The Princes Gate Collection,* Courtauld Institute Galleries, London, from 17 July 1981 (35).
LITERATURE Edith Hoffman, *Kokoschka: Life and Work* (1947), p.238, no.231; Hans Maria Wingler, *Oskar Kokoschka: das Werk des Malers* (Salzburg, 1956), p.319, no.240 (repr.), English edition (Salzburg, 1958), p.319, no.240 (repr.); A.S. [Antoine Seilern], *Paintings and Drawings of Continental Schools other than Flemish and Italian at 56 Princes Gate London SW7,* III (1961), p.142, no.258 (repr.).

In the summer of 1929, between his travels in North Africa and Asia Minor (see no.44 in this exhibition) Kokoschka journeyed to Ireland and Scotland. Three Scottish landscapes, all of the same size, date from this year: *Dolce Bridge Waterfall in Scotland* (both private collections; Wingler, nos.239, 241) and the present view. The *Waterfall,* shown in the same two exhibitions of 1931 as the present painting, is also of Findhorn River, which runs near Inverness and Loch Ness on the east coast. The artist returned to Scotland several times during World War II and painted several further landscapes there (including Wingler nos.324, 332, 335).

KOKOSCHKA, Oskar 1886–1980

46 **Polperro I** 1939–40

Oil on canvas, 61.2 x 81.3 cm

Signed, bottom right: "OK"

PROVENANCE Acquired by Count Seilern 1940/46. Seilern Bequest (Princes Gate Collection no.259) 1978.

EXHIBITED *The Princes Gate Collection,* Courtauld Institute Galleries, London, from 17 July 1981 (36).

LITERATURE Edith Hoffmann, *Kokoschka: Life and Work* (1947), p.335, no.287; Hans Maria Wingler, *Oskar Kokoschka: das Werk des Malers* (Salzburg, 1956), pp.60, 328, no.317, English edition (Salzburg, 1958), pp.59, 328, no.317; A.S. [Antoine Seilern], *Paintings and Drawings of Continental Schools other than Flemish and Italian at 56 Princes Gate London SW7,* III (1961), p.143, no.259 (repr.); J.P. Hodin, *Oskar Kokoschka: the Artist and his Time* (1966), pp.174, 178, 199; Ronald Alley, *Catalogue of the Tate Gallery's Collection of Modern Art other than British* (1981), pp.392f., under no.5251.

Soon after Kokoschka came to England as a refugee he moved, in August 1939, to Polperro, a picturesque fishing village in Cornwall on the south-west coast. War broke out soon after his arrival, when it was forbidden, for security reasons, to paint in the open air. Kokoschka's paintings of Polperro were therefore largely taken from his little house overlooking the sea, known as Cliff End Cottage. These paintings include *Polperro II* (Tate Gallery; Wingler, no.318) and *The Crab* (Sir Edward and Lady Beddington Behrens Collection, London; Wingler, no.319) and at least three preparatory watercolour views including *View of Polperro,* also in the Princes Gate Collection (Inv.no.267) of the Courtauld Galleries. *Polperro II,* the later version of this scene, is viewed slightly further to the right; it shows a group of houses on the right not seen here, and excludes the strip of cliff-face seen to the left of the present canvas as well as the crab in the foreground. Mrs. Olda Kokoschka has kindly given the information that it was painted from the terrace in front of what she described as their small and ugly jerry-built house, and that the rock seen on the left could be climbed with the aid of a rope rail.

A standing figure above the monogram in the lower right corner appears to represent a woman mourning over a prostrate body. Its interpretation remains obscure, but one might be justified in reading it as a figure symbolic of the events of that time. The crab in the foreground is presumably the same crab as in the painting of that title (see above). Kokoschka wrote *(My Life,* 1974, p.161): "In front of our house in Polperro I painted a large foul-smelling crab someone had given me." E. Hoffmann *(op.cit.,* p.233) recounts Kokoschka's comments on *The Crab:* " 'This is Chamberlain after Munich', explains Kokoschka, 'he says "Uah! What have I done!" ' On other occasions he declares that this is 'Hospitality' ".

In the summer of 1940 the whole south coast was declared a defence area from which foreigners were excluded and Kokoschka returned to London.

MAILLOL, Aristide 1861–1944

47 **Standing Female Nude** *c.*1919–23

Pencil, with extensive rubbing; on thin white (now stained) laid paper. The sheet unevenly trimmed at all edges.

29.4 x 16.9 cm

Unsigned.

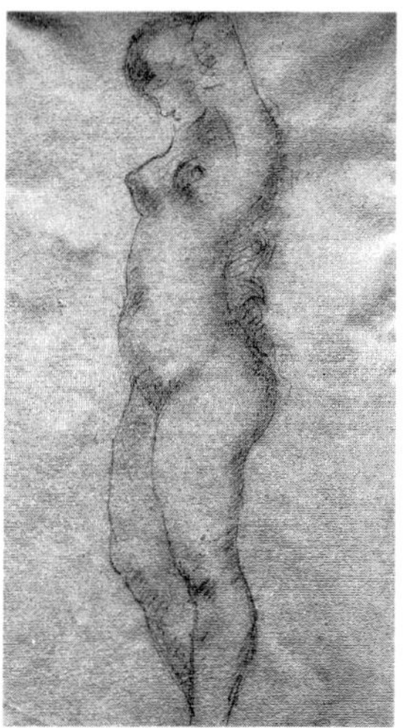

PROVENANCE Purchased by Samuel Courtauld, 1925, possible from E. Weyhe, New York. Courtauld Gift 1935.

EXHIBITED Nottingham University, 1969.

LITERATURE Cooper, 1954, no.136.

John Rewald has made the distinction (*Maillol,* Paris, 1939, p.24) between the two types of drawing executed by Maillol: those drawn direct from the model, which, independent of their degree of finish, display the artist's concern not to go beyond the limits dictated by the body, and those drawn from memory, which still rely on observed rather than imagined form but are composed of simplified contours and generalized volumes.

The present drawing appears to be of the latter type. The head is cursorily indicated, is of a smaller scale when compared to the rest of the body, and is set far back into the shoulders: the buttocks have been moved to the right of the sheet and progressively enlarged to counterbalance the heavy downward curve of shoulders and back; the locks of hair are tightly packed in the back's exaggerated hollow.

A related drawing of a nude with comparable hair and figure, similarly posed, although viewed more strictly in profile, is reproduced in Maurice Denis, *A. Maillol* (Paris, 1925), p.3 (no collection): in contrast to the Courtauld sheet, this drawing suggests that it may have been executed from life.

Cooper (*ibid.*) has assigned to the Courtauld sheet the date of *c.*1918, with no supporting argument. While there is evidence to suggest that the drawing may have been purchased from Weyhe in New York in 1925, there is no indication of the length of time it was in America: at best, this would

have given a *terminus post quem* dating for the work.
The motif of the girl arranging her hair appears in the terracotta sculpture *Standing Girl arranging her Hair* of 1919–20 (illustrated Waldemar George, *Aristide Maillol,* 1965, p.133). A red chalk drawing of a related motif in the collection of Maillol's former model, Dina Vierny, Paris (*Maillol,* Guggenheim Museum 1975, no.129) is a preparatory work for the sculpture *Ile de France (Movement),* and can thus be dated to *c.*1923. It may be tentatively suggested therefore, that the Courtauld sheet and the drawing published by Denis (cited above) both of which were executed prior to 1925, should be grouped with the sculpture and drawing mentioned above, with which they share a common imagery. This would confer on the Courtauld sheet the new date of *c.*1919–23.

MANET, Édouard 1832–1883
48 **Le Déjeuner sur l'Herbe** 1862–63
Oil on canvas, 89.5 x 116.5 cm
Signed, bottom left: "Manet"

colour plate, page 26

PROVENANCE Given by the artist to Commandant Lejosne, Paris; Lejosne family, Maisons-Lafitte (from 1884–1924); with Galerie Druet, Paris; through Percy Moore Turner, London; Samuel Courtauld, June 1928. Courtauld Gift 1932.
EXHIBITED Tate Gallery, 1948 (36); Orangerie, Paris, 1955 (27); Courtauld Centenary, 1976 (23); *Manet at Work. An Exhibition to mark the Centenary of the death of Edouard Manet 1832–1883,* National Gallery, London, 10 August-9 October 1983 (10).
LITERATURE Paul Jamot and Georges Wildenstein, *Manet. Catalogue critique* (Paris, 1932), I, no.78; II, repr.fig.375; A. Tabarant, *Manet: Historie Catalographique* (Paris, 1931), no.63; A. Tabarant, *Manet et ses oeuvres* (Paris, 1947), no.65 and pp.73-74 (and repr.); Jamot-Turner, no.7; Home House catalogue, no.6 (repr); Cooper, 1954, no.32 (repr.); Denis Rouart and Daniel Wildenstein, *Edouard Manet: catalogue raisonné,* I (Paris, 1975), pp.74-75, no.66 (repr.).

This is a smaller version of the famous *Déjeuner sur l'Herbe,* given by Etienne Moreau-Nélaton to the Louvre in 1906, which had been rejected by the official Salon and shown as *Le Bain,* at the Salon des Refusés in 1863. The models in the Louvre picture have been identified as, from left to right, Victorine Meurent (a professional model), either Gustave or Eugéne Manet (brothers of the painter), and Ferdinand Leenhoff, a Dutch sculptor and future brother-in-law of the painter.
The subject caused great controversy when the painting was first exhibited at the Salon des Refusés, and writers and critics still dispute the artist's intentions. Both Françoise Cachin in the Manet centenary exhibition catalogue (Grand Palais, Paris, 1983, no.62) and Michael Wilson in *Manet at Work* (*op.cit.,* pp.22-23, who also discusses the Courtauld painting), summarize the evidence. It appears to have been an attempt by Manet to produce a modern version of the Giorgione *Fête Champêtre* in the Louvre, and Antonin Proust records Manet's wish to work outside the studio in the open air. Others have seen elaborate philosophical meanings, with the two women, one naked, one clothed, as presenting the men with a choice between sensual and spiritual experience (compare, too, Titian's *Sacred and Profane Love* in the Borghese Gallery, Rome). What shocked opinion at the time, however, was the juxtaposition of naked women with men in contemporary dress. Although the river landscape is based on studies the artist made of the Île de Saint-Ouen, the painting was carried out in the studio, and it was not until after he met Monet in 1866 that Manet began to paint *en plein air.*
There are other links with Renaissance painting and classical antiquity besides Giorgione. The poses of the three principal figures in the foreground are borrowed directly from the group of nymphs and river-gods in a Marcantonio Raimondi engraving after a lost composition by Raphael of *The Judgment of Paris.* Just as Daumier had frequently done in his prints, so Manet also parodies classical art and even satirizes it in this "modern" picnic. It may also be noted that Manet was aware of the *fêtes galantes* of French eighteenth century masters such as Watteau and, in his own day, of the popular romantic prints of Devéria and Morlon. The silhouetting of the figures against a landscape backdrop in the *Déjeuner* has also been seen as early evidence of the influence of Japanese art.
The exact status of the Courtauld painting has been debated. Tabarant (*op.cit.,* 1931 and 1947) dismisses the theory that it was painted by Frédéric Bazille, and describes it as a "finished sketch"; while Rouart and Wildenstein *(op.cit.)* describe it as a "reduced version" of the large Louvre painting, and note that the seated female figure in the foreground differs in facial expression and colour of hair from Victorine Meurent (who in the Louvre version has dark hair). However, Manet's portrait of her at the Museum of Fine Arts, Boston, shows her with red hair, and it seems that he changed the colour of her hair in the Louvre painting for purely aesthetic reasons. There are other variations: the poses of Victorine and Ferdinand Leenhoff (who holds a glove in his left hand in the Courtauld sketch) differ from the Louvre version in minor ways, and the draped woman in the background is shown smaller than in the Louvre picture.
The majority of authors think the Courtauld painting comes after the Louvre version, but Alan Bowness ('A note on Manet's compositional difficulties' in *Burlington Magazine,* C111, June 1961,, p.276) and Michael Wilson argue for it being a preliminary study. The matter is complicated by the fact that radiographs recently made of the Louvre *Déjeuner* have revealed that Manet had originally painted a different landscape background than is now visible (information from the Laboratoire de Recherche des Musées de France, kindly conveyed to the compiler by Juliet Wilson Bareau). This might seem to rule out the possibility of the Courtauld painting being a preliminary sketch. But Manet's working methods are notoriously complex, and it can equally be argued that for such an important composition painted at the beginning of his career, Manet may well have done a preliminary sketch, then, when working on the large version, changed his mind about the landscape background only to revert to his original ideas.
A watercolour in the Ashmolean Museum, Oxford, appears to have been done after the Louvre painting, and may in fact have been traced by Manet from a photograph of the Paris picture, with the intention of having it engraved.

MANET, Édouard 1832–1883
49 **A Bar at the Folies-Bergère** 1881–82
Oil on canvas, 96 x 130 cm (on stretcher, 99.8 x 133.5 cm)
Signed, on bottle label, bottom left: "Manet/1882"

colour plate, page 27

PROVENANCE Inventory prepared after Manet's death 1883, no.9; Manet Studio Sale, Drouot, Paris, 4-5 February 1884 (lot 7; 5,850 Frs.) bought Chabrier; Emmanuel Chabrier; Chabrier Sale, Drouot, Paris, 26 March 1896 (lot 8; bought in, 23,000 Frs.); with Durand-Ruel, Paris, May 1897; Auguste Pellerin, Paris; with Bernheim-Jeune, Paris and Paul Cassirer, Berlin; Eduard Arnhold, Berlin; Baron Ferenc Hatvany, Budapest, by 1919; with Justin K. Thannhauser, Munich; Erich Goeritz, Berlin, *c.*January 1924; through Thannhauser, Lucerne; through Percy Moore Turner, London; Samuel Courtauld 1926. Courtauld Gift 1934.

EXHIBITED Salon, Paris, 1882 (1753); Salon, Antwerp, 13 August 1882 (903); *Exposition Posthume Manet,* Ecole des Beaux-Arts, Paris, 1884 (112); *Exposition Manet,* Durand-Ruel, Paris, April 1894 (59); *Manet Exhibition,* Durand-Ruel, New York, March 1895 (3); Exposition Universelle, Paris, 1900 (448); Grafton Galleries, London) January 1905 (93) exhibition organized by Durand-Ruel; *Manet and the Post-Impressionists,* Grafton Galleries, London, 1910–11 (7; lent jointly by Bernheim-Jeune and Paul Cassirer); *Exposition Centennale de l'Art Français,* St. Petersburg, 1912 (405, repr.); exhibitions in Frankfurt-am-Main, Vienna, Dresden, and Copenhagen 1912–14; Galerie Thannhauser, Lucerne, 1926; Tate Gallery, London, June 1926; *French Art,* Royal Academy, London, 1932 (405); *Manet,* Musée de l'Orangerie, Paris, 1932 (82); Tate Gallery, 1948 (40); Orangerie, Paris, 1955 (30); Courtauld Centenary, 1976 (26); National Gallery, London, February-March 1983 (no cat.); *Manet,* Grand Palais, Paris, April-August 1983 (211) and Metropolitan Museum of Art, New York, September-November 1983 (211).

LITERATURE Jamot and Wildenstein, I, no.467; II, repr. fig.327; Tabarant (1931), no.369; Tabarant (1947), no.396 (repr.); Jamot-Turner, no.10 (repr.); Home House catalogue, no.77; Cooper, 1954, no.36 (repr.); Rouart and Wildenstein, I, pp.286-87, no.388 (repr.).

Manet's last great masterpiece, painted in Paris 1881–82, this shows the interior of one of the most fashionable *café concerts* in the city. The artist was already seriously ill with *locomotor ataxy,* and worked slowly and laboriously on this painting in his studio, frequently stopping to rest. Although he had made several oil and watercolour sketches at the Bar of the Folies-Bergère; eye-witnesses, notably the young painter Georges Jeanniot who visited Manet's studio in January 1882, have recorded that Manet used a model posed behind a table laden with bottles and glasses (quoted by Françoise Cachin, *Manet,* 1983, p.482). This model was one of the actual barmaids who worked at the Folies-Bergère, named Suzon.

A preliminary oil sketch in the Stedelijk Museum, Amsterdam (Rouart-Wildenstein 387), shows interesting differences from the finished work; but the lower part of the sketch containing the bar appears less fluently painted and may not be from Manet's hand. In this sketch, the barmaid's head is half-turned to the right and the position of her reflection in the mirror behind the bar is more or less where one would expect it to be; to the right of the composition the reflection of a customer approaching the bar, and lower than that of the barmaid's, has been painted in.

In the final version, Suzon stands impassively in the centre of the composition and looks out at the spectator with a detached, weary, almost melancholy expression. Reflected in the mirror behind her is the auditorium of the Folies-Bergère, and in the dress-circle to the extreme left and just below the legs and feet of the trapeze artist, are the figures of the painter Gaston Latouche and Méry Laurent, while the man at the bar whose reflection we see on the far right is said to be Henry Dupray.

Manet has used the reflected images in the mirror in a totally arbitrary way for aesthetic ends. The reflection of the barmaid's back, for example, is set far too much to the right if we, as spectators, are intended to be standing directly in front of Suzon. Similarly, the customer's reflection has also been shifted across to the right. Unlike Ingres' and Degas' use of mirror images, Manet exploits these reflections to punctuate his composition, and close examination of the paint surface under a raking light, seems to show a *pentimento* which suggests that Manet originally placed Suzon's reflection closer to the central axis.

Radiographs of the painting, taken by the National Gallery, London, in March 1983, confirm that Manet radically altered the composition during the course of execution. Suzon's left arm was originally half bent across her body (and closer to the pose used in the preliminary oil sketch, RW387); and her reflection appears to have been sketched in at least once, if not twice, in positions closer to the central axis, as in the preliminary oil sketch. The radiographs also reveal the figure of the bowler-hatted customer, holding a cane (who appears on the right of the oil sketch), sketched in outline on the right of the Courtauld picture, only to be painted out at a later stage and replaced by the top-hatted customer, who is placed much higher up in the top right-hand corner of the composition.

The contemporary comments by J.-K. Huysmans and Guy de Maupassant about the Folies-Bergère (quoted by Cachin, *op.cit.*) have led some historians, for example T.J. Clark, to interpret this painting as a veiled image of the corruption of a young woman of the people by the bourgeoisie. Cachin finds this too crude an ideological interpretation, and suggests another literary source — Émile Zola's *Le Ventre de Paris,* of which the artist owned a copy dedicated to him. Zola here describes a beautiful pork-butcher, Lisa, who presides over her market stall in the Halles, in terms which correspond to the fresh-faced Suzon.

MANET, Édouard 1832–1883

50 **'Au Bal' ('Marguerite de Conflans en Toilette de Bal')** 1870s

Oil on canvas, 55.7 x 35.5 cm

Unsigned.

PROVENANCE Sale of contents of Manet's studio, Hotel Drouot, Paris, 4-5 February 1884 (lot 42); bought Le Meilleur, Paris, for 170 Frs.; London (label on old stretcher: "J. Chenue, French Packer, 25 Monmouth St. . . ." to "Vienna. Gottlieb"); private collection, Austria; date of acquisition by Count Seilern unknown (but before 1960). Seilern Bequest (Princes Gate Collection, no.206) 1978.

EXHIBITED *The Princes Gate Collection,* Courtauld Institute Galleries, London, from 17 July 1981 (40).

LITERATURE T. Duret, *Histoire d'Edouard Manet et de son oeuvre, avec un catalogue des peintures et des pastels* (Paris, 1902, and subsequent editions, including *Manet and the French Impressionists,* Philadelphia/ London, 1910), no.193; A. Tabarant, *Manet: histoire catalographique* (Paris, 1931), p.256; no.210; P. Jamot and G. Wildenstein, *Manet* (Paris, 1932), no.250 (repr.); A. Tabarant, *Manet et ses oeuvres* (Paris, 1947, 4th ed.), pp.225, 539, no.214 (repr.); A.S. [Antoine Seilern], *Paintings and Drawings of Continental Schools other than Flemish and Italian at 56 Princes Gate London SW7,* III (1961), p.54, no.206 (repr.); M. Bodelsen in *The Burlington Magazine,* June, 1968, CX, pp.341, 344 (as *procès verbal* 166); Rouart and Wildenstein, I, p.174, no.205 (repr.).

This oil sketch was apparently virtually unknown from the time of Manet's atelier sale in 1884 until the death of Count Seilern, by whom it had not been displayed for many years in its then damaged and dirty condition. The reproductions in the literature (except for Count Seilern's catalogue) were evidently based on Lochard's photograph of 1883 (no.86).

In 1981 the painting was restored and cleaning revealed a brilliantly quick and lightly executed sketch of delicate colouring. To the right and slightly below the *profil perdu* there appear to be faint indications of another, perhaps masculine profile, the shoulder possibly to be made out in the area of the bust of the superimposed figure. In the lower left corner brush-strokes appear to form a brief inscription but this cannot be deciphered. Large areas of the ground have been left exposed and a thinned oil paint chiefly used with little impasto. Gold paint from the frame detected under the varnish along the right edge suggests that the painting was initially exhibited in an unvarnished state.

The sale catalogue of 1884 describes the painting as "Au bal, esquisse", and Tabarant was the first, in 1931 *(loc.cit.),* to identify the sitter, without giving evidence, but apparently seeing a resemblance to the known likenesses of Marguerite de Conflans (late Mme. d'Angély), one of which is dated 1873 (now Smith College Museum of Art, Northampton, Mass., Rouart and Wildenstein, no.203). He conveniently dated to the same year the present painting and two other known portraits of the lady (Oskar Reinhart Collection, Winterthur, Rouart and Wildenstein, no.204, and formerly C. Friedman, New York, Rouart and Wildenstein, no.206). In 1947 Tabarant *(loc.cit.)* published another portrait of Mlle. de Conflans, bequeathed to the Louvre at the sitter's wish. Count Seilern *(loc.cit.)* followed Tabarant's proposed identification and Rouart and Wildenstein *(loc.cit.)* appear to suggest that it is a sketch for the full-face portrait at Winterthur. There is no indication in the present profile of the heavy long-jawed features of Mlle. de Conflans, nor does the hairstyle correspond.

Duret *(loc.cit.)* had dated the painting to the period 1875–77 and Jamot and Wildenstein to 1875. It seems that a date in the 1870s is indeed probable, but the exceptionally sketchy quality of the work and the lack of certain identification of the sitter make a more precise dating difficult.

MANET, Édouard 1832–1883

51 **Woman at her Toilet** 1862

Red chalk; on off-white (now stained) laid paper watermarked: "NF." The sheet unevenly trimmed at all sides. The principal contours of figures and pouffe pierced through for engraving.

29.0 x 20.8 cm

Unsigned.

Numbered in pencil, *verso:* "19 large"

PROVENANCE Marcel Guiot; Paris; with the Leicester Galleries, London, from whom purchased by Samuel Courtauld (1928). Courtauld Bequest 1948 (H.H. 206).

EXHIBITED *French Art,* 1200–1900, Royal Academy, London, 1932 (999); Tate Gallery, 1948 (112); *De Fouquet à Cézanne* Brussels, Boymans-van Beuningen Museum, Rotterdam and Orangerie, Paris, 1949–50 (183); *Manet and his Circle,* Tate Gallery, 1954 (18); Orangerie, Paris, 1955 (83); Nottingham University, 1969; London (51); *Manet: L'oeuvre gravé,* Ingelheim-am-Rhein, 30 April-19 June 1977 (Z.7); Arts Council (34); *Manet dessins aquarelles eaux-fortes lithographies correspondance,* Galerie Hugnette Bères, Paris, 1978 (4); British Museum, 1983 (109).

LITERATURE J. Meier-Graefe, *Edouard Manet* (Munich, 1912), fig.19; Vasari Society, 2nd Series (1930), no.XI, p.15, pl.15; Marcel Guérin,

L'oeuvre gravé de Manet (Paris, 1944), p.26; René Huyghe, *Le Dessin français au XIXe Siècle* (Lausanne, 1948), pl.87; Cooper, 1954, no.140; Jacques Mathey, *Graphisme de Manet,* I (Paris, 1961), no.53; A. Mongan, *Great Drawings of All Time* (New York, 1962), no.107; Maurice Sérullaz, *Drawings of the French Masters: French Impressionists* (1963), pp.21, 69; Alain de Leiris, *The Drawings of Edouard Manet* (Berkeley and Los Angeles, 1969), no.185; Jean Leymarie, *Impressionist Drawings from Manet and Renoir* (Geneva, 1969), pp.30, 31; Jean C. Harris, *Edouard Manet. Graphic Works: A Definitive Catalogue Raisonné* (New York, 1970), fig.50, no.78.

The drawing, which Alain de Leiris (*op.cit.,* p.57) suggests dates from 1862, is the preparatory study for the etching *Woman at her Toilet* (see cat.no.52).

The main contours of the drawing have been pierced through with a stylus in order to transfer the design directly to the plate, a method which the artist also employed when transferring the drawing of Philip IV (private coll., France: De Leiris, no.151). Wilson (78,4) notes that such a method of transfer allowed the artist to select the essential lines of the composition, resulting in a more condensed drawing. Grey marks at the top and bottom of the sheet confirm that these edges were folded over the etching plate: the lateral sides were possibly also folded over, although any marks indicating this have been crudely trimmed away.

De Leiris (*op.cit.,* pp.19, 59) suggest that the single, even contours of the bather may be the result of a tracing: the form of the right hand, in which the fingers are not drawn, would suggest this to be the case. (The hand appears in the same form in the first state of the etching.)

Since there is no indication of any medium on the sheet other than red chalk, any initial tracing must also have been executed in that medium. The problem is therefore to distinguish the traced chalk line from that drawn directly on to the sheet: to do so requires examination of those areas where contours are duplicated, which are few, and generally not extensive. Manet evidently followed the tracing closely – except in the area of drapery which curves upward above the bather's left knee. Here, a faintly stated, continuous contour runs alongside and crosses a second, heavier line.

Examination under a lens confirms that the fainter contour has all the characteristics of a traced line: it is unbroken, of even width, and lies flatly on the surface of the paper, in contrast to its counterpart, which is drawn directly on to the sheet, and indicates by the build-up of chalk on the paper's surface and the swelling and thinning of the line, the varying pressure of the artist's hand. The traced contour continues in an unbroken arc over the bather's left knee, terminating above the left thigh in a lozenge shape, which is the initial form of the crease re-stated by the area of hatching to the left of it.

Once the character of the tracing is established, other vestiges of it may be observed, particularly in the drapery on the bather's lap, in the diagonal fold of drapery under her breast, in the right shoulder, and in the angles of drapery at the right, below the elbow and at the thigh.

The upper half of the bather is confidently and boldly delineated, with a dramatic massing of shadows as a form-defining device (De Leiris, *ibid.*). The treatment of the figure below the thighs is more tentative with both contours and areas of shadow more lightly stroked in with a series of curved lines. Upon closer inspection, it can be seen that the more circumspect treatment of this lower area is the result of Manet's drawing of the form with only partial reference to the underlying tracing. The artist's uncertainty regarding the delineation of these forms is suggested by his drawing of the horizontal lines through the bather's knees, indicating an initial intention to terminate the composition at this point. More tentative indications of the lateral extent of an initial pictorial area are visible at the left of the sheet.

Generally, the manner in which the bather is drawn looks back to the style Manet evolved in his early copies after the Old Masters, visible particularly in the sketch after Andrea del Sarto's *Holy Family* (coll. Justin K. Thannhauser, New York: De Leiris 40). In contrast to the bather's laconic hermetic contours other parts of the composition are rapidly indicated by a series of open, cursive strokes. The dislocation between the principal figure and the remainder of the composition which exists in the drawing, is heightened in the etching, where figure and ground are also tonally contrasted.

The interior setting of the composition is implied only by the bowl, pouffe and maid-servant, for whom an initial slight sketch in profile, with arms raised, is located at the extreme left of the sheet. The undulating contours at the upper right of the drawing may be interpreted as vestigial landscape imagery derived from an earlier chalk composition of a bather (private coll., USA: De Leiris 186), of which there is a tracing on mica. Other drawings of related themes which may have preceded the present work are in the Lousada collection (De Leiris 188) and in the Musée du Louvre, Cabinet des Estampes (De Leiris 184). A squared-up study in red chalk of the head of the model in the Courtauld drawing is now lost (De Leiris 182). The initial inspiration for the present composition may perhaps be indebted to an early study of a nude in an interior, derived from an as-yet unidentified painting (Musée du Louvre, Cabinet des Dessins: De Leiris 127).

MANET, Édouard 1832–1883

Selection from an Album of Thirty Etchings 52-62

Catalogue nos.52-62 (inclusive) are taken from an album of thirty etchings by Manet, published posthumously in an edition of 100 by Strölin of Paris in 1905. Strölin's edition repeats that of 1894 printed by Dumont, from whom he purchased the plates. Jean Harris (*Édouard Manet. Graphic Works: A Definitive Catalogue Raisonné* (New York, 1970, p.19), notes that prints from both albums are normally not readily distinguishable, being on ivory-coloured paper, although some of the Dumont edition were printed in brown ink on blue-green paper.

The Courtauld edition of the Strölin album, however, is printed in black ink on grey-blue laid paper. The sheets, of different sizes, were either chosen or cut, according to the dimensions of the plate to be printed: generally, the laid-lines of the paper run vertically, although in certain cases (cat.nos.55, 56, 59, 61) the sheet has been turned so that the laid-lines are horizontal. The paper, of inferior quality, is neither consistent in colour nor in watermark. One of two watermarks appears on the small sheets. Ten are watermarked with three balls in a circle surmounted by a fleur-de-lys, while another seven are watermarked: 'L18/FB'. The design of a bunch of grapes with the letters: "FCj" is watermarked on four of the large sheets, while three others bear the personification of France encircled by: "TIMBRE NATIONAL/RF". Of the remaining large sheets, three are illegibly watermarked and three are blank.

A version of the *Woman at her Toilet,* on comparable paper to that of the Courtauld album, was sold at Sotheby's, London (*Edouard Manet Etchings and Lithographs,* 14 December 1978, lot 12) as one of a series of trial proofs for the Dumont edition. These were printed in black ink, on grey-blue sheets of different sizes, taken from old French departmental ledgers. Clearly, the present album may be identified as a series of trial proofs for the Dumont edition.

However, the portfolio in which the Courtauld etchings are contained, the stamping in red at the bottom right of each sheet with the number of the

etching, and the passe-partout of white wove paper which protects each print, also stamped with the etching's number in red, are characteristics of the Strölin edition (Juliet Wilson, *Manet L'oeuvre gravé,* Ingelheim-am-Rhein, 30 April-19 June 1977, p.137).
It would appear, then that Strölin purchased not only the plates from Dumont, but also any left over proofs from his edition. These were then stamped and mounted by Strölin in a manner consistent with his own edition, and sold as such.
The present album, purchased by Samuel Courtauld from Percy Moore Turner in 1934, was presented as a gift to the Courtauld Institute in the November of that year.
Information concerning states and editions of each print is omitted in the present catalogue, but may be found in Juliet Wilson, *Manet: L'oeuvre gravé.*

Catalogues and other works referred to in the entries:
De L (number): Alain de Leiris, *The Drawings of Édouard Manet,* Berkeley and Los Angeles, 1969. Guérin (number): Marcel Guérin *L'oeuvre gravé de Manet,* Paris, 1944.

Hanson (number); Anne Coffin Hanson, *Édouard Manet 1832–1883,* Philadelphia Museum of Art and Art Institute of Chicago, 1966–67.

Harris (number): Jean C. Harris, *Édouard Manet Graphic Works: A Definitive Catalogue Raisonné.*

Isaacson (number): Joel Isaacson, *Manet and Spain,* The Museum of Art, University of Michigan, January-March, 1969.

JW (number): Paul Jamot, Georges Wildenstein with Marie-Louise Bataille, *Manet* (2 vols.) Paris, 1931.

LM (number): Jean Leymarie and Michel Melot, *The Graphic Works of the Impressionists,* London, 1971.

Melot (number): Michel Melot, *L'estampe impressioniste* Bibliothèque Nationale, Paris, 1974.
M-N (number): Etienne Moreau-Nélaton, *Manet, graveur et lithographe,* Paris, 1906.

R (page number): Léon Rosenthal, *Manet aquafortiste et lithographe,* Paris, 1925 (only the author's principal entry for each etching is cited).

RW (number): Denis Rouart and Daniel Wildenstein, *Édouard Manet, Catalogue Raisonné* (2 vols.), Paris, 1975.

W 77 (number): Juliet Wilson, *Édouard Manet, l'oeuvre grave,* Ingelheim-am-Rhein, 1977.

W 78 (number): Juliet Wilson, *Manet dessins aquarelles eaux-fortes lithographies,* Galeries Huguette Berès, Paris, 1978.

W 83 (number): Juliet Wilson in *Manet 1832–1883,* Grand Palais, Paris, 23 April-1 August 1983.

MANET, Édouard 1832–1883
52 **Woman at her Toilet** 1862
Etching (an uneven 'stipple'-aquatint, sand or salt(?), pressed on to the plate apparently with the palm of the artist's hand, in the area of the bather's legs) over much of the composition; all drawing with the needle (an area of the forehead and nose of the bather almost entirely burnished away) on paper watermarked with the design of a bunch of grapes and: "F C j" (partly cut away). The composition limited at the left, top and right sides by an unevenly bitten ruled etched line. The free-hand lines extending beyond the ruled line at the left, and to the bottom of the plate rigorously wiped.
Platemarks: 28.6 x 22.3 cm
Signed on the plate, within the pictorial area, bottom right: "M"
Stamped in red, bottom right of sheet: "7".

LITERATURE M.N., no.1; Théodore Duret, *Manet and the French Impressionists,* translated by J.E. Crawford-Flitch (1912), p.101; R. p.67; Gotthard Jedlicka, *Manet* (Zurich, 1941), pp.235, 237; Guérin, no.62; Cooper, 1954, no.190/7; Nils Gösta Sandblad, *Manet Three studies in artistic conception* (Lund, 1954), Hanson, no.16; Harris, no.20; LM, no.M 18; RW, II, 360; W 77, no.8; W 78, no.37; W 83, no.25.

The etching which was published in 1862, and was probably executed in that year, reproduces in reverse the figure from the preceding drawing (cat.no.51) set in an interior. Both Rosalind Krauss (*op.cit.,* p.627) and Juliet Wilson (83, *ibid.*) have linked this figure with that in Manet's paintings of *The Surprised Nymph* of 1861, of which there are versions in the Museo Nacional de Bellas Artes, Buenos Aires, the Galerie Charpentier, and the Nasjonalgalleriet, Oslo (JW 55, 53, 54, respectively). The nymph in Manet's paintings is taken from an engraving by Vosterman after a lost painting by Rubens of *Susannah and the Elders,* and is combined with a landscape in such a manner as to evoke Rembrandt's paintings of *Susannah* in the Mauritshuis (The Hague, Krauss, *op.cit.,* p.623).
Rembrandtesque undertones remain in the present etching, although Manet appears to have looked at a more modern prototype for his composition – *Ruega por ella* ('Ask her', or 'Pray for her'), plate 31 of Goya's *Los Caprichos* (Thomás Harris, *Goya Engravings and Lithographs* vol. I, II, Oxford, 1964, no.66). The *Caprichos* has been republished in a French edition of 1855, and it is appropriate that Manet should have turned for inspiration to an original etched composition by a leading and recent European print-maker at a time when he, too, was about to embark on his first etching independent of an oil composition.
The influence of Goya's etching on Manet's work may be observed at many levels: in the pose of the bather, and the treatment of her flesh and drapery as a white silhouette, almost completely detached from a background in which other figures and objects are treated in varying tones of black; in details such as the shallow metal dish at the bather's feet, the patterned braid surrounding the seat of the pouffe, and even in the detached manner

with which both bather and servant regard the spectator. (Krauss, *op.cit.*, p.627, misinterprets the print in suggesting that the maid-servant looks out at the viewer in surprise.) Even the border framing the etching is derived from Goya. Manet has also adopted a recurring feature of Goya's compositions, the contrasting diagonal thrust of overlapping forms.

In drawing many of its formal characteristics from *Ruega por ella,* Manet's etching also allies itself with aspects of the subject matter of that print – a young prostitute groomed by a maid and prayed over by a procuress. Manet substitutes for Goya's grotesque figure of the procuress a canopied bed (upper left), as a more discreet reference to the bather's profession.

The prototype of the freely-sketched maid of the drawing is clarified in the etching, where she removes linen from a chest. A similar motif is employed in Titian's *Venus of Urbino* (Uffizi, Florence), which Manet had copied in *c.*1856. A further reference to Titian's painting can be seen in the unequal division of the background of the etching.

Manet's painting *Olympia* of 1863 deals openly with the subject of the prostitute. Its composition again alludes to Titian's *Venus of Urbino,* while the pale, brittle figure of Olympia, who gazes indifferently at the spectator, is contrasted with the dark silhouette of the negress servant. The painting thus refines many of the formal ideas initially expressed in the etching *Woman at her Toilet,* as well as dealing overtly with the subject matter which was stated in a concealed manner in that print. The *Woman at her Toilet,* then, may be seen to be the crucial link in the chain of thought in which ideas latent in the *Surprised Nymph* series of paintings, which relied on seventeenth-century prototypes, were interpreted into the daring and thoroughly modern *Olympia* of two years later.

MANET, Édouard 1832–1883

53 **Seascape** 1866 (?)

Etching (an uneven 'stipple'-aquatint (sand-grain or salt (?)) underlying the darker areas of the sky, sea and sails; all drawing with the needle, and some stippling with the point of the needle); burnishing away in the sails of the central vessel; on paper watermarked: *"L18/F B".*

The pictorial area enclosed within a ruled and free-hand etched line. Vestiges of ruled etched lines (largely burnished away) beyond the right side of the pictorial area, and below the bottom.

Pictorial area: 12.4 x 18.2 cm

Platemarks: 14.2 x 20.2 cm

Unsigned.

Stamped in red, bottom right of sheet: "17".

EXHIBITED Arts Council (37).

LITERATURE M.N. no.39; R., p.67; Cooper, 1954, no.190/17; Anne Coffin Hanson, "A Group of Marine Paintings by Manet", *Art Bulletin,* vol. XLIV (1962), pp.332-36; Hanson, no.66 and p.85; Harris, no.40; LM., no.M34; R.W., under I 75; *Japonisme: Japanese Influence in French Art 1854–1910* (Cleveland Museum of Art, Rutgers University Art Gallery and Walters Art Gallery, 1975), no.38; W 77, no.47; W 78, no.45.

The etching, datable to 1866 (?), records in reverse, at the left, the sailing vessel from the right of the painting *The Kearsage at Anchor off Boulogne* (coll. Adaline Havemeyar Frelinghysen: JW 88) of 1864, a motif repeated in *The Outlet of Boulogne Harbour* (Art Institute of Chicago: JW 92) of the same year. The boat under full sail, and porpoises, centre, are reworked as unrelated motifs, from the oil, *Ships at Sea* (Museum of Art, Philadelphia: RW 179, Hanson, *op.cit., p.333). The smaller vessels near the horizon of the etching have their prototypes in these paintings. Compositionally, the etching and the paintings mentioned above share with The Battle of the Kearsage and the Alabama* (coll. John G. Johnson, Philadelphia: RW 1, 75) also of 1864, a relatively high horizon near which small vessels are clustered, and below which is an expanse of water relieved only by a solitary boat at the left or right edge of the canvas (Hanson, *op.cit.,* p.332). Such compositions, in which each motif is rendered as a discrete entity — and indeed, the oblong forms of the sails of the boats themselves — owe much to Japanese woodcuts of similar subjects, such as Hiroshige's *Kaijô ichi-ri han funawatashi no zu,* plate 32 of the *53 stages along the Tokaido Highway* (Cleveland, *ibid.).* Hanson's suggestion *(op.cit.,* p.334) that Manet's etching reproduces a lost painting is a moot point.

One feature of the etched composition which appears in none of the paintings mentioned above is the "stepped" horizon-line. In both the *Kearsage at Anchor off Boulogne* and *Ships at Sea,* Hanson notes *(Manet and the Modern Tradition,* New Haven and London, 1977, p.203) how one edge of the vessels' pennants is aligned with an edge of the canvas, in order to stress the pattern of the boats and to secure their forms within the pictorial area.

In the greatly reduced format of the etching, the compositional device of the pennants is abandoned and the artist has to invent a new method to stabilize the discrete motifs of the boats. This is achieved by lowering the horizon, firstly, beyond the bows of the centrally placed vessel, so that its line meets the angle of the fore-sail: the resulting conjunction of lines pins the vessel, as it were, within the composition. The same device is used for similar effect at the right of the etching: the progressive lowerings of the horizon force it into alignment with the top and bottom edge of the sails of the two smaller vessels.

MANET, Édouard 1832–1883
54 **The Spanish Singer** 1861–62

Etching (a sand or salt(?) aquatint underlying much of the figure and ground, and surrounding many of the forms with a corona of tone; all drawing with the needle); on paper, watermarked with the personification of France, encircled by: *TIMBRE NATIONAL/RF*. The sheet blind-stamped, centre left, with the personification of France surrounded by the inscription: ".REP. FRA./ADM. DES. DOM. DE L'ENREG. ET DU TIMBRE". The composition extends vertically to the platemarks, and is limited horizontally by a ruled etched line (at a distance of approx. 0.1 cm. from the platemarks).
Platemarks: 29.8 x 24.4 cm
Signed on the plate, upper right: "éd Manet".
Stamped in red, bottom right of sheet: "2".

LITERATURE M.N., no.4; R, p.62; J.W., under no.40; Guérin, no.16; Cooper, 1954, 190/2; Jean Adhémar, "Notes et Documents: Manet et l'Estampe", *Nouvelles de l'Estampe,* VII (1965), pp.230-31; Hanson, no.47, pp.67-69; De Leiris, under nos.160, 161; Isaacson, no.9; Harris, no.12; L M, no.M 12; Melot, nos.21-24; RW, under I 32, II 458, 459; W 77, no.13; W 78, no.29; W 83, no.11.

The etching reproduces in reverse Manet's painting of the same title of 1860 (Metropolitan Museum, New York: JW40) which received critical acclaim at the Salon of 1861, winning for the artist an honourable mention (George Heard Hamilton, *Manet and His Critics* (New York, 1969), pp.24-27). A watercolour and a tracing (locations unknown: De Leiris 161, 160, respectively) preceded the transposition of the subject on to copper. De Leiris (*ibid.*) notes that the tracing reproduces only the major, simplified contours of the painting, which suggests that it was made either from a drawing or a photograph (both of which are now lost). The tracing was undoubtedly used to transfer the composition to the plate; that the artist did so, without reversing it (thus choosing to make the etched design in the opposite sense to that of the painting), indicates his desire to make of the etching an autonomous work, which would also refer to, and popularize, his painting. Wilson (83, *ibid.*) notes that this "autographic reproduction", fashionable among French artists during the 1860s, lies half way between the reproductive engraving of the artisan and the original etching of the artist-engraver.

Among the many sources cited for this composition, the most convincing is Goya's etching *The Blind Singer* (Tomás Harris, *Goya,* no.35), although Hanson (*op.cit.,* pp.59-60) notes the many paintings of mandolin or lute players by both Ostade and Teniers, in which elements of the present composition can be found.

Harris' misgivings (*ibid.*) that the figure of the guitar-player was executed after a model who was not a musician, are confirmed by the position of the fingers upon the guitar neck; they lie across the strings, rather than pressing on to them, forming a discordant G# and C. A similar convention for the guitarist's hand is found in the etching *The Street Singer* (W 77, 26) also of 1862.

The etching was first published during Manet's life-time by Cadart in September 1862 as one of the album of eight etchings. The artist, however, had worked on the plate since 1861, as a second state which is signed and dated to that year proves.

MANET, Édouard 1832–1883
55 **The Gypsies** c.1862

Etching (all drawing with the needle, and stippling with the point of the needle); apparently some of the zig-zags of the ground, lower left, formed by use of the roulette; on paper, watermarked apparently with the TIMBRE NATIONAL wire (the watermark almost illegible). The sheet blind-stamped twice, centre left, with the personification of France surrounded by the inscription: ".REP. FRA./ADM. DES. DOM. DE L'ENREG. ET DU TIMBRE". The sheet turned so that the laid lines are horizontal. The pictorial area enclosed within a ruled etched line.
Pictorial area: 28.6 x 20.8 cm
Platemarks: 31.8 x 24 cm
Signed on the plate, bottom right of pictorial area: "éd. Manet".
Printed above the pictorial area, right: "4".
Stamped in red, bottom right of sheet: "4".

LITERATURE M.N., no.2; R, pp.22, 63; JW, under no.59; Jedlicka, *op.cit.,* p.236; Guérin, no.21; Cooper, 1954, no.190/4; Adhémar (1965), *op.cit.,* p.231; Hanson, no.32, p.59; Isaacson, no.13; Harris, no.18; Anne Coffin Hanson, "Édouard Manet 'Les Gitanes' and the Cut Canvas", *Burlington Magazine,* CXII (March, 1970), pp.158-66; L M, no.M 16; Janine Bailly-Herzberg, *L'eau-forte de peintre au dix-neuvième siècle. La Société des Aquafortistes, 1862–1867* (2 vols., Paris, 1972), I, p.21, no.4, p.55; RW, under I 41, 44; W, 77, no.17; Anne Coffin Hanson, *Manet and the Modern*

Tradition (New Haven and London, 1977), pp.60, 61; W, 78, no.32; W 83, no.48.
The etching records in reverse the painting of the same title, of 1862, which was cut apart some time between 1867 (after it was included in the one-man exhibition at the Pont de l'Alma), and 1872. The two surviving fragments — each of which, as Hanson has shown (1970, *op.cit.,* p.165), has been repainted to form an independent work of art — are: *The Waterdrinker* (Art Institute of Chicago: JW 59), *The Male Gypsy* (location unknown: JW 60). The oil was probably preceded by the small etching, *The Gypsies* (W, 77, 16) known only from six trial proofs, one of which, in the Bibliothéque Nationale, is squared up.
The centrally-placed male figure repeats a convention for the depiction of provincial types in *Les Français peints par eux-mêmes* (Hanson, 1977, *op.cit.,* p.61), and both he and the landscape setting may also have been inspired by the portrait of Philip IV, attributed to Velázquez, which entered the Louvre in 1851. The group of mother, baby and drinker has its compositional prototype in such subjects as *The Flight into Egypt,* or the *Holy Family* (Isaacson, *ibid.*).
Possible reasons for Manet's cutting of the canvas have been suggested by Hanson (*ibid.*); the artist may have encountered difficulties in painting the head of the gypsy woman, or he may have been dissatisfied with the composition. Hanson (1970, *op.cit.,* p.164) also states that the etching is an exact record of the painted composition. If this is the case, what was it in the etched composition which was acceptable to Manet, in contrast to that of the painting, which was cut up? Manet's satisfaction with the etching is attested to by the fact that he selected it to be his first work in the first album of five etchings by various artists to be published by the Société des Aquafortistes on 1 September 1862 (J. Baily-Herzberg, *ibid.*).
From the photograph of the *Waterdrinker* removed from its stretcher (reproduced Hanson, 1970, *op.cit.,* fig.51) it is possible to measure the distance between the edge of the painting, and the angle formed by the side and base of the jug. Measurement of the same two points in the etching reveals that the space between the end of the jug and the framing edge of the composition is proportionately greater. Similar comparative measurements between other points on the figure and the edge of the composition in both painting and etching, reveal that in the latter, the space between the edge of the figure and the edge of the composition is consistently proportionately larger. Hanson (*op.cit.,* 1970, under no.47) notes that the format of the etching is proportionately wider than that of the painting; it can now be seen that the extra width was added to the side of the composition in which the gypsy drinker and mother and child are situated. The X-ray photograph of the *Waterdrinker* (reproduced Hanson, *op.cit.,* 1970, no.49) shows that the forms of female gypsy and drinker were related in precisely the same way in the painting as they are in the etching. This would indicate that in the narrower oil composition, the female figure was uneasily squashed in to the left side, and was even possibly cropped at the edge (as she appears in the small plate of the subject; see above).
Thus, in making the etching, Manet employed the wider format to accommodate more comfortably the group of the drinker, woman and child, whose formal relationship parallels that in the painting. Manet had, in effect, invented a new composition. It can be argued that his recognition of the etching as such is signalled by his reversal of the motifs from the painting — an act of choice on his part, since as Harris (*ibid.*) notes, the transfer of the image to the plate was by means of a tracing.
The motif of the waterdrinker was isolated from the painting and recombined with other motifs, in a small brush and ink drawing dated: "2 April 1865", (private coll.: De Leiris 117) which illustrated the 8 July edition of *L'Autograph au Salon.* The figure, subsequently related to an extended mountain background of the type visible at the left of *The Gypsies,* appears in the etching *The Waterdrinker* of 1866–67 (W, 77, 44). A variant of the mountainous background alone is the subject of the etching *The Mountain* of 1874 (W, 77, 83) which illustrated Charles Cros's book of poems, *Le Fleuve.*

MANET, Édouard 1832–1883
56 **The Dead Toreador** *c.*1868
Etching (an even, hand-shaken aquatint (through three silks?) in the foreground, an uneven, hand-shaken aquatint (through one silk?) between the Toreador's right arm and leg and underlying the background (and partly burnished away in the cape); all drawing with the needle; a lavis(?) aquatint in the area between the Toreador's right arm and leg largely burnished away; (an 'image drift', top left, where the plate has moved slightly during printing); on paper, apparently watermarked: *"L18/F B"* (the watermark very faint). The sheet turned so that the laid lines are horizontal. The pictorial area limited by a ruled etched line, left and right, and a broken ruled etched line, bottom.
Pictorial area: 9.6 x 19.5 cm
Platemarks: 15.6 x 22.4 cm
Signed on the plate, within the pictorial area, bottom left: *"Manet".*
Stamped in red, bottom right of sheet: "8".

LITERATURE M.N, no.13; R, pp.59-60; Jedlicka, *op.cit.,* p.234; Guérin, no.33; Cooper, 1954, no.190/8; Hanson, no.60, p.81; Gerald M. Ackermann, "Gérome and Manet", *Gazette des Beaux-Arts,* LXX (1907), pp.163-70; Isaacson, no.25; Harris, no.55; Hanson, 1970, *op.cit.,* pp.158-61; L M, no.M49; Melot, no.145; RW, under I 71; W, 77, no.55, W, 78, no.43.

The etching re-works, in the same sense, the painting of the same title (National Gallery of Art, Washington: JW 83), initially the lower portion of a larger picture, *Incident in a Bull-ring,* which, when exhibited at the Salon of 1864, was the subject of severe adverse criticism. After the exhibition, the painting was cut up: the second surviving fragment, *The Bull-fight,* is in the Frick collection, New York (JW 84).
The pose of the bullfighter was taken from that of the figure of the dead Caesar in a painting of that title exhibited by J-L. Gérôme (1824–1906) at the Salon of 1859 (Ackermann, *op.cit.,* p.163). The pose of the Caesar in Gérôme's canvas was derived from that of the dead soldier in the painting *Orlando Muerto* (at that time attributed to Velázquez) in the Pourtalès collection (now Seventeenth-century Italian School, National Gallery, London).
Ackermann (*op.cit.,* p.168) convincingly demonstrates that while painting the *Incident in the Bull-ring,* Manet may have been ignorant of the Pourtalès picture, although by the time he cut his work up, he was certainly acquainted with it. In cutting the dead toreador from the larger oil, Manet deliberately restored the figure to the format of the Pourtalès painting, thus making specific his debt to Velázquez.

The *Dead Toreador* was exhibited again in 1868 at Le Havre, where it won a silver medal. Isaacson (*ibid.*) suggests that this success may have prompted Manet to translate the subject into an etching, which was apparently preceded by a preparatory drawing (location unknown: De Leiris 200). In making the etching, Manet cut down the space surrounding the corpse (Harris, *ibid.*), thereby bringing it towards the viewer. The seven or more widely differing states in which aquatint and "lavis" were employed — a complex operation in which Félix Bracquemond (1833–1919) collaborated – bear witness to Manet's search for a gamut of tone and texture commensurate with the intensified dramatic nature of the subject. In 1871, Manet again had recourse to the pose of the dead toreador: he appears in reverse as the dead French soldier in the lithograph *Civil War* (W, 77, 73).

MANET, Édouard 1832–1883

57 **The Meeting of the Thirteen, *or* The Little Cavaliers** c.1862–67

Etching (an uneven stipple-aquantint (sand or salt(?)) underlying the darkest areas of the composition; all main drawing with the needle); drypoint in the wrist of the fourth cavalier from the right; some use of the roulette to make up the tone of the aquatint, lower left of centre; on paper watermarked with the personification of France and: "TIMBRE NATIONAL/ RF." The sheet blind-stamped, bottom centre, with the personification of France surrounded by the inscription: ".REP. FRA./ADM. DES. DOM. DE L'ENREG. ET DU TIMBRE", and stamped in black ink, bottom centre, with an apparently similar mark (now largely cut away).

Platemarks: 25 x 39 cm

Unsigned. Inscribed by the artist on the plate below the pictorial area, left: "...Cavaliers..." and right: "...Vélasquez..." (now largely burnished away).

Stamped in red, bottom right of sheet: "9".

LITERATURE M.N., no.5; R, p.142; J W, under no.7; Guérin, no.8; Cooper, 1954, no.190/9; Sandblad, *op.cit.*, pp.37, 38, 40, 44; Adhémar (1965), *op.cit.*, p.231; Hanson, no.4, p.40; De Leiris, under no.146 (state with watercolour); Harris, no.5; L M, no.M4; Melot, nos.122, 123; RW, under I 21, II 70 (state with watercolour); W 77, no.10; W 78, no.23; W 83, no.37.

The etching reproduces, in the same sense, the painting *The Meeting of the Thirteen*, or *The Little Cavaliers*, attributed to Velázquez, which entered the Louvre in 1851. Manet had copied the painting in oil in 1858–60 (Private Collection, New York: JW 18) at the same time as J. McN. Whistler (1834–1903) (D. Sutton, *J. McN. Whistler*, 1966, p.30) and it is probably from his own copy that the etching was made.

The date of the etching is uncertain; it was published in the third state (signed below the pictorial area, right: "éd. Manet d'après Vélasquez") by Cadart and Chevalier in 1862. Adhémar (*op.cit.*, p.231) cites a letter (which Harris, *ibid.*, dates to 1867) in which Manet talks of repairing the plate prior to further publication. The possible five states of the etching therefore occupied the artist from 1862 (or probably the year before) to 1867 and later.

The Louvre painting, which the etching reproduces, was attractive to Manet for two reasons: firstly, it was considered to be a genuine work from Velázquez's hand, with all the atmospheric effects and daring composition that this implied, and secondly, it was thought to contain the artist's portrait (extreme left) with that of Murillo (seen in bust-length) (Sandblad, *op.cit.*, p.40). Sandblad has observed *(op.cit.*, p.45) that the unexpressed self-identification between the young artist and the figure of Velázquez in Manet's painted and etched copies was made specific in his first painting of modern life, the *Music in the Tuileries Gardens* (National Gallery, London: JW 36). In this work, whose composition is derived from *The Little Cavaliers*, Manet includes himself at the extreme left.

As well as being the compositional model for *Music in the Tuileries Gardens*, *The Little Cavaliers* provided prototypes of individual figures which were included in other compositions by Manet of *c.*1860. The figure with cane, on the left of the etching, appears on the right of the painting *Scene in a Spanish Studio* (coll. Lorenceau, Paris: JW 9, Isaacson, *ibid.)*, in which a painter, identifiable as Velázquez, is seated before an easel upon which is an unfinished *Little Cavaliers*. The figure in the pale cloak, right of centre of the etching, appears in reverse in *Spanish Gentlemen and Boy with a Tray* (Musée des Beaux-Arts, Lyon: JW 28) (Isaacson, *ibid.)*.

Jean Harris *(ibid.)* has observed the wide value range of the etching, and the different and complex handling of each tonal area: these are disposed rhythmically over the picture surface, unifying the frieze-like composition by their suggestion of the enveloping effects of light and atmosphere.

The importance Manet attached to this etching may be gauged by the number of times it was published during his lifetime (in 1862, 1863 and 1874) and also exhibited: it was included in the Salon of 1863, at the Pont de l'Alma, 1867, and again at the Salon of 1869.

The status Manet accorded to the lightly-bitten first state heightened with watercolour (Museum of Fine Arts, Boston: JW, II 70) is uncertain. Juliet Wilson points out (1978, *ibid.)* that it may have functioned as an exploratory sketch to indicate the direction of further work on the plate, or it may have been regarded as a work of art in its own right. As a tribute to both Manet and Velázquez, a copy of the etching of the *Little Cavaliers* appears in the background of Renoir's painting *Still life with Bouquet*, of 1871 (Museum of Fine Arts, Houston).

MANET, Édouard 1832–1883

58 **Theodore de Banville** (turned to the left) *c.*1874

Etching (an uneven grained, hand-shaken aquatint underlying the upper right area of the plate (partly burnished away, bottom) and all main drawing with the needle); possibly some slight drypoint in the smoke, left; on paper watermarked with three balls in a circle surmounted by a fleur-de-lys.

Platemarks: 24 x 16 cm

Unsigned.

Stamped in red, bottom right of sheet: "18".

LITERATURE M.N, no.42; R, p.65 (as "The Sailor's Dream"); Etienne Moreau-Nélaton, *Manet raconté par lui-même* (2 vols., Paris, 1926) II, pp.14-16; Cooper, 1954, no.190/18; Adhémar (1965) *op.cit.,* p.232; Hanson, no.139, p.153; De Leiris, pp.27, 28, 74, nos.421, 422; Harris, no.82; L M, no.M 64; RW, nos. II 469, 470; W 77, no.92; W 78, m.67; Jean-Paul Bouillon, "Bracquemond, Rops, Manet et le procédé à la plume", *Nouvelles de l'Estampe,* no.38 (March-April 1978), pp.4-10.

The Parnassian poet, Thédore de Banville (1823–91) was a follower of Théophile Gautier (1811–72) and friend of Baudelaire who became acquainted with Manet's friend, the etcher, Félix Bracquemond (1833–1919), after praising in an editorial in *L'Union des Arts* of October 1864 the latter's invention of a "resist" etching process in which pen and ink were used to draw directly on to the plate (Bouillon, *op.cit.,* p.4). Since both Manet and de Banville moved in contiguous circles, it is likely that each may have known of the other from about the mid-1860s.

The first instance of collaboration between Manet and de Banville occurred in June 1874, when the lithograph *Polichinelle* W 77, 90) was published, accompanied by a couplet by the poet. Prior to this, de Banville had praised Manet in an article of 21 June 1872 (George Heard Hamilton, *op.cit.,* p.155) and more importantly, in the review of the Salon of 1873, which appeared in *Le National* of 15 May (Hamilton, *op.cit.,* p.172).

To thank de Banville for the kind reviews and collaboration on the *Polichinelle* lithograph, Manet offered to etch the poet's portrait, as an illustration to *Les Ballades*. (A similar offer to illustrate the poet's *Odes Funambulesques* had been made by Bracquemond in 1857).

The etching was preceded by a preparatory portrait from the model, in pencil on squared note-paper (formerly coll. E. Rouart: De Leiris 421), and by a composition study in ink and wash (Musée du Louvre, Cabinet des Dessins: De Leiris 422) in which the portrait is reversed — although de Banville still holds the pen in his right hand — and the poet is surrounded by images symbolizing the thematic content of the poems, rising in the smoke from his cigarette.

A first etched portrait of de Banville (W, 77, 91) was abandoned, partly as Wilson *(ibid.)* suggests, for technical reasons, but also, it can be argued, because of the unsatisfactory composition, in which the poet is centrally placed and turned to the right within an irregular oval of aquatint.

In this, the second version, de Banville is reversed (apparently transferred from the image on the first plate, since the poet is now left-handed) and is placed at the right of the composition within an area of aquatint whose roughly oblong form echoes that of the plate, leaving at the left an 'L'-shaped space for the possible inclusion of a table of contents.

The figures indicating the principal poems in the ink drawing (see above) are condensed and re-grouped in the etching: the most strongly bitten, and arguably the most important of these (and the only one to appear in the first plate) is the exotic lady. In both plates, she is situated close to de Banvill's head, inclining towards it — a playful personification, in contemporary dress, of the poet's muse.

Harris *(ibid.)* notes Manet's tonal treatment of the poet, which contrasts with the linear treatment of the surrounding images. The short, parallel, diagonal strokes describing the right arm form an open contour which simultaneously detaches the figure from the background, while retaining links with it. A similar convention had been used to describe the contours of the white cat in the etching *The Cats* of 1868–69 (W 77, 58).

Although Manet eventually brought the plate to a successful conclusion, it was with regret that he wrote to de Banville on 2 August 1874, informing him that the work would not be completed in time to meet the publisher's deadline, which was the September of that year.

MANET, Édouard 1832–1883

59 **Profile Portrait of Baudelaire in a Top-Hat (I)** *c.*1862–69

Etching (all drawing with the needle); the rocker dragged over the plate to create the parallel lines on the coat; on paper watermarked: *"L 18/FB"* (partly cut away). The sheet turned so that the laid lines are horizontal.

Platemarks: 13.0 x 7.4 cm

Signed on the plate, upper left: "EM" (in monogram)

Stamped in red, bottom right of sheet: "20".

EXHIBITED Arts Council (38).

LITERATURE M.N., no.40; R, p.51; Guérin, no.30; Jean Adhémar, "Le portrait de Baudelaire gravé par Manet", *Revue des Arts,* 4 (1952), pp.240-42; Cooper, 1954, no.190/20; Sandblad, *op.cit.,* pp.64-66; Hanson, no.36, p.61; Harris, no.21; L M, no.M19; RW, under I 51; W, 77, no.27; Bouillon, *op.cit.,* p.4; W, 78, no.40; W, 83, no.54.

The etching is related to the portrait of the poet Charles Baudelaire (1821–67) in the painting *Music in the Tuileries Gardens* of 1862 (National Gallery, London: JW36).

Sandblad's suggestion (*ibid.*) that Manet may have etched the portrait after a lost preliminary pencil drawing, rather than after the painting, cannot be proved, although the handling of the etching does have a basis in the style of such preliminary sketches for the painting as the *Silhouette of a man in a top hat, viewed from the rear* (coll. A. Santamarina, Argentina: R W II 309) or the *Three studies of men, one of a woman* (Musée de Louvre, Cabinet de Dessins: R W II 314), in which primarily the head and shoulders

of figures are described with slight, rapid pencil strokes. Indeed, the fluidly brushed patch of sombre tone by which Baudelaire's profile is rendered in *Music in the Tuileries Gardens* would be untranslatable into the medium of etching.

The present work is one of five etched portraits of Baudelaire, with whom Manet became friends in *c.*1859. Another similar profile portrait (W. 78, 41) exists, as do three versions of a frontal portrait of the poet without a hat.

A letter from Manet, datable to 1867–68 (quoted in Adhémar, *ibid.*) addressed to the publisher Charles Asselineau establishes the existence of both types of portrait at this date. Adhémar (*ibid.*) has therefore concluded that the present portrait, also one of the versions of Baudelaire bareheaded, was executed at this time specifically to offer Asselineau for inclusion in his book commemorating the dead poet, entitled *Baudelaire, sa vie, son oeuvre.*

When the second version of the profile was published by Aselineau in January 1869, the playful and incidental contours visible in the present work had been refined from it (Sandblad, *ibid.*) to make an equally elegant but less fleeting image, more suited to the requirements of a memorial portrait. Below it was printed: "Peint et Gravé par Manet 1862 Imp A. Salmon". Sandblad (*ibid.*) suggests that the inscription supports the contention that the present, earlier version of the portrait was indeed executed at the same time as the painting *Music in the Tuileries Gardens,* while the later memorial portrait was considered to be merely a repetition of it.

On the other hand, Wilson (77, *ibid.*) argues that the portrait may date from 1869, on the basis of the watermark: "WZ . . . TMAN . . . 69" on the sheet of an impression in a private collection. This impression, however, may be on eighteenth-century Whatman paper (James Whatman established the Turkey Mill in 1731 (Dard Hunter, *Papermaking, The History and Technique of an Ancient Craft,* New York 1943 and 1970, pp.16, 265), or it may be on forged Whatman paper which was produced on the Continent from 1850.

While the date 1867–68 for this portrait cannot be discounted, the passage in Manet's letter in which he offers it to Asselineau ("If a portrait is to be placed at the head of the *Spleen of Paris,* I have a Baudelaire with hat, that is to say as a stroller, which perhaps would not be bad at the beginning of this book . . .") suggests the artist's recognition of the appropriateness to the prospective publication of a portrait which had been in existence for some time, and probably since 1862.

MANET, Édouard 1832–1883

60 **Olympia** (small plate) 1867

Etching: all drawing with the needle; a 'lavis' aquatint in the background (some of which is on the pillow below Olympia's right forearm); printed in black ink (artistic wiping); on pale grey-blue laid paper, watermarked: *"L18/FB"* (very faintly).

Platemarks: 8.8 x 17.7 cm

Unsigned.

Stamped in red, lower right of sheet: "23".

EXHIBITED Arts Council (39).

LITERATURE M.N., no.17, p.3; R, pp.57-58; Guérin, no.39; Cooper, 1954, no.190/23; John Richardson, *Edouard Manet, Paintings and Drawings* (1958), under no.20; Adhémar (1965), *op.cit.,* p.231; Hanson, no.58, p.77; Isaacson, no.23; Harris, no.53; LM, no.M45; Melot, nos.142-44; RW, under II 381 and pp.14-15; Theodore Reff, *Manet: Olympia* (1976), pp.30, 31; W, 77, no.53; David Alston, "What's in a name? Olympia and a Minor Parnassian", *Gazette des Beaux Arts* (April, 1978), pp.148-54; W, 78, no.47; W, 83, no.69.

The etching re-works in the same sense the composition of the oil painting, *Olympia,* of 1863 (Musée de Louvre, Jeu de Paume: JW 82) which was refused at the Salon of 1866, and which was hung in Manet's self-financed retrospective exhibition held at the Pont de l'Alma in 1867, just outside the grounds in which the Universal Exhibition was taking place.

Manet's exhibition was accompanied by a pamphlet in which Zola's combative article in defence of the painter, originally published in the *Revue de XIX siècle* of 1 January 1867 (Hamilton, *op.cit.,* pp.87-107), was reprinted. The present etching was also executed for the brochure, and was published in an original edition of 600.

That Manet chose his most controversial painting to date as the subject for translation into an etching is in accord with the defiant tone of the catalogue, and, as Theodore Reff (*op.cit.,* p.30) points out, demonstrates the importance which the artist attached to that painting as the epitome of his art, and confirms Zola's opinion of it as a masterpiece.

The etching, which dates from the period January-May 1867, was preceded by a drawing on wood of the same subject (Guérin, 88) and another etching (W, 77, 52), both of a squarer format similar to that of the painting. The drawing on wood, which was finally cut by a professional engraver, Moller (Guérin, *ibid.*), reproduces the composition of the painting in reverse. Manet had hoped that it would illustrate Lacroix and Verboekhoeven's *Paris-Guide,* published to celebrate the Universal Exhibition, although it is doubtful whether the wood-engraving was commissioned; a reproduc-

tion of a painting not admitted to the Salon of 1866 would scarcely have received official sanction the following year. Furthermore, the block had not been cut by early 1867, as a letter from Manet to Zola during that period confirms (Wilson, 1978, *op.cit.,* reproduced under no.97), and,, as Juliet Wilson has observed (1983, *ibid.*) the format of the block is in any case too large for the *Guide*.
Wilson (1983, *ibid.*) has established that the figures of Olympia in both woodblock and etchings are of almost identical dimensions, indicating that the motif was transferred from the block to the plates by means of tracing. This may have been the *Study for Olympia* (formerly in the collection of Degas, last recorded at an auction in Zürich in 1925: RW II 378), although it is probable that this drawing, which similarly reverses the oil composition, may also have been produced from the same tracing.
The new, shallow format of the present version of *Olympia* was dictated by that of Zola's brochure, the dimension of which Manet had asked for in the letter of early 1867 (cited above). Manet's initial problems of fitting the design into an over-wide format were overcome by cutting the lateral sides of the plate after the third state. Haris (*ibid.*) has noted that in cutting down the space surrounding the figure and in simplifying the tonal values of the final states, Manet asserts the two-dimensional design of the composition. After the Pont de l'Alma exhibition, Zola confirmed in a reply to a letter from Arséne Houssaye, that Manet would be unwilling to lend the plate of *Olympia* for further publication, and confided to him that the etching was a failure (Adhémar, *op.cit.,* p.231). Zola may have had reservations about Bracquemond's collaboration in the printing of the early states (Moreau — Nélaton, 1906, *op.cit.,* unpaginated).
In November 1867, Manet began to paint Zola's portrait, in the background of which is an etching of *Olympia,* with head slightly turned to achnowledge her champion. For this Olympia, the artist reverted to the earlier version on the larger plate, an indication, perhaps, of his dissatisfaction with the version published in Zola's pamphlet. If this is the case, Zola's confidence to Houssaye regarding the failure of the print, may, in reality, have been merely a transmission of the artist's own opinion.

MANET, Édouard 1832–1883

61 **Berthe Morisot** 1872

Etching (all drawing with the needle, and some stippling with the point of the needle); the rocker dragged over the plate to create a tonal area of parallel lines, lower right; on paper watermarked with three balls in a circle surmounted by a fleur-de-lys. The sheet turned so that the laid lines are horizontal.
The composition limited at the bottom by two ruled etched lines.
Platemarks: 11.9 x 7.9 cm
Unsigned.
Stamped in red, bottom right of sheet: "26."

EXHIBITED Arts Council (40)
LITERATURE M.N., m.41; Duret-Flitch, *op.cit.,* opposite p.103; R, p.72; Jedlicka, *op.cit.,* p.235; Guérin, no.59; Cooper, 1954, no.190/26; Hanson, no.107, p.123; Jacques Mathey, *Graphisme de Manet,* III (Paris, 1966), no.62e; LM, no.M61; RW, under I 179, II 389; W, 77, no.76; W, 78, no.65.

Manet first met the artist Berthe Morisot (1841–95) through the painter Henri de Fantin-Latour (1836–1904) in the Autumn of 1868 (John Rewald, *The History of Impressionism,* 1973, p.192). She agreed to pose for the figure on the left of the balcony in the painting of that title (Musée du Louvre, Jeu de Paume; JW 150) which Manet began at this time (Rewald, *ibid.*), and thereafter was the subject of seven portraits.
The etching reworks in reverse the painting *Berthe Morisot in Black Hat, with Violets,* 1872 (coll. Rouart, Paris: JW 208). A drawing (ex. coll. Roger-Marx: RW II 389) may have preceded it; a second, rather flaccid and schematic drawing of the same subject (location unknown: Mathey, *ibid.*) in chalk and watercolour does not appear to be by Manet.
The etching simultaneously simplifies the painted portrait — the complexities of right ear and earring (which would be on the right of the etching) are eliminated — while adding to it a new urgency and instability: Rosenthal (*ibid.*) was the first to note the impression of movement given by this tragic image. The oil's centrally-positioned, triangular composition is transposed to the left of the etching, leaving a space at the right; the etched composition now appears to be titled towards the right, for the artist has reversed all elements of the oil composition except the shoulders, which remain in the same sense as the painting.
In comparison to the treatment of forms in the painting, the etched forms are rendered freely. The broken, agitated lines which make up the silhouette of the torso become more rhythmical around the head and the hat. Such handling, which clearly displays the influence of Goya's etchings, can also be found, as Wilson has observed (77, 76) in the *Queue in front of the Butcher's Shop* (W, 77, 71).

MANET, Édouard 1832–1883

62 **Jeanne — Spring** 1882

Etching (an uneven-grained, hand-shaken aquatint (visible particularly in the lower half of the plate), and an uneven (sand or salt?) aquatint on the left arm; all drawing with the needle); the paper watermarked: *"L18/F B"*.
The pictorial area enclosed within a ruled etched line (other ruled lines at the top and bottom partly burnished away).
Pictorial area: 15.7 x 10.8 cm
Platemarks: 24.8 x 18.3 cm
Signed on the plate below the pictorial area, left: "Manet".
Stamped in red, bottom right of sheet: "30".

EXHIBITED Arts Council (43).
LITERATURE *Gazette des Beaux-Arts,* XXVII, 1902, opposite p.248; M-N. no.47; R, p.149; Jedlicka, *op.cit.,* p.235; Guérin, no.66; Cooper, 1954, no.190/30; Richardson, *op.cit.,* under no.76; Adhémar (1965), *op.cit.,* pp.234-35; Hanson, no.164, p.175; Carl Chiarenza, "Manet's Use of Photography in the Creation of a Drawing", *Master Drawings,* no.VII (1969), pp.38-45; De Leiris, under no.588; Harris, no.88; LM, no.M66; RW, under I 372; W, 77, no.107; W, 78, no.102; W, 83, no.214.

The etching records in the same sense Manet's painting of 1881, *Jeanne-Spring* (coll. Henry Payne Bingham, New York: JW 470), the first of two canvases in which beautiful and fashionably-dressed women represent the seasons. The second painting, *Méry Laurent — Autumn* (Musée des Beaux-Arts, Nancy: JW 480) also dates from 1881.
The model for *Spring,* the young actress Jeanne de Marsy, had posed for Manet as early as 1875 (Hamilton, *op.cit.,* p.249). For the present portrait, Manet advised her on the choice of costume, and purchased especially for her the bonnet from the celebrated *modiste* Mme. Virot (Antonin Proust, *Édouard Manet, Souvenirs,* Paris, 1913, pp.112-13). The artist had begun to frequent shops selling fashionable dresses, materials and toiletries in 1874, after meeting the poet Stéphane Mallarmé (1842–98), who was at that time both editor and journalist of the ephemeral fashion paper *La Dernière Mode* (Wilson, 1978, *ibid.*).
Richardson (*ibid.*) suggests that Manet may have begun his paintings of the seasons after a similar series had been commissioned from Alfred Stevens (1823–1906) by the King of the Belgians. Manet's handling of the subject, however, owes much to Japanese art. The theme of the four seasons, associated with pretty girls and fashionable clothing, had been treated by Utamaro (1753–1806) in the two small volumes of woodcuts, *Shiki no hana* ('Flowers of the Four Seasons'), published in 1801. In the first volume, a frontispiece of yellow blossom is followed by pages of girls in spring and summer attire, mainly in the open air. A frontispiece of chrysanthemums betokens the autumn and winter scenes of the second volume, in which girls in winter costume are seen in interiors, on verandahs, or being buffeted by the elements (J. Hillier, *Utamaro Colour Prints and Paintings,* 1979, pp.140-41).
Manet's awareness of the Japanese precedents for his paintings is evident in the choice of background screen or wallpaper for the composition *Autumn.* It is clearly of Japanese origin, and is decorated with chrysanthemums — the flowers chosen by Utamaro to herald the cold seasons in the second volume of *Shiki no hana.* This would suggest that Manet also knew of Utamaro's publication of 1801; if this is the case, then Manet's two canvases, *Spring* and *Autumn.* can be seen to parallel Utamaro's two volumes of *Shiki no hana,* each of which presents a conflation of two seasons. Hamilton's suggestion (*ibid.*) that Manet completed only two paintings out of an intended series of four may therefore be erroneous.
The *Gazette des Beaux-Arts* of 1 June 1882 reproduced a drawing by Manet after *Jeanne — Spring* as an illustration to Antonin Proust's article on the Salon of 1882. Carl Chiarenza (*op.cit.,* p.41) has shown that the drawing (now in the Fogg Art Museum: De Leiris 588), was simply traced through from a reversed photograph on the *verso* of the sheet, specifically for reproduction in Proust's article. However, the tonal values and areas of soft-focus of the photograph correspond exactly to those of the etching, suggesting that it may similarly have been traced on to the plate from a photograph (Chiarenza, *op.cit.,* p.40). The Fogg photograph, however, is twice the size of the etched plate, and it is likely therefore that Manet worked from a smaller version of the image for the etching.
The present etching, which may be dated to Spring 1882, was the last Manet made. After the first state, the plate was passed to Henri Guérard for aquatinting and further biting. In a letter of 2 May the artist wrote to Guérard: ". . . labourez moi cette planche d'un bon coup de burin . . ." ("plough up the plate for me with a good cut of the burin"); Michel Melot (Wilson 83, *ibid.*) cites this as evidence of Manet's desire to cancel the plate, rather than to have Guérard bring it to a successful conclusion.
Wilson (1978, *ibid.*) suggests the possibility that Manet executed the etching specifically to illustrate Proust's article in the *Gazette des Beaux-Arts;* the approaching deadline for publication and the artist's failing health may have compelled him to abandon the plate in favour of an easier means of reproduction, that is, the traced photograph in the Fogg Art Museum.

MODIGLIANI, Amedeo 1884–1920
63 **Female Nude** 1916
Oil on canvas (relined), 92.4 x 59.8 cm
Signed, top left: "Modigliani"

PROVENANCE With Léopold Zborowski, Paris; C. Zamaron, Paris; with Zborowski, Paris; Samuel Courtauld by 1931. Courtauld Gift 1932.
EXHIBITED *Modigliani,* Palais des Beaux-Arts, Brussels, November 1933 (22); *Modigliani,* Kunsthalle, Basel, January 1934 (14); Tate Gallery, 1948 (42); Orangerie, Paris, 1955 (31); Courtauld Centenary, 1976 (27); *Modigliani,* Musée Saint-Georges, Liège, October–December 1980 (7), as "Nu assis".
LITERATURE Jamot-Turner, no.54 (repr.); Home House Catalogue, no.21; Cooper, 1954, no.38 (repr.); Ambrogio Ceroni, *Modigliani peintre, suivi des "souvenirs" de Lunia Czechowska* (Milan, 1958), no.29; Joseph Lanthemann, *Modigliani 1884–1920: catalogue raisonné, sa vie, son oeuvre peint son art* (Barcelona, 1970), no.160; A. Ceroni and F. Cachin, *Tout l'oeuvre peint de Modigliani* (Paris, 1927), no.127.

Although dated by Cooper to *c.*1917 on the basis of stylistic affinities with the *Crouching Nude* (Antwerp Museum) which shows the same model, Lanthemann assigns it to the previous year. Ceroni (*op.cit.,* 1958) preferred an even earlier date of 1912–13, which seems much less convincing. Modigliani's nudes apparently caused a scandal when shown at the Galerie Berthe Weill, Paris, in 1917. Léopold Zborowski, an emigré Polish dealer, befriended Modigliani and did much to promote his work.

MONET, Claude 1840–1926
64 **The Seine at Argenteuil, Autumn** 1873
Oil on canvas, 55 x 74.5 cm
Signed, bottom right: "Claude Monet/73"

colour plate, page 29

PROVENANCE With Durand-Ruel, Paris; Erwin Davis, New York, 1886; with Durand-Ruel, Paris, 1901; G. Hoentschel, Paris, 1904; Comte de Rasti, Paris; with Alexandre Rosenberg, Paris; Hodebert; with Bernheim-Jeune, Paris, 1924; acquired by Samuel Courtauld, May 1924. Courtauld Gift 1932.

EXHIBITED (?) *La société des impressionistes,* Dowdeswell and Dowdeswell's (exhibition organized by Durand-Ruel), London, 1883 (16), as "Le petit bras à Argenteuil"; *The Impressionists of Paris,* American Art Galleries, New York, April 1886, and National Academy of Design, May-June 1886 (282); *Monet,* Union League Club, New York 1891 (68); Tate Gallery, 1948 (44); *Impressionism,* Royal Academy, London, 1974 (71); Courtauld Centenary, 1976 (28).
LITERATURE (?) Frederick Wedmore, "The Impressionists" in *Fortnightly Review,* January 1883, p.82; "The Impressionists' Exhibition" in *The Academy,* 28 April 1883, p.300; O. Reutersward, *Monet* (Stockholm, 1948), p.283; Cooper, 1954, no.40; D. Wildenstein, *Claude Monet: biographie et catalogue raisonné,* I: *1840–1881 Peintures* (Lausanne – Paris, 1974), pp.238-39, no.290 (repr.), for full literature 1886–91, not quoted here.

Painted in late summer or early autumn of 1873, the town of Argenteuil is in the background, with the Île Marante on the left, an arm of the River Seine in the centre, and on the right bank, Colombes. Wedmore (*loc.cit.*) gives a description of a picture shown at Dowdeswell's gallery in 1883 which seems to refer precisely to this picture: "... palpitating light and glowing hue. The whole one side of the canvas is filled with flame-coloured autumn trees which throw their bright reflection of a rosier flame-colour upon a broad river water otherwise turquoise and opal" (quoted Wildenstein, *op.cit.*).
The painting has been known as *Effet d'Automne à Argenteuil,* and the location occasionally mistakenly identified as Vétheuil. Stylistically, it shows Monet working in his early Impressionist manner, where the whole composition is constructed in "terms of contrasts of clear colour, which model the forms without relying on tonal contrasts" (John House, *Impressionism,* Royal Academy, 1974, p.42). The same view had been painted by Daubigny as early as 1850, and both Renoir and Sisley worked from this site. A year after this picture was painted, the Impressionists were to hold their first group Exhibition in Paris (see also no.75 in this exhibition).

MONET, Claude 1840–1926
65 **Vase of Flowers** *c.*1881–82
Oil on canvas, 100.4 x 81.8 cm
Signed, bottom right: "Claude Monet"

colour plate, page 33

PROVENANCE With Bernheim-Jeune, Paris; with Alex. Reid, Glasgow; bought by Samuel Courtauld, August 1923. Courtauld Gift 1932.
EXHIBITED *French Art,* City Museum and Art Gallery, Birmingham, October 1947 (no cat.); Tate Gallery, 1948 (49); *Monet,* Edinburgh and London 1957 (59); Courtauld Centenary, 1976 (31).
LITERATURE Jamot-Turner, no.17 (repr.); Home House Catalogue, no.24; O. Reuterswärd, *Monet* (1948), p.280; Cooper, 1954, no.43 (repr.); D. Wildenstein, *Calude Monet,* I (1974), pp.382-83, no.626 (repr.).

Described by Wildenstein (*op.cit.*) as "Bouquet des Mauves", the flowers are Common, or Wild Mallow (*Malva silvestris*). Wildenstein also notes that the artist's signature has been added later, presumably on the basis of the orthography. Monet probably began to paint still-lifes of flowers under the influence of Renoir, and first exhibited studies of dahlias at the second Impressionist exhibition of 1876. Several oils of chrysanthemums date from 1878–80.

MONET, Claude 1840–1926
66 **Antibes** 1888
Oil of canvas, 65.5 x 92.4 cm
Signed, bottom left: "Claude Monet 88"

colour plate, page 31

PROVENANCE (?) bought from the artist by Boussod Valadon et Cie., June 1888; (?) with Georges Petit 1888; Mme. Vve. Barbedienne, Paris, 1894; sold Drouot, Paris, 24 February 1894 (lot 39), bought Durand-Ruel; Decap, Paris, 1894; with Bernheim-jeune, Paris, 1907; Baron Caccamisi, Paris, 1907; Mrs. Blanche Marchesi, London, *c.*1910; with Paul Rosenberg, Paris; with Knoedler, London; bought by Samuel Courtauld, August 1923. To Sir John Atkins, London (with a life interest), thence to Home House Society Trustees, a year before Sir John's death, in 1962.
EXHIBITED (?) *Monet,* Boussod Valadon et Cie., Paris, 1888; *Monet et Rodin,* Georges Petit, Paris, June 1889 (103); *Tableaux* par *Besnard, Cazin, etc.* Georges Petit, Paris, 1899 (51); *International Society of Sculptors, Painters and Gravers,* Grafton Galleries, London, 1910 (133); *19th Century French Painters,* Knoedler, London, July 1923 (35); Tate Gallery, 1948 (47); *Impressionism,* Royal Academy, 1974 (77); Courtauld Centenary, 1976 (32).
LITERATURE (?) Gustave Geffroy, "Dix tableaux de Cl. Monet" in *La Justice,* 17 June 1888, p.1; (?) A. de Calonne, "L'Art contre nature" in *Le Soleil,* 23 June 1889, p.1; Arsène Alexandre, *Claude Monet* (Paris, 1921), pp.87-88 (repr.pl.37); Jamot-Turner, no.18 (repr.); L. Venturi, *Les Archives de l'Impressionisme,* I (Paris, 1939), p.236; Cooper, 1954, no.44 (repr.); John Rewald "Theo Van Gogh, Goupil, and the Impressionists" Parts I and II, *Gazette des Beaux-Arts,* LXXXI (January-February 1973), p.25 (repr.), Appendix I, (?) pp.92-93 and 99; D. Wildenstein, *Claude Monet,* III (1974), pp.110-11, no.1192 (repr.), as "Montagnes de l'Esterel".
Painted in the spring of 1888. Monet worked at Antibes from February until May 1888 and on his return exhibited ten paintings of Antibes at Boussod and Valadon (formerly Goupil) in Paris, then run by Theo Van Gogh. Wildenstein (*op.cit.*) considers the Courtauld picture to have been among those exhibited, and catalogues it as *Montagnes de l'Esterel.* He identifies the location from which Monet painted the subject as Pinède, close to the site of another picture (Wildenstein 1188), but looking south-west across the Golfe Juan to the Montagnes de l'Esterel. The peaks of Rastel d'Agay and Souvières can be seen, framing in between the Pic d'Ours and the summit of the Grues. On the far left, is the peak of Bataiguier on the island of Sainte-Marguerite.
This painting is discussed in "Japonisme" in the exhibition catalogue, *Japanese Influence on French Art 1854–1910* (Cleveland Museum of Fine Art, Ohio, 1971; repr.fig.42, p.130), where it is noted that Monet enters a new phase of Japonisme. He becomes increasingly interested in dramatic compositional elements and it is suggested that among the more obvious Japanese sources he may have turned to are the prints by Utagawa Kuniyoshi, *Fifty-Three Stages and Four Post Towns Along the Tokaido.*
In this painting, Monet uses vivid colour-contrasts, echoed again in the more muted harmonies of the background, to convey the brilliant light of the Mediterranean. John House (*Impressionism,* Royal Academy, 1974, p.43) has noted that the tree trunk, which makes an arabesque across the foreground, has been moved by Monet a little to the right during the execution of this picture.

MORISOT, Berthe 1841–1895
67 **Portrait of the Artist's Sister, Mme. Edma Pontillon** Early 1870s
Oil on canvas, 56 x 46.1 cm
Signed, top left: "B. Morisot"

PROVENANCE Prague (label on back of frame: "K.K. Hauptzollamt Prag"); with Galerie Miethke, Vienna; 1904/13 acquired Baron Adolf Kohner, Budapest; sold Musée Ernst, Budapest, 26ff. February 1934, lot 60 and p.7, bought Count Seilern. Seilern Bequest (Princes Gate Collection, no.210) 1978.
EXHIBITED *Les grands maitres de l'art français du XIXeme siècle,* Musée Ernst, Budapest, 1913; *Exposition des oeuvres d'art socialisées,* Palais des Beaux-Arts, Budapest, 1919; *Nineteenth Century French Paintings,* National Gallery, London, 1942 (21); *The Princes Gate Collection,* Courtauld Institute Galleries, London, from 17 July 1981 (46).
LITERATURE A.S. [Antoine Seilern], *Paintings and drawings of Continental Schools other than Flemish and Italian at 56 Princes Gate London SW7,* III (1961), p.59, no.210 (repr.); M.-L. Bataille and G. Wildenstein, *Berthe Morisot* (Paris 1961), p.24, no.21 (repr.); [Antoine Seilern], *Corrigenda and Addenda to the Catalogue of Paintings and Drawings at 56 Princes Gate London SW7* (1971), p.61.

The sitter in this portrait was unidentified early in this century and Bataille and Wildenstein *(loc.cit.),* for unexplained reasons, called her Mme. Heude; her resemblance to known likenesses of Mme. Edma Pontillon is however so striking that the identification by Count Seilern *(loc.cit.)* can scarcely be doubted.

Berthe Morisot had two older sisters, Yves and Edma. Yves took an early dislike to art lessons, but Edma was Berthe's inseparable companion in painting until the time of her marriage in 1869 to Adolphe Pontillon, a naval officer then stationed at Cherbourg, when she virtually gave it up. The two girls had been pupils of Corot, who preferred Edma's work, finding Berthe too independent; they enjoyed painting in the open air, and they exhibited at the Salon. Their separation in 1869 and the sacrifice of Edma's occupation was a source of distress which is recorded in their correspondence. Mme. Morisot wrote in March 1869: "Berthe says she is waiting for you to know whether what she is doing is good or bad"; in September Edma wrote to Berthe: "My passion for painting has not yet left me" *(The Correspondence of Berthe Morisot,* ed. D. Rouart, 1957, pp.29, 39).
The following winter Edma stayed at her parents' home in Passy to await her first confinement. During the week preceding the birth in 1870 she sat with her mother for her most celebrated portrait in *Mother and Sister of the Artist* (National Gallery of Art, Washington; Bataille and Wildenstein, no.20), on the basis of which, chiefly, the present sitter is identified. Berthe Morisot wrote an account to her sister of Manet's visit to touch up the portrait before exhibition at the Salon. The horrified nature of her account is such that, contrary to what has often been suggested, it is doubtful whether she ever encouraged such assistance before or after. At the end of 1871, when Edma came to Passy for the birth of her second daughter, her sister made the careful pastel portrait now in the Louvre (Bataille and Wildenstein, no.419) which confirms the identity of the present sitter. She appears in numerous other works, but these are mainly figure compositions, not revealing details of physiognomy.
Mme. Pontillon looks a year or two older in this portrait, which must still, however, date from the early 1870s. Although it is unlikely that Manet participated directly it was undoubtedly painted under his influence, as the colours and their application show. The artist wrote in 1871 to Mme. Pontillon, of a portrait she was painting of her sister Yves: "as a composition it resembles a Manet. I realize this and am annoyed" *(Correspondence,* p.71). The pose is unusually formal, the details painted lovingly. The delicacy of the tones has recently been revealed by cleaning (1983). The background and parts of the dress are thinly painted, the pale priming showing through, but the details of the collar and the asters (?) at the breast, reminiscent of Berthe Morisot's violets in Manet's celebrated portrait of 1872 (private collection; D. Rouart and D. Wildenstein, *Edouard Manet,* Lausanne/Paris, 1975, no.179), are impasted highlights. X-rays show the reworking of the contours of shoulders and arms, which originally presented a broader image. As in the case of Manet's *Au Bal* (no.50 in this exhibition), examination reveals that the painting was initially exhibited in an unvarnished state. (Technical information, as for nos.15, 26, 44 and 50, from Department of Technology records.)

MUNCH, Edvard 1863–1944
68 **Self-portrait** 1895–1902
Lithograph (the head with crayon alone, all other areas with crayon and wash); printed in black ink; on cream (now unevenly discoloured) wove-paper.
Stonemarks: 48.7 x 35 cm
Signed in pencil, below the pictorial area, within the stonemarks, right: "Edvard Munch".
Inscribed in a different hand in pencil, lower left of sheet: "No.13. 3 die tilstand", and in other hands in pencil, *verso:* "Selbabildnis/Berlin 1895" and: "1902", and: "42" and: "258nd"
PROVENANCE In a German collection? (cf. inscriptions); Samuel Courtauld (no date of acquisition). Courtauld Gift 1938.
EXHIBITED *Expressionist Exhibition,* St. George's Gallery, London, February 1950 (50); Nottingham University, 1969.
LITERATURE Cooper, 1954, no.222.

This, the second state of Munch's first self-portrait in the graphic medium, was unknown to the compiler of the catalogue raisonné of Munch's graphic work, Gustav Schiefler (cf. *Edvard Munch das graphische Werk 1906–1926* (Berlin, 1927) no.31, first state only), and is unrecorded by Werner Timm *(The Graphic Work of Edvard Munch,* Berlin 1969). That it is a reworking of the signed and dated self-portrait executed in Clot's workshop in Paris in 1895 (Schiefler, *ibid.*) is confirmed by vestiges of the earlier date and signature, visible top left and right.
The first state of the *Self-portrait,* which included a skeletal arm across the

bottom foreground – clearly a *Memento mori* – was executed during a period in which Munch first encountered literary symbolism in Paris (Timm, *op.cit.,* p.101): Timm *(op.cit.,* p.37) has observed the debt of the initial composition to Félix Vallotton's (1865–1925) woodcut portrait of Dostoiewsky (M. Vallotton and C. Goerg, *Félix Vallotton Catalogue raisonné of printed graphic work,* Paris and Lausanne, 1972, no.163) – one of Munch's favourite authors – which was completed in 1895.
In Berlin in 1902, Munch recovered the stones upon which the Parisian lithographs were drawn, reprinting them in colour by adding new stones. During this year, the present state of this lithograph was probably executed: confirmation of this appears in the corrected inscription on the *verso* of the Courtauld example (see above).
The new isolation of the pale head against a dark background, reminiscent of portraits by Eugène Carrière (1849–1906), aligned the image formally and psychologically with Munch's other portraits of 1902, in various media (for example, the lithograph *Double Portrait of the Leistikows* (Schiefler, *op.cit.,* no.170), or the drypoint *Head of Girl* (Schiefler, *op.cit.,* no.162)).
The example of reworking a portrait after an interval of several years is repeated later in Munch's career: in 1925–26, he drew the lithograph *Self-portrait with a Bottle* (not in Schiefler), which re-examines the artist's appearance as it is depicted in an oil painting of the Weimar period of 1906.

MUNCH, Edvard 1863–1944
69 **Ibsen in the Grand Café, Kristiania** 1902
Lithograph (crayon); printed in black ink; on thick off-white (now unevenly discoloured) wove paper.
Signed in pencil below the pictorial area, right: "Edvard Münch", and numbered by the artist in pencil below the pictorial area, left: "338".
Inscribed and dated in different hands in pencil, *verso:* "Henrik Ibsen au Grand Café Oo C/Litho Le presse detruit/A peu pres 50 epreuves.", and :" nur 50 Exemplare/Hendrick Ibsen/350", and: "1902".

PROVENANCE ? in French and German collections (see inscription, *verso*); Samuel Courtauld (no details of acquisition). Courtauld Gift 1938.
EXHIBITED *Expressionist Exhibition,* St. George's Gallery, London, February 1950 (50); Nottingham University, 1969; Arts Council (54); *20th Century Portraits,* National Portrait Gallery, London, 1978 (48).
LITERATURE Gustav Schiefler, *Verzeichnis des graphischen Werks Edvard Munchs* (Berlin, 1907),no.171; Gustav Schiefler *Edvard Munchs Graphische Kunst* (Dresden, 1923), pl.48; Gustav Schiefler, *Edvard Munch das Graphische Werk* (Berlin, 1927), no.171; Pola Gauguin, *Edvard Munch* (Oslo, 1946), p.142; J.P. Hodin, *Edvard Munch* (Stockholm, 1948), pl.188; Cooper, 1954, no.223; Otto Benesch, *Edvard Munch* (New York, 1960), p.29; Werner Timm, *The Graphic Art of Edvard Munch* (1969), no.77, pp.42-43.

Munch first made contact with the literary Bohemian circle of Kristiania (renamed Oslo after 1924) in 1894 (Timm, *op.cit.,* p.36): in the autumn of the following year, at his one-man exhibition at Blomquist's, Munch met the playwright Hendrick Ibsen (1828–1906).
During the latter part of this year, or possibly in 1898, he painted the first portrait of Ibsen in the Grand Café, the meeting place of the Bohemians (ex. coll. Fritz Jonas; Benesch, *op.cit.,* no.40). A more stylized version of this work (Kommunes Kunstsamlinger, Oslo) was painted in *c.*1902.
The present lithograph, drawn in 1902, records in the same sense the latter painting. The bright star-like form of Ibsen's head, observed by Benesch (*op.cit.,* p.29) is suggestive of the playwright's power to illuminate a complacent society. The close-up head is juxtaposed with a sketchy street scene of Kristiania, whose bourgeoisie were the subject of many of Ibsen's literary attacks: the contrast of head and city-scape suggests a debt to similar compositions by Félix Vallotton, particularly his woodcut *Self-Portrait* of 1891 (M. Vallotton and C. Goerg, *Vallotton, op.cit.,* no.82).
A similar, but more obvious, suggestion of Ibsen's powers of enlightenment is conveyed by Munch's lithograph *Ibsen with Lighthouse* (Schiefler 1927, *op.cit.,* no.171 (a)) in which the playwright's head appears, mask-like, superimposed on the beams of a lighthouse which cut through the darkness of a Norwegian coastline. This lithograph, originally executed in 1897 as a poster to advertise the play *John Gabriel Borkman* at the Théâtre-de l'Oeuvre, Paris (Timm, *op.cit.,* p.43), was also reworked in 1902. In this print, however, Ibsen's head appears almost as a caricature.
Benesch (*ibid.*) has suggested that the body of Ibsen in the present lithograph is "totally ignored". This is not true, for a *pentimento* in the window-sill, right, which continues through to the mutton-chop whiskers, and the paler angle of the right shoulder, clearly indicate an initial intention to draw a bust-length portrait. Although the precise contours of the shoulders are now largely obliterated, the mass of the torso is acknowledged by the swift, downward-curving stroke of the crayon.
The lithograph was printed by Lassally of Berlin in an edition of 50: there is a unique impression in black ink on grey paper.

PICASSO, Pablo 1881–1973
70 **Child with Dove** 1901
Oil on canvas, 73 x 54 cm
Signed, centre left: "Picasso"

colour plate, page 60

PROVENANCE With Paul Rosenberg, Paris; with Alex. Reid, Glasgow; Mrs. R.A. Workman, London; through Reid and Lefèvre, London; Samuel Courtauld, 1928; bequeathed to Lady Aberconway 1947. On long loan to the National Gallery, London, since 1975.

EXHIBITED *French Painters of Today,* Alex. Reid, Glasgow, October 1924 (24); *French Painters of Today,* Lefèvre Galleries, London, November 1924 (24); Opening Exhibition, Modern Foreign Gallery, Tate Gallery, June 1926; *A Century of French Painting,* Knoedler, New York, November 1928 (47); Tate Gallery, 1948 (50); Orangerie, Paris, 1955 (36); Courtauld Centenary, 1976 (33); *Pablo Picasso. A Retrospective,* Museum of Modern Art, New York, 22 May–16 September 1980 (repr. p.43).
LITERATURE Jamot-Turner, no.50 (repr.; date wrongly given as "about 1907"); C. Zervos, *Picasso, Oeuvres,* I (Paris, 1932), no.83 (plate 41); Cooper, 1954, no.46 (repr.); Pierre Daix, Georges Boudaille, and Joan Rosselet, *Picasso: The Blue and Rose Periods. A Catalogue Raisonné of the Paintings* (Greenwich, Connecticut, 1966), VI, no.14.

Painted in Paris in the autumn of 1901, this picture has also been called "Child with Pigeon". The present title is a more accurate description. The painting belongs to the early part of Picasso's so-called "Blue Period", and in the use of strongly-defined, non-naturalistic outlines, and the flattening of the perspective stems directly from the tradition of Gauguin and the Symbolist painters. There is also a lingering trace, in the asymmetrical composition and rhythmic curves of the child's body, of the conventions of Art Nouveau, which Picasso had admired and absorbed as a young student in Barcelona. The somewhat sentimental treatment of the subject-matter may also owe a little to English book illustrators of the late 19th century. *Lent anonymously.*

PICASSO, Pablo 1881–1973
71 **Seated Female Nude** 1923
Pen and black (Indian?) ink; on off-white (now unevenly discoloured) wove paper. The sheet unevenly trimmed, top and bottom.
35 x 26.1 cm
Signed in pen and black (Indian?) ink, bottom right: *"Picasso"*
Numbered in a different hand in pencil, verso: "35".

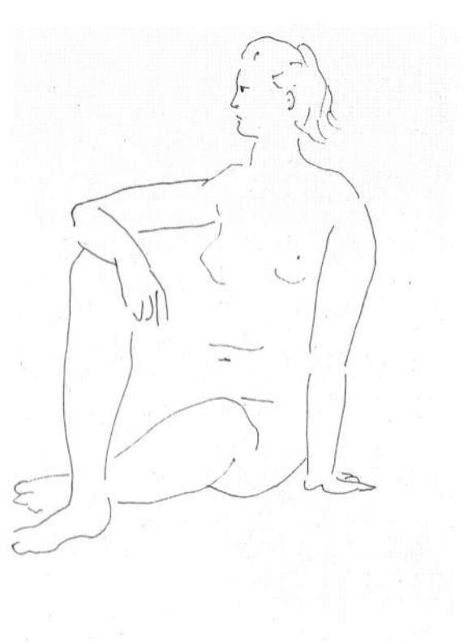

PROVENANCE Paul Rosenberg, Paris; Samuel Courtauld (purchased 1926). Courtauld Gift 1932 (H.H.63).
EXHIBITED *Picasso,* The London Gallery, London, 1939; Tate Gallery, 1948 (113); *France 1850–1950,* the Art Gallery, Kettering, June 1950 (57); Orangerie, Paris, 1955 (86); Manchester, 1962 (97); Nottingham University, 1969, Centenary, 1976 (73); Arts Council (55).
LITERATURE Home House Catalogue, no.63; Christian Zervos, *Pablo Picasso, Oeuvres,* (Paris, 1952), no.48; Cooper, 1954, no.145; Mervyn Levy, *The Human Form in Art* (1961), p.83.

The present work is one of a series of 31 drawings depicting bathers, either individually or in groups, which Picasso executed at Cap d'Antibes during the summer holiday of 1923 (Zervos, *ibid.*). Four drawings of a related subject were made in Paris prior to moving to the coast, and the Courtauld drawing is analogous in both treatment and pose to the figure in the sheet *Seated Woman with Elbow on her Knee* of this period (Zervos, *op.cit.,* V, p.13, no.20).
Of the drawings made in Antibes, all but nine are of identical format, indicating that probably the same sketchbook was in use most of the time. The seashore setting of the majority of drawings is specific, although in certain works it is so abstracted as to be ambiguous: the Courtauld sheet is one of four drawings in the series in which no background at all is indicated.
The sensitive contour which so precisely defines the forms and volumes of the figure in the present sheet is ultimately derived from Greek white figure vases, although Zervos (*op.cit.,* p.X) has noted Picasso's thoroughly modern interpretation of this style: this is particularly evident in the short-hand convention used to describe the heel of the left palm.
Anthony Blunt ("Picasso's Classical Period (1917–1925)", *Burlington Magazine,* CX, April, 1968, p.189) has noted in certain of Picasso's classical paintings and drawings an awareness of the work of artists much nearer his own time. A similar observation has been made by Timothy Hilton (*Picasso's Picassos,* Hayward Gallery, 1981, p.59) who suggests that the paintings and drawings of the summer of 1923 also contain reminiscences of Picasso's own paintings of *c.*1905–06. The Courtauld drawing would appear to be a work of this type: in pose and monumentality, the female figure is reminiscent of sculpture by Maillol, for example, *The Mediterranean* of 1901, a marble version of which Picasso could have seen in the Tuileries Gardens, while it also looks back to the pose of the seated women in the artist's own gouache of 1905, *Nude with Hair tied back,* (Zervos, *op.cit.,* I, p.113, no.259), which is in turn dependent upon certain nudes by Gauguin, for example, the seated figure in *And the Gold of their Bodies,* (1901) (Wildenstein, *Gauguin, op.cit.,* no.596).

PISSARRO, Camille 1830–1903
72 **Lordship Lane Station, Dulwich** 1871
Oil on canvas, 44.5 x 72.5 cm
Signed, bottom right: "C. Pissarro 1871"

colour plate, page 30

PROVENANCE With Alexandre Rosenberg, Paris; Lazare Weiller, Paris; Lazare Weiller Sale, Paris, 29 November 1901 (lot 34; 1,750 Frs.); with Tavernier, Paris; Pearson, Paris; Pearson, Sale, Berlin, 18 October 1927 (lot 53); Anonymous Sale, Paris, 23 June 1928 (lot 82; 51,000 Frs); with Schoeller, Paris; Morot, Paris; with Durand-Ruel, Paris; with Arthur Tooth & Sons, London; acquired by Samuel Courtauld, June 1936. Courtauld Bequest 1948 (Home House Trustees, no.233).
EXHIBITED *Flèche d'Or,* Tooth's Gallery, London, May 1936 (20); Tate Gallery, 1948 (51); *The Impressionists in London,* January-March 1973 (32); Courtauld Centenary, 1976 (34); *Pissarro,* Hayward Gallery, London, October 1980–January 1981 (16), and Grand Palais, Paris, January-April 1981, Museum of Fine Arts, Boston, May-August 1981.
LITERATURE L.-R. Pissarro and L. Venturi, *Camille Pissarro, Catalogue de son Oeuvre* (Paris, 1939), no.111 (repr.); Cooper, 1954, no.47 (as "La Station de Penge, Upper Norwood"; repr.); M. Reid, "Camille Pissarro: three paintings of London. What do they represent?", *Burlington Magazine,* CXIX, April, 1977, pp.251-61.

Formerly known as "Penge Station, Upper Norwood", the correct location has been established by Martin Reid (*op.cit.,* pp.254-57). Pissarro painted this picture when living in London in 1871 as a refugee from the Franco-Prussian War and the Commune, and it shows Lordship Lane Station (now demolished) on the old Crystal Palace (High Level) Railway, seen from the footbridge across the cutting to the south of the station. The line was opened in 1865 and closed in 1954.
Radiographs and infra-red photographs, taken in January 1983 by Ruth Bubb of the Department of Technology of the Courtauld Institute, reveal a *pentimento,* of the figure holding what appears to be a scythe. He is standing half-way up the railway embankment on the right of the painting, immediately above the point where the diagonal of the division between the ballast and the grass bank meets the bottom edge of the picture.
Railways feature as a subject in the work of several Impressionist painters, notably Daubigny, Pissarro, and pre-eminently Monet. Pissarro's *Lordship Lane Station* is the first fully elaborated treatment of a train in Impressionist art, and, as many writers have observed, it may have been inspired by J.M.W. Turner's *Rain, steam and speed: the Great Western Railway* (1844: National Gallery, London). Here, however, Pissarro has been more dispassionate, and Dr. John Gage sees a closer link in treatment with the early prints of railways.

PISSARRO, Camille 1830–1903
73 **The Quays at Rouen** 1883
Oil on canvas, 46.3 x 55.75 cm
Signed, bottom left: "C. Pissarro, 1883"

colour plate, page 32

PROVENANCE Private collection, Berlin; with Paul Cassirer, Berlin; Samuel Courtauld 1926. Courtauld Gift 1932.
EXHIBITED British Institute of Adult Education, Silver End, Essex, March 1935; Tate Gallery, 1948 (52); Orangerie, Paris, 1955 (38); Courtauld Centenary, 1976 (35).
LITERATURE Jamot-Turner. no.6 (repr.); Home House Catalogue, no.18; L.-R. Pissarro and L. Venturi, *Pissarro* (1939), no.601 (repr.); C. Pissarro (ed. L. Pissarro and J. Rewald), *Lettres à son fils Lucien* (Paris, 1950), pp.59-70 (English ed., London and New York, 1943, pp.40-48), especially the letter of 1 December 1883.

Painted at Rouen between September and November 1883, the view looks east along the river Seine from the Isle Lacroix, and beyond the river are the factories on the Quai de Paris, while on the top of the hill behind, appears the silhouette of Notre Dame de Bonsecours. Pissarro spent three months at Rouen in the autumn of 1883 in a hotel run by Eugène Murer. Murer, a professional pastrycook, was a childhood friend of the painter Armand Guillaumin, who had introduced him to other Impressionist painters. Both Renoir and Pissarro painted his portrait. Gauguin, having abandoned his career as a stockbroker a few years earlier, to take up painting, joined Pissarro in Rouen in November 1883.
Mr. Christopher Lloyd (Ashmolean Museum, Oxford) has called the compiler's attention to the fact that this painting appears in the background of the *Bouquet de Fleurs* (Pissarro and Venturi 1064) now in the California Palace of the Legion of Honor, San Francisco.

PISSARRO, Camille 1830–1903
74 **Festival at L'Hermitage (Les Boutiques)** *c.*1876–78
Oil on canvas, 46.5 x 55.1 cm
Signed, bottom left: "Pissarro"

PROVENANCE With Durand-Ruel, Paris; bought 3 April 1913 by Paul Cassirer, Berlin (their inventory no.5611 on label on back of stretcher); Louis Ullstein, Berlin; with Cassirer; acquired by Count Seilern. London, 1941. Seilern Bequest (Princes Gate Collection, no.205) 1978.
EXHIBITED *The Princes Gate Collection,* Courtauld Institute Galleries, London, from 17 July 1981 (51).
LITERATURE L.-R. Pissarro and L. Venturi, *Pissarro* (1939), p.144, no.449 (repr.); A.S. [Antoine Seilern], *Paintings and Drawings of Continental Schools other than Flemish and Italian at 56 Princes Gate London SW7,* III (1961), p.53, no.205 (repr.); Leopold Reidemeister, *Auf den Spuren der Maler der Ile de France* (Berlin, 1963), p.53.

The picture was once known as *La Fête à Osny,* and Cassirer's label of 1913 on the back of the stretcher is inscribed "Fête at Jouy"; the identification of the scene by the artist's son, however, is certainly correct. It represents the former Rue du Fond de l'Hermitage, now rue Maria Deraisme, at L'Hermitage, the suburb of Pontoise to which Pissarro moved in 1866. His first home there was in that same street, and an early painting of the scene is *The Hillsides of L'Hermitage, Pontoise, c.*1867 (Solomon R. Guggenheim Museum, New York, Thannhauser collection; Pissarro and Venturi, no.58). In about 1872–73 Cézanne painted a scene strikingly similar to the present one (Paris, Mme. Bénatov collection; Reidemeister, *op.cit.,* p.52), also with a market in the foreground and evidently viewed from almost the same spot.
Pissarro spent most of the 1870s at Pontoise, now inseparably associated with his paintings; its scenes, particularly those of L'Hermitage where he habitually stayed, portrayed repeatedly over the years. He paid his last visit in 1882. Cézanne copied his work and often painted beside him in the earlier 1870s. Pissarro wrote to his son Lucien: "he [Cézanne] was influenced by me at Pontoise and I by him" (22 November 1895; *Camille Pissarro's Letters to his son Lucien,* ed. J. Rewald, 1943, p.276). Pissarro and Venturi (*loc.cit.*) dated the present view to *c.*1878; John House (verbally) to, probably, *c.*1876, noting that its rapid execution and summary details show it to be a sketch rather than a fully finished painting. Typical of the second half of the 1870s are the clear bright colours, the concentration on trees and foliage portrayed with a flickering touch, and an increased interest in the complexity of space which was to be explored further by Cézanne.

RENOIR, Pierre-Auguste 1841–1919
75 **La Loge** 1874
Oil on canvas, 80 x 63.5 cm
Signed, bottom left: "A. Renoir 74"

colour plate, page 35

PROVENANCE Bought from the artist by Père Martin, Paris, (425 Frs.) in 1874; M. Fleurnois, Paris, sold by him to Durand-Ruel, 9 February 1899 (8,500 Frs.); with Durand-Ruel, Paris, sold to Percy Moore Turner 1925; bought from P.M. Turner by Samuel Courtauld 1925. Courtauld Bequest (H.H.210).
EXHIBITED First Impressionist Exhibition, Galerie Nadar, Paris, 15 April-15 May 1874 (142); *Renoir,* Galerie Durand-Ruel, Paris, April 1899 (74); Exposition Internationale Universelle, Grand Palais, Paris 1900 (562); *La Libre Esthétique,* Brussels, February 1904 (128); Grafton Galleries, London, January 1905 (251); *French Art,* Royal Academy, London, 1932 (415); *Renoir,* Orangerie, Paris, 1933 (17); Tate Gallery, 1948 (56); *Renoir,* Tate Gallery, 1953 (6); Orangerie, Paris, 1955 (39); Courtauld Centenary, 1976 (36); National Gallery, London, 1983 (no cat.).
LITERATURE Jamot-Turner, no.29 (repr.); Cooper, 1954, no.51 (repr.); François Daulte, *Auguste Renoir. Catalogue raisonné de l'oeuvre peint,* I (Lausanne, 1971), pp.26, 29, 37-38; no.116 (repr.).

The artist's brother Edmond Renoir, and a Montmartre model Nini, posed for this picture. Renoir found it hard to sell this painting for 500 Frs., and only succeeded in persuading Pére Martin to buy it for 425 Frs. — money which he desperately needed to pay the rent (Rewald, *History of Impressionism,* 2nd ed., New York, 1961, p.334). Another, smaller, version of this picture was once in the Jean Dollfus collection from 1875–1912. The Tate Gallery acquired Renoir's *La première Sortie* (1875–76) through the Courtauld Fund in 1924, and this also shows a pretty young girl in a theatre box, but seen in profile and looking out at other members of the audience. *La Loge* is a work of the artist's early maturity, and he uses here a technique of composing by patches of pure colour without any precise drawing. After a visit to Italy in the winter of 1881–82, he began to place more emphasis on firm draughtsmanship and carefully built-up modelling of forms.

RENOIR, Pierre-Auguste 1841–1919
76 **Portrait of Ambroise Vollard** 1908
Oil on canvas, 81.6 x 65.2 cm
Signed, top left: "Renoir. 08"

colour plate, page 34

PROVENANCE Given by the artist to the sitter; bought from Vollard by Samuel Courtauld, June 1927. Courtauld Gift 1932.
EXHIBITED *Portraits par Renoir,* Durand-Ruel, Paris, June 1912 (48); *Exposition Renoir,* Durand-Ruel, Paris, November 1920 (21); Tate Gallery, 1948 (48); Orangerie, Paris, 1955 (43); Courtauld Centenary, 1976 (40); *20th Century Portraits,* National Portrait Gallery, London, 1978 (30).
LITERATURE Jamot-Turner, no.30 (repr.); Home House Catalogue, no.15 (repr.); A. Vollard, *La Vie et l'Oeuvre de Renoir* (Paris, 1919), p.217; Cooper, 1954, no.56 (repr.).

This portrait of Ambroise Vollard (1865 or 1867–1939) was painted in Paris in 1908, and shows the Parisian dealer who befriended the Impressionists, and Cézanne and Gauguin. He is here depicted examining a terracotta statuette by Aristide Maillol. Vollard was of part Creole origin, and had established his business in the rue Lafitte, where the chief picture dealers then were, in the mid-1890s. His first major venture was a show devoted to Cézanne in 1895, which caused much comment, most of it hostile to the artist. He was an extremely shrewd business man and connoisseur, but became something of a recluse in his later years. He died in a road accident shortly after the outbreak of war with Germany (P.M. Doran (ed.) *Conversations avec Cézanne,* 1978, p.5).
Renoir had by this time begun to suffer from arthritis which gradually so crippled his fingers that he could only paint with the brushes either stuck between them or strapped to his wrist. In this portrait, and in the *Woman tying her Shoe* (no.77), appear the warm pink and red harmonies, and the pearly flesh tones, which characterize the work of the last twenty-five years of his long career.

RENOIR, Pierre-Auguste 1841–1919
77 **Woman Tying her Shoe** *c.*1918
Oil on canvas, 50.5 x 56.5 cm
Signed, bottom left: "Renoir"

colour plate, page 36

PROVENANCE Atelier Renoir, Cagnes; with Galerie Barbazanges, Paris; through Percy Moore Turner, London; Samuel Courtauld, September 1922. Courtauld Gift 1932.
EXHIBITED Galerie Barbazanges, Paris, June 1922; Independent Gallery, London, September 1922; Tate Gallery, 1948 (61); Orangerie, Paris, 1955 (44); Courtauld Centenary, 1976 (39).
LITERATURE Jamot-Turner, no.33 (repr.); Home House Catalogue, no.13; Cooper, 1954, no.57 (repr.).

One of the first two French pictures bought by Courtauld for his private collection (see Introduction), this was probably painted in 1918 at Cagnes in the South of France, where Renoir had moved in 1906 to escape from the cold northern winters which would only have aggravated his arthritis.

RENOIR, Pierre-Auguste 1841–1919
78 **The Outskirts of Pont-Aven** *c.*1888–90
Oil on canvas, 54.5 x 65 cm
Signed, bottom left: "Renoir"

PROVENANCE Ambroise Vollard, Paris; Capt. S.W. Sykes, Cambridge; with Alex. Reid and Lefèvre, London 1942; acquired by Count Antoine Seilern 1942. Seilern Bequest (Princes Gate Collection, no.211) 1978.
EXHIBITED *French Paintings of the XIXth and XXth Centuries,* Alex. Reid and Lefèvre, London, August 1942 (8); *Renoir,* Edinburgh and London, 1953 (24); *The Princes Gate Collection,* Courtauld Institute Galleries, London, from 17 July 1981 (56).
LITERATURE A. Vollard, *Tableaux, pastels & dessins de Pierre-Auguste Renoir* (Paris, 1918; reprint 1954), I, no.481 (as *Paysage;* repr. only); A.S. [Antoine Seilern], *Paintings and Drawings of Continental Schools other than Flemish and Italian at 56 Princes Gate London SW7,* III (1961), pp.60f., no.211 (repr.).

The present painting has been confused on a number of occasions with a similarly entitled landscape of identical size which also belonged to and was published by Vollard (*op.cit.* II, repr. twice, pp.8, 94). In the exhibitions of 1942 and 1953 (see above) it was thought to be identical with that painting, which was shown at Knoedler's, New York, in 1933 (31); the latter was sold at Parke-Bernet, 26 April 1961 (64; *Near Pont-Aven*) with a history which combined the provenances of both paintings, including, erroneously, "Comte Antoine Seilern, Paris". Its present location is unknown.
The two scenes could well show the same group of farm buildings, seen in the middle-distance from different viewpoints. Trees stand to the front in each; in the present painting, more successfully, they present a foreground screen through which the sun casts a dappled light on the grass, partly shading a scene of luminous summer heat.
The richness of the colours might well reflect the influence of Gauguin, whom Renoir certainly met at Pont-Aven. Vollard recorded Renoir's account (*La Vie et l'oeuvre de Pierre-Auguste Renoir,* 1919, p.155): "Vers 1892, j'allai avec Gallimard à Pont-Aven. On m'en avait parlé comme d'un des plus jolis coins de Bretagne . . . en arrivant à Pont-Aven je tombai en pleine *Exposition Internationale de peinture!* . . . on pouvait voir des peintres venus de toutes les parties du monde. J'avais remarqué . . . Émile Bernard. Il y avait là aussi, Gauguin . . . de Hann . . . Pendant le temps que je restai á Pont-Aven, je ne fis guère que du paysage."
In 1892 Bernard was still at Pont-Aven, but Gauguin was in Tahiti, to return just once more (in 1894), and Meyer de Haan was only there (and with Gauguin at le Pouldu some fifteen miles distant) in 1889–90. It appears therefore that Vollard's date is erroneous and that this visit by Renoir took place *c.*1889. From letters to Durand-Ruel (L. Venturi, *Les Archives de l'Impressionisme,* 1939, I, pp.149ff.) we know that Renoir also visited Pont-Aven in 1892 and 1893, when he wrote in August, "Je suis à Pont-Aven . . . je suis bien ici. Je m'y plais beaucoup . . ."
On the back of the stretcher is a note, "Pont-Aven. 1887"; the painting may, however, date from several years later. On grounds of style, John House suggests (verbally) a date of *c.*1888–90. This style and brushwork is not dissimilar to Gauguin's first views of Pont-Aven, in 1886 and even 1888, but his *Haymaking* (no.30 in the present exhibition) painted at Pont-Aven in the following year illustrates his departure towards the new aims of the School of Pont-Aven.

RODIN, Auguste 1840–1917
79 **Recumbent Female Nude** *c.*1905
Soft pencil, with rubbing, or use of the stump; on cream (now stained) wove paper.
24.8 x 32.5 cm
Signed in pencil, bottom right: "A *Rodin*"

Numbered in a different hand in pencil, *verso:* "4", with direction to a picture mounter.

PROVENANCE ? ; Sir Robert Witt (acquired as a gift from Paris, no date, but apparently 1949). Witt Bequest 1952 (no.4205).
EXHIBITED *Rodin Drawings: True and False,* National Gallery of Art, Washington, and Solomon R. Guggenheim Museum, New York, 1971–72 (96).
LITERATURE *Hand-list of the Drawings in the Witt Collection* (1956), no.4205; J. Kirk T. Varnedoe, "True and False" *Rodin Drawings* (New York, 1971), no.139.

The present composition, an example of Rodin's developing late manner of draughtsmanship which first emerged during the period 1897–1900, is datable to *c.*1905 (Varnedoe, *ibid.*). It displays Rodin's increasing preoccupation with the rendering of the interior modelling of form by use of rubbing, either with the fingers, or less probably, with the stump, which gives to many drawings of this period an overall silvery greyness. Also characteristic of this type of drawing is the lack of distinction between initial indications of form and the heavier contours, which may be interpreted as the final description of the image. The constant repetition and variation of line represents a multiple essay in the totality or portion of the form in question (Varnedoe, *op.cit.,* p.162): such repetitious contours,

which may appear incoherent within the context of the final image, nonetheless always add supplementary information concerning the position, weight or structure of the form they describe.
The pose of the Witt nude is dictated by Rodin's detached concern to master a difficult foreshortened view of the human body, and displays, as Varnedoe (*ibid.*) has observed, the "uncompromising specificity" of the artist's curiosity concerning every feature of the body.
Indented and abraded contours over the sheet indicate vestiges of a head, left leg, and modelling across the hips and stomach, comparable in both size and location within the pictorial area to the pencil lines describing the same areas of the body in the drawn nude. This indicates that a version of the same subject had been executed on paper lying on top of the present sheet: such a drawing, probably preceding the Witt version, is as yet unlocated.
Traces of very dilute flesh-coloured watercolour splashed at the top left and right of the present sheet suggest the possibility of its having been among a group of drawings, possibly executed at a similar date and of a related subject (?), which the artist tinted.

ROUSSEAU, Henri ('Le Douanier') 1844–1910
80 **The Customs Post** *c.*1900
Oil on canvas, 40.6 x 32.75 cm
Signed, bottom right: "H Rousseau"

colour plate, page 47

PROVENANCE Wilhelm Uhde, Paris; Dr. Hartwich, Berlin; with Alfred Flechtheim, Berlin; Samuel Courtauld, 1926. Coutauld Bequest 1948.

EXHIBITED Wiedereröffnung der Galerie Flechtheim, Düsseldorf, December 1919 (repr.); *Henri Rousseau,* Galerie Flechtheim, Berlin, March 1926 (12); Tate Gallery, 1948 (62); *Rousseau Exhibition,* Venice Biennale, 1950 (4); Orangerie, Paris, 1955 (45); Courtauld Centenary, 1976 (41).
LITERATURE W. Uhde, *Henri Rousseau* (Paris, 1911), pl.20; Uhde, *Rousseau* (Berlin, 1914), pl.19; Jamot-Turner, no.51 (repr); Cooper, 1954, no.58 (repr.).

Cooper (*op.cit.*) comments that the date of this painting cannot be precisely determined, but he considers it not to be a late work, nor to be earlier than 1895.
Rousseau had served first in the army from 1863–68, then as a low-ranking customs official from 1871–93, and had manned toll-gates on the outskirts of Paris. He began painting, untaught, in his spare time, probably *c.*1880. Rejected by the official Salon in 1885, he began exhibiting with the free, jury-less Société des Artistes Indépendants from 1886. He gradually became known in avant-garde circles, meeting Gauguin and the playwright Alfred Jarry in the 1890s, and Picasso and his friends in the last years of his life.
This painting is a characteristically *naif* rendering of a subject that would have been very familiar to him. Although he had never, apparently, travelled abroad, he also painted ambitious jungle scenes of a fantastic kind, figure pieces, and portraits of compelling directness such as that of the writer Pierre Loti. He seems to have derived some of his exotic subject matter from visits to the zoological and botanical gardens in Paris.

SEURAT, Georges 1859–1891
81 **Man Painting a Boat** 1883
Oil on panel, 15.9 x 25 cm
Unsigned.

colour plate, page 42

PROVENANCE Mme Seurat, the artist's mother, Paris; Félix Fénéon, Paris; through Percy Moore Turner, London; Lord Ivor Spencer-Churchill, London; Lord Berners, London; through Percy Moore Turner, London; Samuel Courtauld, 1928. Courtauld Bequest 1948 (H.H.212; on loan to Lord (R.A.) Butler until 1983).
EXHIBITED *Seurat,* Bernheim-Jeune, Paris, 1909 (14); *Seurat,* Bernheim-Jeune, Paris, January 1920 (9); *Ingres to Cézanne,* Independent Gallery, London, May 1925 (20); *19th and 20th Century French Masters,* Independent Gallery, London, June 1928 (31); Tate Gallery, 1948 (64); Orangerie, Paris, 1955 (48); Courtauld Centenary, 1976 (44),
LITERATURE Inventaire Posthume Seurat, Panneaux, no.44; Jamot-Turner, no.43 (repr.); Cooper, 1954, no.62 (repr.); H. Dorra and J. Rewald, *Seurat, l'oeuvre peint, biographie et catalogue critique* (Paris, 1959) p.80, no.82 (repr.); C.M. de Hauke, *Seurat et son oeuvre* (Paris, 1961), no.66 (repr.); Roger Fry, *Seurat,* with Foreword and Notes by Anthony Blunt (1965), p.78 (repr. colour pl.8).

Seurat was the son of a property owner and began to study art under a pupil of Ingres at the École des Beaux-Arts, Paris, 1877–79. He made small studies of urban and suburban subjects before 1884.
This small oil sketch (or "croqueton"), although still in the Impressionist style, is composed of separate touches of colour put on in criss-cross brushstrokes, which suggests that Seurat was already interested in the

ideas about outdoor colour published in Ogden Rood's *Modern Chromatics* (1881). A French edition of this book by Rood (of the University of Columbia, USA) appeared shortly after and was read by Seurat.

The formal construction of the sketch is perhaps more rigorously thought-out than a typical Impressionist picture, note particularly the strong vertical emphases of the post and fence in the centre of the picture.

SEURAT, Georges 1859–1891
82 **The Bridge at Courbevoie** 1886
Oil on canvas, 46.4 x 55.3 cm
Signed, bottom left: "Seurat"

colour plate, page 46

PROVENANCE Arsène Alexandre, Paris (1887); Alexandre Sale, Paris, 18 May 1903 (lot 57; 630 Frs.); with Georges Petit, Paris; with L.W. Gutbier, Dresden; with Bignou, Paris; through Reid and Lefèvre, London; Samuel Courtauld, 1926. Courtauld Bequest 1948 (H.H.185).
EXHIBITED 3me Exposition de la Société des Artistes Indépendants, Paris, 1887 (442); *Exposition Commémorative Seurat,* Salon des Artistes Indépendants, Paris, March 1892 (1090); *Georges Seurat* (organised by *La Revue Blanche),* Paris, 1900 (25); *Seurat,* Bernheim-Jeune, Paris, 1909 (64); *Georges Seurat,* Lefévre Gallery, London, May 1926 (4); *French Art,* Royal Academy, London, 1932 (541); Tate Gallery, 1948 (69); Orangerie, Paris, 1955 (52); Courtauld Centenary, 1976 (48).
LITERATURE Jamot-Turner, no.47 (repr.); Cooper, 1954, no.67 (repr.); Dorra and Rewald, pp.204-06, no.172 (repr.); de Hauke, no.178 (repr.); Fry and Blunt (1965), p.82 (repr. colour pl.29).

A view upstream along the Seine, seen from the north bank of the Ile de la Grande Jatte and looking towards the Courbevoie bridge, which appears in the background. The bridge also appears in the background of the large *Une Baignade, Asnières* (National Gallery, London).
The *Baignade* (1883–84) also shows Seurat experimenting with the technique of pointillism, that is, the stippling of dots of pure, unmixed complementary colours in juxtaposition, especially on the back of the central figure of the bathing boy. This technique was an application of the theory of "divisionism", which was a codification, in quasi-scientific terms, of the principles underlying Impressionsim. In the *Bridge at Courbevoie,* the pointillist technique has been brought to a high degree of refinement, where in all areas the small dots or "points" are added over broader strokes of paint to create an effect of colour vibration. Even so, there are delicate variations of colour within the picture, so as to take account of reflected light in the water or to suggest the softness of tree foliage. Henri Dorra (*op.cit,* pp.XC-XC11, and 204–06) notes that Seurat has become a little more arbitrary in his use of colour. The sail in the foreground is a superb mosaic of colour painted more to delight the artist and spectator, than to observe the strict division of colours.
By the spring of 1886, Seurat had met the scientist Charles Henry, whose mathematical and aesthetic theories were deeply to influence him, especially the psychological properties of line. Broadly summarised, Henry propounded (in *Theory of Directions,* and *The Scientific Aesthetic,* both 1885; and in 1886, a "study of numerical aesthetics", *Law of the Evolution of Musical Sensations);* that horizontal lines express repose and tranquillity; ascending lines, gaiety and joy; whilst descending lines evoked melancholy and sorrow. Following Henry's theories, Seurat constructed and sub-divided his compositions so as to observe laws of mathematical proportions such as the "golden section".
Bridge at Courbevoie has been constructed on a plan of interlocking triangles, and the balance he has struck between verticals, horizontals, and diagonals, in this composition, produces a satisfying sense of repose and timelessness.

SEURAT, Georges 1859–1891
83 **Study for 'Le Chahut'** 1889
Oil on panel, 21.8 x 15.8 cm

colour plate, page 44

(The painted border on the right of the panel cut away by a (?) later hand.)
Unsigned.

PROVENANCE Mme Seurat, the artist's mother, Paris; Félix Fénéon, Paris; through Percy Moore Turner, London; Samuel Courtauld, by 1931. Courtauld Bequest 1948 (H.H.186).
EXHIBITED *Seurat,* Bernheim-Jeune, Paris, January 1920 (29); Tate Gallery, 1948 (70); Orangerie, Paris, 1955 (53); Courtauld Centenary, 1976 (49).
LITERATURE Jamot-Turner, no.46 (repr.); Cooper, 1954, no.68 (repr.); Dorra and Rewald, p.253, no.197 (repr.); de Hauke, no.197 (repr.); Fry and Blunt (1965), p.84 (repr. colour pl.41).

A preliminary study for the large picture *Le Chahut* ("The Can-Can") in the Rijks-museum Kröller-Müller, Otterlo, which contains more figures and additional details. A more advanced study is in the Albright-Knox Art Gallery, Buffalo, USA. The final picture was first exhibited at the Salon des Indépendants in March 1890.
The picture is surrounded on three sides by a border painted by the artist

(at left side, approx. 4 mm. wide; at top 7 mm., and along the bottom, 6 mm. wide). Seurat seems to have begun to introduce painted borders (and painted frames) into his pictures during 1887, as a deliberate attempt to preserve the integrity of the total effect of his painted harmonies and composition.
It has already been noted (cat.no.82) that Seurat deliberately sought to suggest a specific emotional mood by formal means. In this study for *Le Chahut,* with its relatively coarse stipplings of colour, and strongly accented rising diagonals (e.g. the neck of the double-bass, the high-kicking legs of the dancers), Seurat conveys the frenetic, artificial gaiety of the music-hall. There is also more than a hint of satire (see also cat.no.84).

SEURAT, Georges 1859–1891
84 **A Young Woman Powdering Herself** 1889–90
Oil on canvas, 95.5 x 79.5 cm (with painted border in pointilliste technique on all four sides, approximately 2.25 to 2.5 cm wide)
Signed, on painted border, bottom right: "Seurat"

colour plate, page 45

PROVENANCE Mlle Madeleine Knobloch, Paris; Félix Fénéon, Paris; Dikran Khan Kélékian, Paris; Kélékian Sale, American Art Association, New York, 31 January 1923 (lot 154, repr., $5,200); with Eugene O.M. Liston, New York; through Percy Moore Turner, London; John Quinn, New York; with Paul Rosenberg, Paris; through the French Gallery, London; Samuel Courtauld, 1926. Courtauld Gift 1932.
EXHIBITED 6me Exposition de la Société des Artistes Indépendants, Paris, 1890 (727); *Exposition Seurat,* Musée Moderne, Brussels (9me Exposition des XX), 1892 (14); *Exposition Commémorative Seurat,* Société des Artistes Indépendants, Paris, March 1892 (1085); *Georges Seurat* (organised by *La Revue Blanche),* Paris, 1900 (35); exhibitions at Munich, Frankfurt-am-Main, Dresden, Karlsruhe (1906) and at Stuttgart (1907); *Seurat,* Bernheim-Jeune, Paris, 1909 (73); Sezession, Berlin, 1913; Brooklyn Museum, USA, 1921 (not in catalogue); Brummer Gallery, New York, 1924 (18); French Gallery, London, February 1926 (41); *French Art,* Royal Academy, London, 1932 (503); Tate Gallery, 1948 (71); Orangerie, Paris, 1955 (54); Courtauld Centenary, 1976 (50); *Post-Impressionism,* Royal Academy, London, November 1979–March 1980 (204); National Gallery, London, February-March 1983 (no catalogue).
LITERATURE Jamot-Turner, no.45 (repr.); Home House Catalogue, no.11 (repr.); Cooper, 1954, no.69 (repr.); Dorra and Rewald, pp.247-49, no.195 (repr.); de Hauke, no.200 (repr.); Fry and Blunt (1965), pp.16, 84 (repr. colour pl.42; and detail, facing p.10); John House, "Meaning in Seurat's Figure Paintings", *Art History,* III (Sept. 1980), 345-56.

This is a portrait of the artist's mistress Madeleine Knobloch at her toilette, and according to Paul Signac and Charles Angrand, dates from the winter of 1888–89 (G. Coquiot, *Seurat,* 1924, p.39). Madeleine was pregnant in the winter of 1889–90. The more usual dating of 1889–90 has been followed here. An oil study (Dorra and Rewald, no.194, ex-coll. Mr. and Mrs. Leigh Block), is now at the Museum of Fine Arts, Houston, Texas. Dorra and Rewald (*op.cit.,* pp.LXIX-LXXI, XCVI-XCVIII) analyse the composition and note that the painted border on the right appears to be composed of two superimposed bands, according to evidence revealed by radiographs taken when this picture was exhibited at the Art Institute of Chicago, 1958 (147).
Seurat's face originally appeared in the imitation bamboo frame on the wall behind Madeleine's head, but a friend had warned him this might appear ridiculous, and he replaced it with a still-life of flowers on a table, placed at an angle and thus made impossible to read as a reflection. (Traces of the painted-out face are dimly discernible in radiographs.)
The composition consists of a counterpoint between rounded and angular forms. The massive solidity of the woman is contrasted with the spindly little dressing table (the "poudreuse" by which the picture has sometimes been incorrectly called), the curves of which are echoed in Madeleine's ample shape and both are contrasted with the angles of the mirror. Roger Fry (*op.cit.*) remarked on the absurdity of the pseudo-18th century table and the ironic intentions of the artist. Seurat appears here to be commenting on the artificiality of the trappings of urban life which surround his mistress, rather than attacking her personally.
The motif of lines rising from a point ↨which appears as a repeat decoration on the walls and in the bottom left hand side of the picture, was used by Seurat to symbolize gaiety (see also cat.no.82), following the ideas of Charles Henry about the emotive power of line. These forms appear again in the bow rising from the mirror on the dressing table and the bamboo frame top, but their effect is to some extent cancelled out by the heavy form of the sitter and her impassive expression. This reinforces the supposition that Seurat's intention was ironic, but not satirical as has been made out by Signac. William Bradford has suggested to the compiler that Seurat may also have been inspired by Manet's *Nana* (Kunsthalle, Hamburg), which shows a young woman at her toilet. There could well be an element of parody of the Manet painting.

SEURAT, Georges 1859–1891

85 **Beach at Gravelines** 1890

Oil on panel, 16 x 24.5 cm (with painted border in pointilliste technique on all four sides, irregular, approximately 2 mm. to 4 mm. wide)
Unsigned.

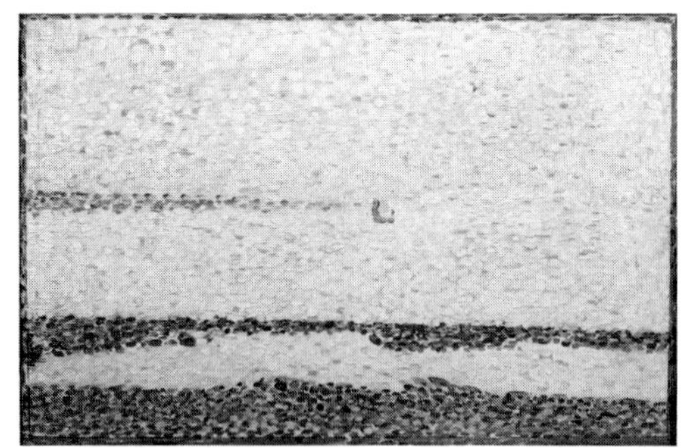

colour plate, page 43

PROVENANCE Mme Seurat, the artist's mother, Paris; Alfred Tobler, Paris; with Bernheim-Jeune, Paris; Alphonse Kann, St. Germain-en-Laye; with Bignou, Paris; through Reid and Lefèvre, London; Samuel Courtauld, 1928. Courtauld Bequest 1948 (H.H.187).

EXHIBITED *Seurat,* Bernheim-Jeune, Paris, 1909 (78); *Seurat,* Bernheim-Jeune, Paris, 1920 (31); 12th International Biennale, Venice, 1920 (56); Van Wisselingh et Cie, Amsterdam, April 1928 (59); Tate Gallery, 1948 (293); Orangerie, Paris, 1955 (55); Courtauld Centenary, 1976 (51).

LITERATURE Jamot-Turner, no.49 (repr.); Cooper, 1954, no.70; Dorra and Rewald, p.261, no.201 (repr.); de Hauke, no.204 (repr.); Fry and Blunt (1965), pp.84-85 (repr. colour pl.46).

Painted at Gravelines, on the Channel coast near Dunkerque and the Belgian border. Seurat made regular visits to the coast and spent the last summer of his life at Gravelines, between May-October 1890, the date of this picture.

He told Émile Verhaeren that he made this visit "to cleanse his eyes of the days spent in the studio and to translate as exactly as possible the luminosity of the open air, with all its nuances" (Verhaeren essay of 1891, in *Sensations,* 1927, pp.199; quoted J. House, *Post-Impressionism* 1979–80, p.135). This picture, with its emphatic horizontals, conveys the flat tranquillity of this part of the coastline in calm weather. The coarse stippling technique used here was later to be more freely adapted by Signac and other former Neo-Impressionists, and is an element in the development of Fauvism (see cat.no.87).

SEURAT, Georges 1859–1891

86 **Standing Female Nude** 1879

Drawing with the stump impregnated with pencil for the areas of shadow on the left of the head and body; black (Conté?) crayon; slight scraping with the point of a knife (?) to lighten some of the more densely crayoned areas (e.g. around the left knee, and lower left of centre); on off-white (now unevenly discoloured) laid paper, watermarked: "MICHALLET". All edges of the sheet uneven, the lower corners torn away. A tear repaired right side. The sheet an irregular shape.
63.2 x 48.2 cm
Unsigned.
Inscribed in pencil, *verso:* "de Georges Seurat/felF" and numbered in red crayon: "381".

PROVENANCE With the Seurat family (?); ?; Samuel Courtauld (no date of acquisition). Courtauld Bequest 1948.

EXHIBITED *Georges Seurat,* Galerie Bernheim-Jeune, Paris, 15-31 January 1920 (40); *Les Dessins de Georges Seurat,* Galerie Bernheim-Jeune, Paris, 29 November-24 December 1926 (78, as from collection "X"); London (76); Courtauld Centenary, 1976 (78); Arts Council (62); *Drawing Technique and Purpose,* Victoria and Albert Museum, 28 January-26 April 1981 (100); British Museum, 1983 (111).

LITERATURE Gustave Kahn, *Les Dessins de Seurat* (2 vols., Paris, 1928), pl.61; Robert L. Herbert, *Seurat's drawings,* (1965), no.23 and pp.25, 26.

The drawing was first published in 1928 by Gustave Kahn (*ibid.*), the plates for whose book were selected by Seurat's friend and champion, the critic Félix Fénéon (1861–1944). Kahn's publication is a folio reproduction of the drawing exhibited at Bernheim-Jeune, Paris in 1926. The Courtauld sheet, no.78 in this exhibtion, had previously been shown at the same gallery in 1920: its inclusion in both Bernheim-Jeune exhibitions, arranged by Fénéon, is a guarantee of its authenticity. Further confirmation that the work is genuine is gained from Fénéon's inscription on the *verso* of the sheet, discovered in 1982 (see above).

Inexplicably, Douglas Cooper omitted the drawing from his catalogue (*op.cit.*) as did César de Hauke (*op.cit.*) who must have known it.

The provenance of the work is uncertain: in 1926, it was one of twenty-one sheets attributed to collection "X", seven of which de Hauke traced to Seurat's family, while a further thirteen later entered Fénéon's collection.

R.L. Herbert dated the sheet to *c.*1879, noting its reliance upon a small contour sketch (location unknown: photograph from de Hauke: Herbert, *op.cit.*, no.22). In comparison to the figure in this work, that of the Courtauld sheet is treated in an idealized manner. Seurat has thickened the tops of the model's legs, reworked the curves of buttocks, back and shoulders, and eliminated some of the hair to produce a continuous contour from ear to ankle at the right side of the body (Herbert, *ibid.*). The left side is similarly treated: the lower abdomen curves less sharply into the body, the left forearm is repositioned in the same diagonal line as the right leg, while the line of the upper left arm is parallel to that of the breast. Individuating features of the body are eliminated, while both contours and interior musculature are simplified. The merging into shadow of the figure's hands and lower legs is anticipated in the preliminary sketch by the slight and tentative notation of these extremities.

In making a preliminary line sketch for the Courtauld drawing, Seurat was following the procedure taught at the École des Beaux-Arts for producing an academic nude: a similar line sketch (coll. Mr. and Mrs. John Rewald, New York: Herbert, *op.cit.*, no.17) preceded the academic study of *c.*1877, *Man standing with his palms out* (private coll., Paris: Herbert, *op.cit.*, no.16). While both the pose of the Courtauld figure and the initial modelling of head, breast and abdomen with the stump suggest links with such earlier academic studies as the *Nude with a Baton* (de Hauke, *op.cit.*, no.267), the choice of buxom model whose form emerges from a shadowed background suggests a debt (as Herbert (*ibid.*) notes) to the lithographs of Henri de Fantin-Latour (1836–1904) an artist at the height of his fame in the late 1870s.

SIGNAC, Paul 1863–1935

87 **Saint-Tropez** 1893

Oil and pencil on panel, 18.8 x 27.1 cm

Signed, bottom left: "P. Signac"; and on back: "P.S St Tropez" (Von der Heydt-Museum, Wuppertal).

colour plate, page 58

PROVENANCE With Alfred Gold, Berlin; Samuel Courtauld, 1928. Courtauld Bequest 1948 (H.H.234).

EXHIBITED Tate Gallery, 1948 (74); Orangerie, Paris, 1955 (57); Courtauld Centenary, 1976 (53); *Post-Impressionism,* Royal Academy, London, November 1979–March 1980 (213).

LITERATURE Cooper, 1954, no.72 (and dated "c.1895").

John House (*Post-Impressionism,* 1979–80, p.139) points out that this is a preliminary study for *The Port of Saint-Tropez* (Von der Heydt-Museum, Wuppertal), first exhibited in December 1893; its forms are transposed quite precisely into the final painting.

This is one of many small studies in oil or watercolour, executed out of doors, which Signac made during the 1890s for compositions which were subsequently worked up into finished pictures entirely in the studio. Unlike the final paintings, which are precisely handled, these sketches are highly improvisatory and executed in the Impressionist tradition, with bright patches of colour freely set against a white ground, or priming, as in this work.

This type of boldly-executed sketch, with its bright colours and summary forms, influenced the Fauve style evolved by Matisse and Derain at Collioure in 1905. In the previous year, Matisse had worked with both Signac and Derain at Saint-Tropez.

SIGNAC, Paul 1863–1935

88 **Still Life with Carafe and Watermelon** 1918

Extensive preliminary drawing in pencil; extensive drawing with black (?Indian) ink, both over and under the painted areas; gouache (?) of varying strengths, and coloured inks, with drawing with the flat of the brush; on off-white (now unevenly discoloured) wove paper. The sheet apparently trimmed at all sides, and backed with tissue.

34.4 x 39 cm

Signed and dated in pencil, bottom left: "P. Signac 1918".

PROVENANCE With Percy Moore Turner (Independent Gallery, London) by 1920, from whom purchased by Samuel Courtauld 1924. Courtauld Gift 1932.

EXHIBITED *Modern French Paintings and Drawings,* Independent Gallery, London, May 1920 (84); on loan to City Art Gallery, Wakefield, 1946–47; Tate Gallery, 1948 (120); *France 1850–1950,* The Art Gallery, Kettering, June 1950 (84); Orangerie, Paris, 1955 (90); Nottingham University, 1969.

LITERATURE Home House Catalogue, no.69; Cooper, 1954, no.152.

Still-lifes are scant in Signac's work when compared to the landscape and marine subjects. The present example, dated to 1918, was executed in Antibes where Signac had lived since 1913.

A composition of sliced water-melon and its segment, arranged almost identically to those motifs in the Courtauld sheet, upon the same shallow dish or tray, appears in an undated watercolour, *Still-life (Melon)* (coll. Mr. and Mrs. William Preston Harrison, USA: illustrated in *P. Signac Watercolours and Paintings,* Los Angeles County Museum, 1953–54, no.22). In this drawing, whose final form is the result of extensive initial pencil work, the diagonal edge of the table, melon stalk, and background wall are more tentatively yet laboriously rendered than in the Courtauld watercolour, while the composition is placed uncomfortably high on the sheet; similar oblong brushstrokes to those employed in the Courtauld sheet are disposed over the picture surface, but in a less assured and rhythmical manner. It may be argued that this composition probably preceded the more confident and elaborate Courtauld picture.

Lucy Cousturier (*P. Signac,* Paris, 1922, p.26) has noted that Signac's watercolours are always preparatory studies for oil compositions; if her observation is correct, both the Harrison and Courtauld sheets ought to relate to a painting.

The relevant work in this case would appear to be the oil composition, *Still-*

life with Watermelon (private coll.: France), which shares with the drawings discussed above common motifs in an analogous arrangement, and comparable handling. Here, the watermelon is again placed on a shallow dish similar to that in the Courtauld drawing; the line of the melon's core, the result of cutting away a wedge of the fruit, is placed diagonally as in the Courtauld sheet, while the form of the cut segment is similarly contrasted with that of the remainder of the watermelon, but is placed behind it. The fruit is juxtaposed with a jug, right, and with the forms of aubergines and peppers. The oil paint is applied to the canvas in discrete oblong patches, again comparable to those in the Courtauld drawing.

Lemoyne de Forges assigned to the oil composition the date of 1914, without justification (*Signac,* Musée du Louvre, 1963–64 (76)): it had previously been dated to 1915 (under no.20, *Signac retrospective exhibition* Marlborough Galleries, London, March-April 1954), but was initially exhibited as a work of 1919 (*Signac,* Musée d'Art Moderne, Paris, 1951 (31)). This original dating of the oil would appear to be confirmed by its connections with the dated Courtauld sheet, and by its links with a watercolour of a similar subject in which the flat dish of the Courtauld drawing also appears. This is dated by the artist: "1919" (cf. *Still-life with a Jug,* Metropolitan Museum of Art: George Szarbo, *Paul Signac (1863–1935) Paintings Watercolours Drawings and Prints,* Metropolitan Museum of Art, New York, 1977, no.12).

Cousturier reproduces a brush and ink drawing of a sliced watermelon on a shallow dish, contrasted with aubergines and peppers (*op.cit.,* p.12), and a more elaborate watercolour in which peppers, lemons, and tomatoes are juxtaposed with a shallow dish and jug (*op.cit.,* no.30). Both drawings can be dated to prior to 1922 (the date of Cousturier's publication), while both compositions are characterized by the intricate placing of a large number of elements, observed from a viewpoint higher than that employed in the works discussed above. Such compositions anticipate that of the ambitious watercolour of 14 July, 1926 (coll. Mr. and Mrs. Jack E. Butler, New York: illustrated in R.L. Herbert, *Neo-Impressionism* (Solomon R. Guggenheim Museum, New York, 1978), no.106), in which a jug is contrasted with fruit and vegetables, again placed on the shallow dish repeated from the Courtauld work.

The Courtauld watercolour may thus be regarded as a work not only related to the oil *Still-life with Watermelon,* but also as part of a larger group of still-life subjects, spanning the period *c.*1918–*c.*1926, in which Signac restated or made variations of motifs, apparently arranged in increasingly complex and intricate compositions.

SISLEY, Alfred 1839–1899

89 **Snow at Louveciennes** 1874

Oil on canvas, 46.3 x 55.8 cm

Signed, bottom right: "Sisley"

PROVENANCE Ch. de Hèle, Brussels; de Hèle Sale, Amsterdam, 13 June, 1911 (lot 13; 2,750 florins); with Bernheim-Jeune, Paris; with Durand-Ruel, Paris; with Paul Rosenberg, Paris; through Percy Moore Turner, London; Samuel Courtauld, June 1926. Courtauld Gift 1932.

EXHIBITED *Exposition Sisley,* Durand-Ruel, Paris, February 1902 (6); *Sisley,* Durand-Ruel, Paris, January 1922 (9); *Masterpieces of French Art of the 19th Century,* Agnew, London, July 1923 (1); Tate Gallery, 1948 (75); Orangerie, Paris, 1955 (58); Courtauld Centenary, 1976 (54).

LITERATURE Jamot-Turner, no.5 (repr.); Home House Catalogue, no.17 (repr.); Cooper, 1954, no.73 (repr.); Francois Daulte, *Alfred Sisley. Catalogue raisonné* (Lausanne, 1959), no.150 (repr.).

This painting has also been known as "Hiver: Route de Village". The village of Louveciennes lies on the river Seine, a few miles west of Paris, and Sisley painted many views in and around this location during the 1870s. Of English birth, Sisley lived in France and studied at Gleyre's studio, where he met Monet and Renoir. He exhibited at the First Impressionist Exhibition in 1874.

SISLEY, Alfred 1839–1899

90 **Boats on the Seine** 1877

Oil on canvas, laid down on plywood, 37.2 x 44.3 cm

Signed, bottom right: "Sisley"

PROVENANCE ?; Richard Samson, Hamburg; with Matthiesen Gallery, London; Samuel Courtauld, 1947. Courtauld Bequest 1948 (H.H.201).

EXHIBITED Tate Gallery, 1948 (77); Courtauld Centenary, 1976 (55).

LITERATURE Cooper, 1954, no.75; Daulte, no.273.

This has been dated by Cooper to *c.*1888, but by Daulte to 1877. It is much more freely painted than *Snow at Louveciennes* (see above), and the artist has blocked in the forms with bold brushstrokes.

TOULOUSE-LAUTREC, Henri de 1864–1901

91 **Jane Avril in the Entrance of the Moulin Rouge, Drawing on her Gloves** 1892

Pastel and oil (peinture à l'essence), on buff millboard, laid down on panel. The painting made up of three sheets of millboard.
Overall dimensions: 102 x 55.1 cm
Lower sheet of millboard, 35 x 55.1 cm; strip of millboard inserted into upper left side of painting, 66.7 x 2.7 cm
Signed, bottom left, the initials in monogram: "T-Lautrec"

colour plate, page 38

PROVENANCE Murat, Paris; Eugene Blot, Paris; Blot Sale, Paris, 9 and 10 May 1900 (lot 161; 1,250 Frs., bought in); Blot Sale, Paris, 10 May 1906 (lot 74; 6,600 Frs.); Mancini, Paris; Prindonoff, Paris; with J. Seligmann, New York; through Percy Moore Turner, London; Samuel Courtauld, November 1929. Courtauld Gift 1932.
EXHIBITED Galerie Goupil, Paris, 1893 (18); International Society, London, 1898 (5); *Exposition Toulouse-Lautrec,* Durand-Ruel, Paris, May 1902 (72); Salon d'Automne, Paris 1904 (19); *Toulouse-Lautrec,* Musée des Arts Décoratifs, Paris, 1931 (95); *French Art,* Royal Academy, London, 1932 (551); Tate Gallery, 1948 (79); *Toulouse-Lautrec,* Orangerie, Paris 1951 (37; wrong provenance); Orangerie, Paris, 1955 (60); Courtauld Centenary, 1976 (56).
LITERATURE Maurice Joyant, *Henri de Toulouse-Lautrec, Peintre* (Paris, 1926), pp.136-40, 274; Jamot-Turner, no.38 (repr.); Home House Catalogue, no.3 (repr.); Cooper, 1954, no.79 (repr.).

Jane Avril was a well-known dancer of her day. She was born in Paris in 1868 and was said to be the illegitimate daughter of an Italian nobleman and a Parisian *demi-mondaine.* She first appeared at the Moulin Rouge in 1889, and first appears in a Toulouse-Lautrec painting, *Au Moulin Rouge: La Danse* of 1890 (Henry P. McIlhenny collection, Philadelphia). She was known by the jocular nickname 'La Melinite', under which title this picture has been exhibited. Melinite was a high-explosive of French invention. The Moulin Rouge was a Parisian dance-hall, and at the time of this picture enjoyed considerable fame. It had just been sold to a new owner and re-opened in September 1892, when Jane Avril was one of its star performers. This picture has hitherto been known as *Jane Avril sortant du Moulin Rouge et mettant ses gants,* and was so catalogued by Joyant. However, she seems to be walking down a corridor away from the street, and thus more likely to be entering the Moulin Rouge rather than leaving it. The present title follows that first published by Cooper (*op.cit.,*). There are *pentimenti* around Jane Avril's jawline and on the left side of her nose. Over her shoulders there are traces of a cape, part of a top coat, which have subsequently been painted over by the artist.

TOULOUSE-LAUTREC, Henri de 1864–1901

92 **Tête-à-Tête Supper** 1899

Oil on canvas, 55.1 x 46 cm
Signed, top right, the initials in monogram: "T-Lautrec"

colour plate, page 39

PROVENANCE G. Séré de Rivières, Paris; with Georges Bernheim, Paris; Caressa, Paris; through Percy Moore Turner, London; Samuel Courtauld 1928. Courtauld Bequest 1948 (H.H.188).
EXHIBITED *Exposition Toulouse-Lautrec,* Durand-Ruel, Paris, May 1902 (38); *Exposition Rétrospective Toulouse-Lautrec,* Galerie Manzi-Joyant, Paris, June 1914 (34); *Toulouse-Lautrec,* Galeries Paul Rosenberg, Paris, 1914 (21); *30 Ans d'Art Indépendant,* Paris, February 1926 (3252); *French Art,* Royal Academy, London, 1932 (513); Tate Gallery, 1948 (80); Orangerie, Paris, 1955 (61); Courtauld Centenary, 1976 (57); National Gallery, London, February-March 1983 (no catalogue).
LITERATURE Joyant, 1926, p.298 (repr. facing p.176); Jamot-Turner, no.40 (repr.); Cooper, 1954, no.80 (repr.).

The picture has been catalogued as *En Cabinet Particulier,* by Cooper who also lists other titles by which it has been known (*op.cit.*). It probably shows a tête-à-tête supper in a famous Parisian restaurant, *Le Rat Mort,* formerly 7 Rue Pigalle. There seems to be no evidence to support the statement that the man is the painter Charles Conder, and anyway, too little of his face is visible for identification. The woman has been identified as Lucy Jordan.

TOULOUSE-LAUTREC, Henri de 1864–1901

93 **A Woman Lying in Bed** 1896

Soft pencil; touches a very dilute pale grey watercolour wash (apparently mixing in part with the pencil) restricted to parts of the head only; on off-white (now unevenly discoloured) laid paper, watermarked: "P L BAS". The sheet unevenly trimmed at the bottom.

30.3 x 48 cm

Signed in pencil, lower left: "H T-Lautrec" (the initials in monogram).

Inscribed in different hands in pencil, *verso,* with directions to a picture mounter, and: "Mr. Claude Sayle".

PROVENANCE Gustave Pellet (? probably purchased direct from the artist); (? with Claude Sayle, cf. inscriptions); with the Leicester Galleries, London, from whom purchased by Samuel Courtauld, 1922. Courtauld Bequest 1948 (H.H.193).

EXHIBITED *French Art 1200–1900,* Royal Academy, London, 1932 (976); Tate Gallery, 1948 (121); *De Fouquet à Cézanne,* Brussels, Museum Boymans-van Beuningen, Rotterdam, and Orangerie, Paris, November 1949–February 1950 (215); *French Drawings,* Arts Council, 1952 (156); Orangerie, Paris, 1955 (91); Nottingham University, 1969; Courtauld Centenary, 1976 (79); Arts Council (69); British Museum, 1983 (112).

LITERATURE *Royal Academy Commemorative catalogue,* 1932, no.931: Réne Huyghe, *Le Dessin français au XIXe Siècle* (Lausanne, 1948), pl.134; Graham Reynolds, *19th Century Drawings, 1850–1900* (1949), pl.31; *Art et Style,* no.14 (1950), pl.48; Edouard Julien, *Lautrec, Dessins* (Paris, 1951) pl.13; *The Illustrated London News,* Christmas 1953; Cooper, 1954, no.154; *T-Lautrec* (Génies et Réalités Séries, Paris, 1962) p.138; M.G. Dortu, *Toulouse-Lautrec et son oeuvre* (New York, 1971), VI, D.4.264.

This sheet is one of a group of drawings, comprising the *Woman in Bed, Asleep* (coll. C. Roger-Marx: Dortu, *op.cit.,* D.4. 265), two designs entitled *Dozing* (coll. Boymans-van Beuningen Museum, Amsterdam; coll. Wildenstein, Paris: Dortu, *op.cit.,* D.4. 266 and D.4. 267, respectively) and *Woman in Bed* (Bibliothèque Nationale, Paris: Dortu, *op.cit.,* D.4. 270) which precede the lithograph *Woman with a Tray* (Adriani, *Toulouse-Lautrec, op.cit.,* no.179) from the album *Elles,* published in April 1896, for which there are two preparatory designs (private coll., France; and Matthiesen Gallery: Dortu, *op.cit.,* nos. D.4. 271, and D.4. 272, respectively).

The model in the Courtauld sheet, who appears in the works mentioned above, is identifiable by her broad face and low forehead from which hair rises vertically, as Pauline (Mlle Popo) whose mother, Mme Baron, owned a brothel in the rue des Moulins. Mlle Popo is also the subject of the lithograph *Woman in Bed: waking up* (Adriani, Toulouse-Lautrec, *op.cit.,* no.180).

The Courtauld sheet, distinguished by the rapidity and vigour of its notation, shares with the works mentioned above a mood of quiet, mundane domesticity which borders on tenderness – a feeling not normally present in Lautrec's work.

TOULOUSE-LAUTREC, Henri de 1864–1901

94 **Miss Ida Heath, the English Dancer** 1894

Lithograph (crayon); printed in olive-green ink; on off-white (now unevenly discoloured) wove paper.

No visible stonemarks or registration marks.

Sheet: 37.5 x 28 cm

Signed on the stone, upper left: "HT-L" (in monogram, encircled).

Inscribed in pencil, bottom right: "N° 27 Ida Heath/danseuse anglaise", and numbered in different hands in pencil, top right: "D.155" and: "5". Numbered in pencil, *verso:* "24205" and: "D169".

Stamped with the artist's mark (Lugt 1338), lower right.

PROVENANCE Percy Moore Turner, from whom purchased by Samuel Courtauld, 1923. Courtauld Gift, 1935.

EXHIBITED Tate Gallery, 1948 (132); Nottingham University, 1969; Arts Council (74).

LITERATURE *Le Figaro Illustré,* April 1902; H. Esswein, *H. de Toulouse-Lautrec* (Munich, 1912), pp.6-7; Loys Delteil, *Le peintre-graveur illustré: H. de Toulouse-Lautrec* (Paris, 1920), no.165; P. Leclercq, *Autour de Toulouse-Lautrec* (Paris 1921), p.12; Maurice Joyant, *Henri de Toulouse-Lautrec, Dessins, Estampes, Affiches* (Paris, 1927), p.92; *Oeuvre graphique de Toulouse-Lautrec* (Bibliothèque Nationale, Paris, 1951), no.143; Cooper, 1954, no.204; Jean Adhémar, *Toulouse-Lautrec His complete lithographs and drypoints* (1965), no.104; Götz Adriani, *Toulouse-Lautrec. Das gesamte graphische Werk* (Cologne, 1976), no.66; Frances Carey and Antony Griffiths, *From Manet to Toulouse-Lautrec* (British Museum, 1978), no.102.

This lithograph, executed in 1894 and published by Kleinmann, Paris, is the only print by Lautrec of the English dancer.

A rapid pencil sketch of Ida Heath high-kicking, in reverse to the present composition (ex. coll. Ludwig Charell, sold Sotheby's, 6 October 1966, lot 121: Dortu, *op.cit.,* no.D.3. 840) has been dated to 1895, although it is certainly a preparatory drawing for this unique image of the dancer.

Neither Delteil (*ibid.*) nor Adriani (*ibid.*) record this lithograph printed in olive-green ink: the total edition of sixty appears to have been printed largely in black.

TOULOUSE-LAUTREC, Henri de 1864–1901

95 **Marcel Lender, Bust-Length** 1895

Lithograph (crayon, and ink with drawing with the brush and use of the 'crachis' technique); printed in dark green, pale green, yellow-green, yellow, red, pink, blue and grey inks; on off-white (now unevenly discoloured) wove paper. The pictorial area enclosed within a border printed in dark green ink.

No visible stonemarks: registration marks at the centre, above and below the pictorial area, and at the upper right and lower left.

Pictorial area (maxima): 32.5 x 24.4 cm

Signed on the stone within the pictorial area, upper left: "H T-L" (in monogram, encircled). Printed in black, bottom of sheet: "ORIGINAL-LITHOGRAPHIE IN ACHT FARBEN VON H. DE TOULOUSE-LAUTREC. PAN 1/3".

PROVENANCE Bellier, Paris; with the Leicester Galleries, London, from whom purchased by Samuel Courtauld 1928. Courtauld Gift 1935.

EXHIBITED Tate Gallery, 1948 (129); Arts Council (72).

LITERATURE Delteil, *H. de Toulouse-Lautrec,* no.102 (1st and 2nd states only); Joyant, *Toulouse-Lautrec ... Estampes ...,* pp.92, 99; *Oeuvre graphique de Toulouse-Lautrec,* no.95; Cooper, 1954, no.202; Adhémar, *Toulouse-Lautrec,* no.131 (as 3rd state); Adriani, *Toulouse-Lautrec,* no.118 (a variant of state IV b); Carey and Griffiths, *From Manet to Toulouse-Lautrec,* no.108.

Lautrec first depicted the actress Marcel Lender (1863–1927) in 1893 (in the lithograph *Lender et Baron:* Adriani, *op.cit.,* no.45). In 1895, however, the artist became captivated by Lender's dancing in the rôle of Galswinthe, in Hervé's operetta *Chilpéric* (Francis Jourdain and Jean Adhémar, *T-Lautrec,* Paris, 1952, p.98), and thereafter she began to figure more prominently in his work.

The present lithograph was commissioned by the German art-critic Julius Meier-Graefe in 1895 for the magazine, *Pan,* of which he was co-editor: as a result of the lithograph's publication (1st year, 3rd volume, opposite p.196), Meier-Graefe was dismissed from the editorial board (Carey and Griffith, *ibid.*).

The prototype for the composition of this print may be found in the lithograph *Lender bowing* (Adriani, *op.cit.,* no.117), although here Lender is seen against a background of figures. A small pen portrait of the actress in profile to the left (private coll., France: Dortu, *op.cit.,* D.4. 242) is dated to 1896, although this would also appear to precede the prints mentioned above.

In the Courtauld lithograph, in which Lender is seen on stage, as the lighting from below confirms, the drawing is crisper, the contours more angular, while the figure is more rigorously cropped and set diagonally within the pictorial area in a composition reminiscent of those depicting actors in Japanese woodblock-prints.

Lender's hairstyle is more exaggerated than in the earlier print: similar extravagant coiffures, reminiscent of Japanese hairstyles in which large pins or combs are prominent, had been the subject of at least two sketches by Lautrec in 1894 (Göteborg Konstmuseum, Sweden; private coll., France: Dortu, *op.cit.,* D.3. 725 and D.3. 732, respectively), while the frontal portrait sketch of Lender of 1895 (coll. Mr. and Mrs. Bertel Hintze, Helsinki: Dortu, *op.cit.,* D.3. 898) had concentrated on a similar exotic hairstyle at the expense of the facial features.

In the present print, *pentimenti* indicate that the artist has extended the forehead and hair to the right, in order to link the plume of hair to the right framing edge of the composition. A mobility of facial expression and movement of the head is suggested as a result of the redrawing, for the upper area of the head now appears inclined towards the spectator, in contrast to the strict profile of nose and chin.

The lithograph was published first as a contour drawing in olive-green: colour was introduced in the fourth state, its disposition over the sheet having been explored in a first state heightened with watercolour. The print conforms to the state described by Adriani (*ibid.*) under IV b, except that it lacks the "PAN" blindstamp.

TOULOUSE-LAUTREC, Henri de 1864–1901
96 **The Jockey**
Lithograph (crayon); printed in black ink; on white (now unevenly discoloured) laid paper.
No visible stonemarks or registration marks.
Sheet: 51.6 x 36.1 cm
Signed and dated on the stone, bottom right: "H T-L/1899" (the initials in monogram, encircled, the date reversed).
Numbered in a different hand in pencil, bottom right (now almost completely erased): "18842", and inscribed in pencil, *verso,* with directions to a picture-mounter.

PROVENANCE With Marcel Guiot, Paris; with the Leicester Galleries, London from whom purchased by Samuel Courtauld 1928. Courtauld Gift, 1935.
EXHIBITED On loan to the City Art Gallery, Wakefield, 1946–47; *History of Lithography,* Victoria and Albert Museum, London, October 1948; Tate Gallery, 1948 (135).
LITERATURE Delteil, *Toulouse-Lautrec,* no.279; Joyant, *Toulouse-Lautrec ... Estampes ... ,* p.100; *Oeuvre graphique de Toulouse-Lautrec,* no.189; Cooper, 1954, no.209; Adhémar, *Toulouse-Lautrec,* no.365; Adriani, *Toulouse-Lautrec,* no.356 (I); Carey and Griffiths, *From Manet to Toulouse-Lautrec,* no.139.

This lithograph, one of the last to be made by Lautrec, was executed in 1899 for a projected album of racetrack subjects. The artist's ill-health prevented him from completing the series, although four plates were published in May by Pierrefort (Adriani, *op.cit.,* nos.356-59 inclusive).
This lithograph was published in two editions of a hundred, the first of which was printed in black, the second with the addition of colour stones. The effect of the colour is questionable: it plays almost no positive rôle, unlike that in the lithograph *Marcel Lender* (see cat.no.95), and it can be argued that its addition was an afterthought. Confirmation of this appears to lie in the detailed drawing of the first edition, in which all tones are completely and finally stated. Here, the dark silhouettes of the large horses are finely balanced against the almost unrelieved white of the racecourse, while smaller silhouettes of the solid forms of jockeys' caps are wittily contrasted with each other, and with the arcs of space between the jockeys' legs. The rather dull colour of the second state tends to confuse such contrasts.
The jockeys in the present lithograph are formally related to that on the right of *The Good Jockey – Is it enough to want something passionately?,* one of two racecourse scenes published in *Le Figaro Illustré* of July 1895 (illustrated in Philippe Huisman and M.G. Dortu, *Toulouse-Lautrec* (1971), pp.60-61, nos.1 and 2). The subtitles of both earlier racetrack scenes make parallels between the career of the jockey and that of the artist: although there are no subtitles to indicate a similar meaning for the series of 1899, it may nevertheless have been intended.

UTRILLO, Maurice 1883–1955
97 **Street at Sannois** 1912
Oil on canvas, 54 x 81 cm
Signed, in pen, bottom right: "Maurice. Utrillo. V"

PROVENANCE With Libaude, Paris; through Reid and Lefèvre, London; Samuel Courtauld by 1931. Courtauld Gift, 1932.
EXHIBITED Tate Gallery, 1948 (82); Orangerie, Paris, 1955 (62); Courtauld Centenary, 1976 (58).
LITERATURE A. Tabarant, *Utrillo* (Paris, 1926), p.94; Jamot-Turner, no.53 (repr.); Home House Catalogue, no.31; Cooper, 1954, no.82 (repr.); Paul Petrides, *Maurice Utrillo* (4 vols., Paris, 1959), I, p.358, no.299 (repr.).

The painting can be dated to 1912 from its subject-matter. Sannois is on the outskirts of Paris, close to Argenteuil, and Utrillo spent some months there in 1912 at a home for inebriates run by Dr. Revertégat.
The pigment in this picture has a "dried-out" appearance, not only in the areas of masonry, but also in the foliage of the trees. This chalky quality may have been achieved by the use of white spirit as a medium.

VAN GOGH, Vincent 1853–1890
98 **Peach Blossom in the Crau** 1889
Oil on canvas, 65 x 81 cm
Unsigned.

colour plate, page 56

PROVENANCE With Bernheim-Jeune, Paris; through Percy Moore Turner, London; Samuel Courtauld 1927. Courtauld Gift 1932.
EXHIBITED *Van Gogh,* Marcel Bernheim, Paris, January 1925 (32); *Ingres to Cézanne,* Independent Gallery, London, May 1925 (26); *Dutch Art, A.D. 1450–1900,* Royal Academy, London, 1929 (454); Tate Gallery, 1948 (32); Orangerie, Paris, 1955 (66); Courtauld Centenary, 1976 (60); National Gallery, London, February-March 1983 (no catalogue).
LITERATURE Jamot-Turner, no.28 (repr.); Home House Catalogue, no.12 (repr.); J.-B. de la Faille, *L'Oeuvre de Vincent Van Gogh* (Paris and Brussels, 1928), no.514; J.-B. de la Faille (revised ed., London, Paris and Toronto, 1939), no.531 (repr. in both eds.); Cooper, 1954, no.86 (repr.); J.-B. de la Faille (rev. ed. by A.M. Hammacher and others), *The Works of Vincent Van Gogh: His Paintings and Drawings* (Amsterdam, 1970), no.F.514 (H.531).

Painted in Arles in March-April 1889, this shows a view in the Crau near Arles. It was one of the last pictures Van Gogh painted before he left Arles for Saint-Rémy. He painted the subject many times, and a rough pen sketch of this composition appears in a letter to Signac of between 5-11 April 1889 (repr. in G. Coquiot, *Vincent Van Gogh* (Paris, 1923), as facsimile).
Van Gogh refers to this landscape several times in his letters to his brother Theo and to Signac. In early April he writes to Theo: "Just now I have on the easel an orchard of peach trees beside a road with the Alpille foothills in the background" (Letter 583, quoted de la Faille, 1970 ed.).
To Signac (Letter 583b, *loc.cit.*): "I have just come back with two studies of orchards. Here is a crude sketch of them — the big one is a poor landscape with little cottages, blue skyline of the Alpille foothills, sky white and blue. The foreground, patches of land surrounded by cane hedges, where small peach trees are in bloom — everything is small there, the gardens, the fields, the orchards, and the trees, even the mountains, as in certain Japanese landscapes, which is the reason why the subject attracted me."
Further references to this and other paintings occur in a letter written between 13 and 16 April, and on 29 July 1889, Theo writes from Paris to acknowledge receipt of this and other works, saying: ". . . the fields with the gardens in spring are very beautiful" (Letter T13, *loc.cit.*).
An earlier related picture, *Harvest at La Crau, with Montmajour in the Background* (F.412), which was painted in June 1888, now belongs to the Rijksmuseum Vincent Van Gogh, Amsterdam. It shows the Alpille in the distance, but is taken from a slightly different viewpoint, and there are other important differences in composition.

VAN GOGH, Vincent 1853–1890
99 **A Tile Factory** 1888
Extensive preliminary drawing with hard and soft pencil, both freehand and ruled; drawing with reed pens of varying nib thicknesses with brown (iron gall?) ink of varying strengths; some strengthening of contours in soft pencil; on very pale buff (now stained) wove paper. The sheet unevenly trimmed at the left (? a page from a sketchbook, the spine to the left).
25.6 x 34.8 cm
Unsigned.
Numbered by the artist (?) in pen and brown ink, *verso:* "174".

colour plate, page 57

PROVENANCE (Mevr. J. van Gogh — Bonger, Amsterdam; V.W. van Gogh, Laren; with the Leicester Galleries by November 1923, from whom purchased by Samuel Courtauld 1927. Courtauld Bequest 1948 (H.H.194).
EXHIBITED *Van Gogh,* Stedelijk Museum, Amsterdam, July-August 1905 (408); *Vincent van Gogh Teekeningen uit de verzameling mevr. J. van Gogh — Bonger en V.W. van Gogh,* Stedelijk Museum, Amsterdam, December 1914–January 1915 (169); *Vincent van Gogh Teekeningen collectie van mevr. J. van Gogh — Bonger,* Vereniging Voor de Kunst, Utrecht, and Kunstkring, Rotterdam, January-April 1923 (48); *Vincent van Gogh,* Leicester Galleries, London, November-December 1923 (37); Tate Gallery, 1948 (100); Orangerie, Paris, 1955 (92); Manchester, 1962 (21); Courtauld Centenary, 1976 (80); Arts Council (77); British Museum, 1983 (108).
LITERATURE *Lettres de Vincent van Gogh à Émile Bernard,* ed. A. Vollard (Paris 1911), pl.LXVIII; J.B. de la Faille *The Works of Vincent van Gogh His Paintings and Drawings* (Paris and Brussels, 1928; revised edition Paris and Toronto, 1939; second edition, 1970), no.1500; Fritz Novotny, "Reflections on a Drawing by Van Gogh", *Art Bulletin,* XXXV (March 1953), pp.35-43, pl.1; Cooper, 1954, no.155; Jan Hulsker, *The Complete Van Gogh* (New York, 1977), no.1373.

The drawing is dated by Hulsker (*ibid.*) to March 1888, on the basis of that date inscribed by Van Gogh on a drawing of comparable size, subject matter and technique, the *Landscape with Path and Pollard Trees* (Rijksmuseum Vincent van Gogh, Amsterdam: Hulsker, *op.cit.,* 1372). Two other drawings of related technique and format are similarly dated by Hulsker (1374, 1375).

Confirmation that the Courtauld sheet dates from no earlier than March is found in Van Gogh's letters to his brother, Theo. (*Complete Letters of Vincent van Gogh* (New York, no date)): at the beginning of March, the countryside was under freezing snow (*Letters,* 463-67), although by the 10th (*Letters,* 468) it had cleared. At this time Van Gogh ventured out of doors, although he was prevented from serious work by the force of the mistral.

By approximately the middle of the month (*Letters,* 489) the almond trees had begun to blossom, and Van Gogh had executed three drawings from nature, for which he had used a perspective frame. The perspective frame, which the artist had had made in the summer of 1882, and a drawing of which appears in a letter to Theo of late August of that year (*Letters,* 223), was a wooden structure bisected horizontally, vertically and diagonally by wires: it could be pinned at either side, and at the required height, into two posts which the artist sank into the ground.

An initial ruled pencil drawing of the frame, with subsequent freehand reductions of size to allow for the format of the sheet, appears faintly in the Courtauld drawing. The frame's bisecting vertical lies at the centre of the sheet, the horizontal halfway up the pictorial area, coinciding with the tops of the palings.

It would appear that the drawing was executed in two stages: the first, the underdrawing, was carried out from nature with a broad pencil — perhaps one of the carpenter's pencils which the artist had used since 1882 (*Letters,* 180): the second, the more selective and decorative pen drawing, was almost certainly executed in the studio.

The pen strokes are grouped over the surface of the paper in a manner influenced by Japanese drawings and woodcuts, a collection of which Van Gogh had formed by 1887.

Contrary to the Japanese practice, however, Van Gogh concentrates the vertical penstrokes of the foreground into lateral zones, the strokes of each of which diminish in size as they approach the horizon line, suggesting the effects of spatial recession which the artist was able to assimilate rapidly by using the perspective frame. The diagonal strokes near the horizon closely follow those which radiate from the central vanishing point of the perspective frame.

The composition of the Courtauld sheet looks back to drawings from the Paris period such as *Street with People Walking and a Horsecar near the Ramparts,* and its cognate sketch (Rijksmuseum Vincent Van Gogh, Amsterdam: Hulsker, 1283 and 1282, respectively), and *Factories at Asnières* (St. Louis Art Museum, USA: Hulsker, 1287). A similar composition is reversed in the drawing, also of March 1888, *Landscape with Two Trees, Plowman and Horses* (Rijksmuseum Vincent van Gogh, Amsterdam: Hulsker, 1374), although here the scene is conventionally framed by overhanging trees at either side.

The sheet of the Courtauld drawing is unevenly trimmed at the left, suggesting that it was perhaps taken from a sketchbook, the spine of which was on the left: across the centre of the sheet are deep impressions of hatching moving diagonally from upper right to lower left, probably transferred from the sheet above, which may have been that of the *Landscape with Path and Pollard Trees* (mentioned above). This work was almost certainly the first of two drawings (the other is Hulsker, 1375) dating from March 1888 in which the vanishing point and the emphasis of the composition is at the upper right.

By 1 May 1888, Van Gogh had sent a dozen small pen and ink drawings to Theo (*Letters,* 480): the Courtauld drawing was probably one of this number, since its first recorded owner (cf. PROV:) was Joanna van Gogh-Bonger, wife of the artist's brother.

VUILLARD, Edouard 1868–1940

100 **Interior with a Screen c.1909–10**

Oil (peinture à l'essence) over charcoal drawing, on grey-buff card. The card laid down on panel, 35.8 x 23.8 cm

Signed, bottom right: "E Vuillard"

colour plate, page 59

PROVENANCE With Paul Gemetti, London; through the Leicester Galleries, London; Samuel Courtauld, July 1927. Courtauld Bequest 1948 (H.H.190).

EXHIBITED Tate Gallery, 1948 (83); Orangerie, Paris, 1955 (69); Courtauld Centenary, 1976 (61).

LITERATURE Jamot-Turner, no.55 (repr.); Cooper, 1954, no.89 (where dated "c.1912") as "Intérieur: Le Paravent".

A similar sketch, formerly in the Robert von Hirsch collection, Basel, was sold at Sotheby's, London, 26 June 1978 (lot 740) as *Femme nue à sa toilette (Nu au paravent),* 28.2 x 23.5 cm, and dated *c.*1909. The von Hirsch picture had been purchased by Bernheim-Jeune from the artist in October 1910, and shown in a Vuillard exhibition at Bernheim-Jeune's in February 1911. It seems very likely that the Courtauld picture should be redated to *c.*1909–10.

After the dissolution of the Nabis in about 1900, Vuillard continued to paint intimate domestic scenes, but like his great friend Bonnard, turned towards greater naturalism. This delicate sketch, with its subtle tonal graduations and the use Vuillard makes of the background colour as a unifying element, is characteristic of his work of the period.

Bibliographical references and abbreviations

All publications are in London, unless otherwise stated.

Publications relating to the Courtauld Collection

Home House Catalogue	*A Catalogue of the Pictures and Other Works of Art at Home House, 20 Portman Square, London.* (Published by the Home House Society Trustees, London, 1935.)
Jamot-Turner	*Collection de Tableaux Français, faite à Londres, 20 Portman Square, par Samuel et Elizabeth Courtauld, 1914-31:* Texte par Paul Jamot et Percy Moore Turner. (50 copies, privately printed, London, 1934.)
Tate Gallery, 1948	*Catalogue of the Samuel Courtauld Memorial Exhibition,* held at The Tate Gallery, London, May-June, 1948.
Cooper, 1954	Douglas Cooper, *The Courtauld Collection. A Catalogue and Introduction,* with a Memoir of Samuel Courtauld by Anthony Blunt. (University of London, The Athlone Press, 1954.)
Orangerie, Paris, 1955	*Impressionistes de la Collection Courtauld de Londres,* Musée de l'Orangerie, Paris, October, 1955.
Courtauld Centenary, 1976	*Samuel Courtauld's Collection of French 19th Century Paintings and Drawings.* A centenary exhibition to commemorate the birth of Samuel Courtauld, organised by the Courtauld Institute and the Arts Council, (Arts Council of Great Britain, 1976.)
National Gallery, London, 1983	*Paintings from the Courtauld,* National Gallery, London, 10 February-27 March 1983 (no catalogue).
R.A. Commemorative Catalogue	*Commemorative Catalogue of the Exhibition of French Art 1200-1900* Royal Academy of Arts, London, January-March 1932 (1933).
Lugt	Frits Lugt, *Marques de Collections* (Amsterdam, 1921, reprinted with the *Supplement,* The Hague, 1956).

Exhibitions referred to under the drawings

Manchester, 1962	*Master Drawings from the Witt and Courtauld Collections,* Whitworth Art Gallery, Manchester, 17 November-22 December 1962.
Nottingham University, 1969	*Watercolours, Drawings and Engravings from the Courtauld,* Nottingham University, 15 October-15 November 1969 (a selection of 40 works without catalogue).
London	*The Nude,* Morley Gallery, London, 1975.
Arts Council	*Drawings from the Courtauld,* Arts Council travelling exhibition to: Graves Art Gallery, Sheffield 29 October-11 December 1977; Wolverhampton Art Gallery, 17 December 1977-28 January 1978; Bolton Museum and Art Gallery, 4 February-18 March 1978; Laing Art Gallery, Newcastle-on-Tyne, 28 October-10 December 1978; Ferens Art Gallery, Hull, 16 December 1978-28 January 1979; Portsmouth Museum and Art Gallery, 3 February-18 March 1979.
British Museum, 1983	*Mantegna to Cézanne: Master Drawings from the Courtauld,* British Museum January-June 1983.

Index

(Catalogue entries and colour plates in the text, in italics.)